For Hawkeye Fans Only

Rousing Toasts from Loyal Sons

By Rich Wolfe

Published by Lone Wolfe Press

ISBN: 0-9748603-3-6

Interior photos of all University of Iowa stadiums, arenas, and Nile Kinnick are from the University Photo Service and Special Collections Division of the University of Iowa Library
Back cover photo: University Photo Service
Cover Design: Dick Fox
Photo Editor: Dick Fox
Cover Copywriter: Dick Fox
Interior Design: The Printed Page, Phoenix, AZ
Author's Agent: T. Roy Gaul

The page count skipped 16 pages on page 192 to reflect the number of full-page photos.

The author, Rich Wolfe, can be reached at 602-738-5889 or at www.fandemonium.net.

Page Two. In 1941, the news director at a small radio station in Kalamazoo, Michigan hired Harry Caray away from a station in Joliet, Illinois. The news director's name was Paul Harvey. Yes, that Paul Harvey! "And now, you have the rest of the story...... ➡

DEDICATION

To my parents, Melvin and Frances Wolfe,
who had the foresight to make sure I was
born in Iowa and the thoughtfulness not to
name me after my father.

Preface

Could my mother be serious? What she just told me was preposterous. It was the fall of 1953. Iowa was playing in South Bend, Indiana against the number-one team in the country, Notre Dame. Iowa, a huge underdog, was ahead 7-0 just before halftime. Notre Dame had the ball, but they were out of timeouts. The only way a team could stop the clock in those days—when you were out of timeouts—was by injury. With just a few seconds to go in the half, a Notre Dame player faked an injury to stop the clock. On the final play of the first half, Notre Dame quarterback Ralph Guglielmi threw a touchdown pass to tie the game at 7-7. I'm in the kitchen of our farmhouse in eastern Iowa—going crazy! There was a man from **Toronto, Iowa,** named Jim McDivett, who was working on the cabinets in the kitchen that day—the only day in the hundred-year history of that house that anyone ever worked on the cabinets.

My mother was in the dining room. She called me in. Whenever she said, "Richard," I knew I was in trouble. I go in there, not imagining what I had done—well, actually, I imagined a lot of things I had done, but I didn't think she knew about any of them. I go into the dining room. There was a swinging door that closed behind me so McDivett supposedly couldn't hear what we were saying. She said, "Richard, you must root for Notre Dame." I said, "What did you say?" She said, "You must root for Notre Dame." Fortunately, at that stage of my life, I had not yet heard the old adage: "If you can't laugh at yourself, laugh at your mother!" I thought she was just playing a joke on me because I was so upset about what had happened. It became apparent she was serious. I said, "Why would I possibly root for Notre Dame? You know what an Iowa fan I am." She said, "You'll root for Notre Dame because you're Irish and you're Catholic." I

In October, 1992, *Cedar Rapids Gazette* columnist, Mike Hlas informed his readers that he was going to Toronto to cover the World Series between the Blue Jays and the Atlanta Braves. He drove 50 miles east to tiny Toronto, Iowa, watched the game in a tavern there and filed a hilarious report from "Toronto."

said, "What does that have to do with the price of tea in China? I don't care about that. I'm an Iowa fan. I'm rooting for Iowa." She said, "No, you won't." I said, "Yes, I will. I'm rooting for Iowa." In those days, it was very unusual to disobey your mother. I had not only just committed a venial sin; I was well on the way to a mortal sin on this deal. No amount of Hail Marys, indulgences or donations to pagan babies could rescue me now. I had said my piece and counted to three.

In the second half, Iowa goes ahead 14-7. With seven seconds remaining in the game, Notre Dame has the ball. Once again, they're out of timeouts. One of their linemen, Frank Varrichione, fakes an injury. On the last play of the game, Guglielmi throws another touchdown pass to tie the game 14-14. By this time, I'm completely unglued. My mother's ready to shoot me. McDivett's smirking.

That night we're watching the news. The TV station had a taped interview with Coach Forest Evashevski as he disembarked the airplane in Cedar Rapids. The interviewer asked, "Coach, what do you think about what happened in South Bend today?" Evashevski, paraphrasing the famous Grantland Rice poem, said, "When the one Great Scorer comes to mark against your name, He'll mark not if you won or lost, but how you got screwed at Notre Dame." I turned to my mother and said, "What does that word mean?" She said, "Nothing. He's just a sore loser." I said, "But we didn't lose." She said, "Well, I don't want to talk about it." The next day in the Des Moines Register, there was a cartoon in the Peach Section. It showed the clock atop Notre Dame Stadium, indicating seven seconds to go in the game. Underneath the clock, was an old man—the timekeeper—with a long beard leaning back in a chair snoring. You look at the clock, and there are cobwebs in the clock where the seven seconds were marked.

Fast forward to 1982. At that time I had lived in Scottsdale, Arizona for seven years. Iowa was playing the University of Arizona. Not only was I rooting for Iowa, I was doubly rooting for them because I'm an Arizona State fan, and we just don't like the University of Arizona. We head to Tucson. One of my brothers from Davenport is a big supporter of the Hawkeyes, and he was flying out on the team plane.

In Tucson, we're in the Iowa hotel, in one of the announcer's rooms. Among other people there were Ron Gonder, Mike Reilly, both Iowa announcers, Sharm Schuermann, also an Iowa announcer, my brother and some of his friends. It was late, and we are playing black-jack. About three o'clock in the morning, one of the players said, "Hey, while we're playing cards, let's play sports trivia, too." Someone asked, "Who won the first Heisman Trophy?" Right away, I said, "Too easy. Where did he go to school?" Mike Reilly piped up and said, "Jay Berwanger, of the University of Chicago, won the first Heisman Trophy, and he went to Senior High in Dubuque, Iowa." That was Mike's home town. I said, "Jay Berwanger was from Dubuque, but he went to St. Columkille's school." Reilly said, "No, he didn't. He went to Senior High. We have his trophies right in the trophy case. That's where he went to school." I said, "I don't care what kind of trophies you have at Senior High, Jay Berwanger went to St. Columkille. I was reading a story about him one time, and he said that was where he went to school. He told stories about going to school there." One thing leads to another, and pretty soon, there's a total of $480 bet on where Jay Berwanger went to school. Someone said, "Let's call the Tucson paper and get the answer." I said, "Call the Tucson paper? It's three o'clock in the morning. There hasn't been anyone there for five or six hours." Someone else said, "Well, how are we going to settle this. There's almost $500 at stake. We need an answer." I said, "Let's call him up." A chorus replied, "Call who up?" I said, "Let's call Jay Berwanger up." "Where does he live?" "I'm pretty sure he lives in Oak Brook, Illinois." So we go over and grab the telephone. Long distance information was twenty-five cents in those days. The announcer whose room we were in was having a heart attack when he thought we were going to make that phone call. I flipped him a dollar and said, "We might be making more than one of these babies." We called information, and the only listing they had in Chicago for a Berwanger was a Dr. George in Oak Lawn, Illinois. I figured how many Berwangers could there be—they've got to be related. I said, "That's fine. Give us that number." So we dialed that number…it's five o'clock in the morning in Chicago…this elderly-sounding lady answered the phone…. "H-e-l-l-o." I said, "Hey, is Dr. George there?" She said, "No, my George passed six months ago." I said, "Oh—no, I hate hearing that. George was a good man." Then, I decided I'd take a gamble. I said, "I better call Jay and give him my condolences. Do you have Jay's number?" Dr. George's widow gave me the number off the top of her head, right at 5:02 in the morning. Then, we called Jay Berwanger. The phone rang and rang and rang, and finally this elderly man answered. I said, "Jay?" He said, "Yeah." I said, "We're calling you from Tucson, Arizona. We have $480 bet on where you went to school." He said, "Who are you, and what did you say?" I told him my name and that I grew up fifty miles south of Dubuque and said, "I bet that you went to St. Columkille's." He said, "Who are you betting with?" I said, "I'm betting with a guy named Mike Reilly." He said, "The Mike Reilly who played with the Chicago Bears?" I said, "Yes." He said, "What did Reilly say?" Reilly is not going to take my word for Berwanger's answer. He's got his ear pressed so close to my ear that he's pushing the phone receiver into my middle eardrum. I said, "Reilly said you went to Senior High School." He said, "Well…" Now, Reilly is about tipping me over—his ear is tilting the side of my head so hard. "Well, you're both right. I actually went to both schools—no harm, no foul. Keep on having fun, boys. I'm going back to bed."

Now, let's go to the spring of 2000, I had done a book with my good friend, Dr. Bob Margeas in Des Moines and was looking for another subject: Dr. Bob said, "Do Bob Knight." Right at that time was when Indiana University put Bob Knight on "zero-tolerance probation." By the time I would finish the book, Knight would be in the news—either because he had been fired, or because the media would be watching him like a hawk—no pun intended—every game. The book was called *Oh, What a Knight!* It was 130-pages of wonderful, really neat, really nifty Bobby Knight stories. Then, you turned the book over—it had a new cover and a new title called *Knightmares*. That side had a similar amount of stories in a very negative style about Knight.

Knight was fired in September of that year, and nobody saw him for three months. He was spotted playing **golf in Europe** with Norman

> **While playing golf in 1567, Mary Queen of Scots was informed that her husband, Lord Darnley, had been murdered. She finished the round.**

Schwarzkopf and the elder President Bush, but no one had seen him in this country. The book came out in November and sold like hot cakes—although I've never really seen hot cakes sell that well. The book became the best-selling book throughout the state, far outselling the Beatles Anthology, which was the top-selling book in the rest of the country at that time. On December 9, a Monday afternoon, I was in Bloomington, Indiana, delivering books to a Barnes and Noble bookstore. I said to the manager, "There are two more cartons out in the truck—the only two left. You might as well take them 'cause you know you're going to sell them." He said, "You're right. Let's go get them. I'll help you bring them in." That particular day, it was snowing. It was coming down hard and had been coming down all day long. We go through the snow-laden parking lot, get the two cartons of books and were headed back toward the entrance to Barnes and Noble. Walking in front of the bookstore were two men, the taller of whom yelled, "I'll get the door for you guys." The taller man, the guy who yelled, was wearing a golf cap. When we got up by the door, I looked up to see the logo on his golf cap. It wasn't a golf cap. It was a hunting cap. This man is squinting down at me. I realized it was Bobby Knight. I said, "Hey, coach, how are you doing?" He said, "I'm doing great. How are you doing?" I said, "Well, if I was any better, I'd have to be twins." The manager and I carry the cartons into the store, turn to the right and put them down. Knight and the friend who I later recognized as Bob Hamel, the long-time sports editor of the Bloomington newspaper, walked straight ahead to the back of the store. The manager was almost speechless. He said, "Holy cow. Did you see who held the door open for us?" I said, "Yes." He said, "Do you think he knew who you were?" I said, "Pal, if he knew who I was, I'd be in that snowbank out there, and you'd be leading off SportsCenter tonight."

Years before, I talked a friend of mine into hitchhiking to Iowa City for a football game. We were about eleven or twelve years old and had no trouble getting rides. We certainly looked harmless, and hitchhiking was widespread in those days. We finally made it to Iowa City, but the problem was: we didn't know they charged admission. We had no money. We just had no idea that you had to pay money for a ticket to get into those games. We wandered around outside until just before halftime when we were able to sneak in. They were play-ing Minnesota that day.

After the game, we headed for the parking lot and looked for license plates that had the Jackson County number on them—#49. In those days, license plates didn't have the name of the county printed on them…they started with the alphabetical numerical number of the county. Jackson County was the county northeast of where we lived, so we knew that if somebody was going to Jackson County they had to go pretty close to our hometown. The very first people we found with Jackson County plates gave us a ride, not to the door—we didn't want to be dropped off at the front of the farm by strangers—but right near town where we were able to walk home.

I relate these stories because they are the genesis of this book. When-ever they were told, the listeners would always volley with similar tales of their own. I tried to interest publishers to do a series of books involving the fans of certain teams. They laughed; said no one would be interested in other fans' stories.

When I became my own publisher five years ago, I knew I would test this idea. The first book, *For Yankee Fans Only*, sold out. The second, *For Red Sox Fans Only*, sold out immediately. Twenty thousand more were reprinted, and it is being featured in a Drew Barrymore/**Matt Damon** movie, *Fever Pitch*, to be released next summer. The book *For Cub Fans Only* not only became the best-selling book in the his-tory of the Cubs, it sold over three times the previous record. It is my feeling that the football "fans" books will do even better, and there was never a question that the first of many football books would be on the Iowa Hawkeyes and our incredible fans.

I have no idea how I became such a rabid Hawkeye fan. It started when I was about nine years old. In the wintertime, I would sit on the warm radiator in the kitchen and listen to Iowa basketball games, making sure I was keeping score in my Big Chief notebook. We lis-tened to 600-WMT, Cedar Rapids and, occasionally, WHO-Des

> **Matt Damon and Ben Affleck made their movie debuts as extras in *Field of Dreams*.**

Moines. Tait Cummings always did the play-by-play. I'd never been to the Iowa Field House, but I always got excited when I heard Tait say, "Sharm Scheuerman, across the Big I in the center jump circle."

For a while, you couldn't hear the Iowa buzzer at the end of the quarter or the half. The team was good, and as the crowds got bigger, the noise got louder. Besides using the buzzer, they also would fire off a gun. In one game, some wiseacre—don't look at me, I was too young, or I would have done it—brought a dead, undressed chicken. With about two seconds to go in the half, he threw the chicken at the Big I in the center jump circle. Right when the gun went off, the chicken came flying through the air, plopped down at mid-court, and the arena went sideways.

They replaced the gun with a loud horn. It was the greatest horn ever invented. Most of my memories of Iowa Field House revolve around that horn. I've been in hundreds of gyms and arenas and field houses over the years but no horn had the distinctive sound of that old horn in the Iowa Field House. There was no better venue for basketball.

After basketball indoctrinated me into being a big Iowa fan, obviously, I became a huge Iowa football fan. Starting when I was nine years old, I listened to every Iowa football game for years. In order to accomplish this, I had to figure out chores to do around the farm where there was an electrical socket so I could plug in the radio. On one Saturday, I would clean the basement. On the next Saturday, I would clean the chicken house. Then, I would rotate. We had the cleanest basement and the fattest chickens in Iowa.

After the game, WMT had this wonderful scoreboard show. They would give about eight scores and then play a fight song. They would play the Big Ten fight songs, and the Notre Dame or Southern Cal, Georgia Tech or Alabama fight songs. It ingrained a love for these fight songs. To this day, I love college fight songs, particularly the Big Ten songs. The Big Ten easily has the best songs of any conference…especially The University of Iowa, which has two of the best songs—not just one, but two great songs. Also, the WMT scoreboard show would always give the Slippery Rock score. Today, I have exactly one tape in my car…a tape of college fight songs. It has the two Iowa songs twice—on each side!

Every Saturday night, we would watch the highlights on NBC-WOC, Channel 5, in Davenport, with their sportscaster, Hal Hart. That station now is KWQC, Channel 6 in Davenport.

In 1953, I finally got to see the inside of the Iowa Field House. The problem was it wasn't for an Iowa game—it was for the **Harlem Globetrotters**. Every year, the Globetrotters had a tour against the College All-Stars. These were really big-time college players. That was a real treat to finally see the Field House and to hear the horn.

The best thing about the Hawkeyes is the memories they give you over the years…When I was thirteen years old, a friend of one of my older brothers, Jack Marlowe, of Preston, Iowa, had access to a car. We had heard about a man in Davenport named Dick Lamb, who had this incredible sports collection, including a lot of Hawkeye memorabilia. One night, Jack got his dad's car. We drove down and saw Dick Lamb. What a guy and what a collection! He had an unbelievable collection. He was an old guy—probably about forty then. Ironically, he died just a few years later. He was on the board of the National Football Foundation and had written a book on Iowa football. He was really a neat guy. He would let us borrow Iowa programs and take them back to the farm provided we brought them back in perfect shape, which we always would, a month or two later…

I was in seventh grade, and we're at a girls' sectional basketball game in Calamus, Iowa. There was a nicely dressed man sitting next to me. He was by himself. I would steal glances at him and knew he looked familiar, and, finally, I figured it out—the guy sitting next to me was the athletic director from The University of Iowa, Paul Brechler. I turned to him and said, "You're Paul Brechler, aren't you?" He said,

In 1972, Bill Cosby signed a lifetime contract with the Globetrotters for one dollar per year. In 1986, the Globetrotters gave him a nickel raise. Cosby made several appearances with the team and is an honorary member of the Basketball Hall of Fame.

"Yes." I asked, "What are you doing here?" He said, "I'm dating a teacher at one of these schools." For the next hour, we talked Hawkeye sports non-stop. He later married the teacher...

The first really important Iowa game that I saw in person was Ohio State in 1956. That victory sent Iowa to the Rose Bowl. The stadium was going crazy. There was an excellent freshman player from Anamosa named Don Norton. Norton later had a great career at Iowa and with the **San Diego Chargers**, but in those days freshmen could not play varsity sports. The students were going crazy and were trying to tear down the goal posts. Don Norton climbed up and was sitting astride the crossbar. Some fans threw him up a cable, which he looped around the crossbar. Immediately, the fans started pulling hard on the cable. The problem was that Norton's thumb was still underneath the cable. We could see him screaming but didn't realize he was in great pain. His thumb was all but severed, and he would have lost it had there not been a hospital across the street. The doctors didn't think they could save it, but, fortunately, they did. It's ironic that years later, Iowa was the first school to have collapsible goal posts...

Going to those Iowa games as a youngster in the 1950s was an incredible experience. One game in 1957, a back-up Iowa running back named Geno Sessi, from Weirton, West Virginia, caught a Randy Duncan pass and ran eighty yards against Utah State. In order to score that touchdown, he actually traversed about 130 yards. It was the longest pass play in Iowa history at the time. To this day, it's the greatest run I've ever seen on a football field. A few years later, his brother, Tom Sessi, from Weirton lived next door to me in college, which proves that it's a small world—even though I wouldn't want to paint it...

We were at the 1982 Rose Bowl where Washington beat Iowa 28-0. The seats in the Rose Bowl are about three inches wide. After every

> The Chargers were originally the Los Angeles Chargers in 1960, the first year of the AFL. They were owned by Baron Hilton of the Hilton Hotel chain. Hilton owned the Carte Blanche credit card company and named the team, the Chargers, to promote the card.

Washington touchdown, their band played this great, upbeat song. I turned to my starter wife (of 25 years) and said, "Wow, Washington's got a great fight song." She looked at me, and then looked again, and she said, "That's not their fight song. That's the number one song in the country." The song was "Celebration" by Kool & the Gang. To this day, I still think it would be a great fight song. Perhaps, it's a good thing that music is not my life.

All small towns take pride when one of their own can make it on the sports scene. My hometown of Lost Nation is no exception. In Lost Nation, there once was a hardware store owned by a man named Delbert. Delbert sold the store and moved forty miles away to Miles, Iowa and opened up another hardware store. Then, when he sold that one, he moved to Clinton. It was a good thing Delbert moved to Clinton because that gave his son a chance to play football—and that boy was Kenny Ploen, who later became the Big Ten's Most Valuable Player, while leading the Hawks to the Rose Bowl. Also, three of my schoolmates at the time later had Hawkeye connections: Jim McAndrew played varsity baseball at Iowa and had a wonderful major league career. Another with an Iowa tie was Tony McAndrews who became a valued assistant to Lute Olson, both at Iowa and at Arizona. Rich O'Hara was a stellar tight end at Iowa in the mid-sixties and a second-round draft pick of the Minnesota Vikings. At the end of sixth grade, McAndrews moved to Davenport and O'Hara to Maquoketa.

Now is a good time to answer a few questions that always arise. The most often asked is, "Why isn't your name on the book cover, like other authors?" The answer is simple: I'm not Stephen King. No one knows who I am, no one cares. My name on the cover will not sell an additional book. On the other hand, it allows for "cleaner" and more dramatic covers that the readers appreciate, and the books are more visible at the point of sale.

The second most frequent query is, "You sell tons of books. Why don't they show up on the best seller list?" Here's how the book business works: Of the next 170 completed manuscripts, 16 will eventually be published, and only one will ever return a profit. To make the *New York Times Bestseller List*, you need to sell a total of 30,000 copies nationally. Sales are monitored at certain stores, at big book chains, a few selected independent book stores, etc. My last nine books have averaged well over 60,000 units sold, but less than 15,000 were sold in bookstores. Most are sold regionally, another deterrent to national rankings. While I'm very grateful to have sold so many books to the "Big Boys," I'm a minority of one in feeling that a bookstore is the worst place to sell a book. Publishers cringe when they hear that statement. A large bookstore will stock over 150,000 different titles. That means the odds of someone buying my book are 150,000-1. Those aren't good odds; I'm not that good of a writer. For the most part, people who like Mike Ditka or Dale Earnhardt—previous book subjects of mine—don't hang around bookstores. I would rather be the only book at a hardware chain than in hundreds of bookstores.

Example: My *Remembering Dale Earnhardt* hardcover sold several hundred thousand copies, mostly at Walgreens and grocery chains; places not monitored for the "best selling" lists. I sold the paperback rights to Triumph Books, Chicago. They printed 97,000 paperbacks—all sold through traditional channels. My hardcover did not appear on any bestseller list. Meanwhile, Triumph had a paperback on Earnhardt that made number one on the New York Times non-fiction trade list. Go figure. Also, I never offer my books directly to Amazon.com because I can't type, I've never turned on a computer and I keep thinking that Amazon is going out of business soon. For years, the more customers they recruited, the more money they lost…so sooner or later, when the venture capital is gone, the bookkeeping shenanigans are recognized, and the stock plummets, look out. Meanwhile, maybe I should call them.

Since the age of ten, I've been a serious collector of sports books. During that time—for the sake of argument, let's call it 30 years—my favorite book style is the eavesdropping type where the subject talks in his or her own words—without the "then he said" or "the air was so thick you could cut it with a butter knife" waste of verbiage that makes it so hard to get to the meat of the matter. Books such as Lawrence Ritter's *Glory of Their Times* and Donald Honig's *Baseball When the Grass Was Real*. Thus, I adopted that style when I started compiling oral histories of the Jack Bucks and Harry Carays of the world. I'm a sports fan first and foremost—I don't even pretend to be an author. This book is designed solely for other sports fans. I really don't care what the publisher, editors or critics think. I'm only interested in Iowa fans having an enjoyable read and getting their money's worth. Sometimes a person being interviewed will drift off the subject but if the feeling is that Hawkeye fans would enjoy the digression, it stays in the book.

In an effort to get more material into the book, the editor decided to merge some paragraphs and omit some of the commas, which will allow for the reader to receive an additional 20,000 words, the equivalent of 50 pages. More bang for your buck…more fodder for English teachers…fewer dead trees.

Every summer, I make it back to my hometown to visit my parents' graves, followed by a trip to the family farm. No one lives there now. The granary burned down years ago and the other buildings have crashed on the jagged shores of modern farming realities. The house is history—burned to the foundation this spring in a training exercise for the local volunteer fire department. It was a shock standing there looking down at the foundation and the cellar. How could that cellar appear so small when the farmhouse seemed so big? How was I able to bluff my parents for six hours of "cleaning" every Saturday? After all these years, it suddenly dawned on me that they knew how much I loved the Hawks and had simply played along with my otherwise non-existent cleaning fetishes.

It would be so great to turn back the hands of time and return to those halcyon days of Bucky O'Connor and Forest Evashevski…but the sun doesn't back up for anyone. Sometimes, the things we want most are the things we once had. There was only one thing to do: go back to the car, reposition the tape cassette, open the windows and sunroof, turn up the volume and return to the edge of the basement. Here came The Iowa Fight Song…and the memories. Over there by the furnace was where Purdue quarterbacks Dale Samuels and Lenny Dawson ruined three of my Saturdays and Wisconsin's Harlan Carl and Ohio State's Bob White destroyed two apiece. The coal bin? That was Kenny Ploen to Jim Gibbons; the shower room was Ohio State '52; where the freezer once reigned, that was Jerry Reichow territory.

The fight songs wafted through the warm summer breeze. I closed my eyes, and—in my mind—I was a little boy again.

It was easy to do because Hawkeye memories—like Hawkeye heroes—never grow old.

Rich Wolfe

Chat Rooms

WISCONSIN: COME SMELL OUR DAIRY AIR!

Chapter 1

The Land of Ahs

Sweet Home Kinnick

HE COULD HAVE BEEN A MINNESOTA FAN BUT THE DOG BEAT HIM OVER THE FENCE

Mike McGregor

Mike McGregor is, arguably, the number one Hawkeye fan in Arizona. He left his hometown of Manson, Iowa in 1976 to attend Arizona State University. Except for five years in Texas, he has lived in Arizona where he became a titan in the chemical business.

I was nine years old, and I was at Iowa Stadium—I was used to going to small-town fields where players wear patched-up uniforms—just looking down at the variations in the color of the grass, just from the way they mowed it. It was like magic to me. That was the first thing I noticed. In rural Iowa at that point in time, our high school had sharp uniforms. We did, but they were plain—purple and white. Sometimes, something…say, socks or shoes…wouldn't be matched. To see the Iowa uniforms with the gold helmets, the gold pants, the black jerseys—everything, was just great. Going to that Big Ten game—everything was perfect. I was amazed that everything could be so perfect, the field, the grass, the uniforms—everything was together.

The following Monday, I remember telling the kids at school about the game. We had to do some sort of drawing in Art, and what did I draw—Iowa Stadium, with the stands. There was one kid who said he had gotten to go to a college game that Saturday, also. I asked him which one, and he said Morningside. His sister was a student there. Big deal!

Then, in fifth grade my parents took us down for the Ohio State game. My brother, Chuck, was selling programs, cushions, pennants and concessions before the game so we had to get there early. He lived in the Quadrangle Dorm, so I got to stay in the dorm with him the night before the game. There were lots of parties going on up and down the hallways. It was just cool.

Then, we went down to the stadium early the next morning. It was a November game so it was chilly. Chuck's booth was underneath the East grandstand. Big buses came rolling in, and you heard the whistle of their airbrakes. The first guy off the bus was **Woody Hayes**. The people who were standing around started booing him and yelling at him. Then, they opened up the compartments of the bus and brought out these cases with their equipment in them. It was just neat to be there and to see the real deal. Iowa lost the game 14-10.

Bob Anderson was the Iowa kicker, and he hit a field goal early on. Every year for the games, they'd sell helium-filled balloons. They were gold with a black "I" on them and were on a long string. The capacity then was around 60,000, and the place was packed. The first time Iowa would score, everybody would let their balloon go. I remember Bob Anderson lining up for the kick. The ball got tipped at the line of scrimmage, but it went through and put us ahead 3-0. Iowa had scored first and the balloons were released into the air all at once. They just floated up into the sky. They'd block out the sun. They were gold so they just glittered. If the sky was blue, it just looked that much better. To a small-town kid like me, that was so unbelievable, a magical moment getting to be at a game like that.

When I was in junior high, I remember this one guy in Manson named Chuck Dana. He was a bachelor and he had several tickets to all the home games. He'd always take people with him to the games as his guest. One time, I wrote to the university about tickets. They sent me the forms, which I filled out and sent in with my money and got a ticket for one of the games. Chuck Dana knew I had a ticket so he invited me to ride down with him and the group he took with him. He drove a big Chevy Caprice. We'd leave about six in the morning. He'd pick me up at my folks' house, and away we'd go. The car would

> **Bob Knight once had Woody Hayes as one of his instructors in a class at Ohio State...Richard Nixon gave the eulogy at Woody Hayes' funeral.**

be full, and we'd be reading the *Des Moines Register* sports page. We'd drive straight through Ft. Dodge, through Webster City and there was a truck stop he liked along the way. We stopped, and he'd buy everybody breakfast. I thought I should order something cheap like oatmeal and not spend too much of his money. He'd look at me and say, "You don't want a bowl of oatmeal. Here, look at this T-bone and eggs. Get that." You'd walk out of there, get back in the car, and you'd get on I-35 and go south to I-80 and over. When you got down to I-80, you'd start seeing cars filled with other people going to the game. It was just a parade of cars with people wearing their colors and with banners hanging off the cars. A long procession going into Iowa City! There was so much anticipation. We'd go park in one of the lots, and the first thing I'd do was go buy a program. Lord, it was exciting to a young sports fan.

If I was there an hour and a half before kickoff, I would be in the stands watching them warm up, watching everything. I liked to watch the kickers warm up—to see their perfection at what they did. The kickers and holders would always come out early to get ready. They'd put a towel down on the ground. They'd put the footballs on it. The center would snap the ball—and it wasn't like watching some kid in high school in a little town snap it. These hikes were fast—like passes. It was so impressive to see that ball go up into the air. I just sucked it all in—just couldn't get enough.

After games—on the way home—you always had the radio on listening to WHO. It was always better after a win to be just driving around town through the traffic. My favorite thing after a game, as far as getting something to eat, was to go to the Amana Colonies. To go up there and eat until it hurt again. I remember Bill Zuber's Dugout. There was a story up on the wall. He told about growing up in the Amana Colonies. He threw onions from the field where he was working up against a big backboard at the end of a big wagon, and the onions would fall into the wagon. There was a scout from the New York Yankees who saw this kid, with his tremendous arms, out in this field, throwing baseball-sized onions up against that board and into the wagon. The story on the restaurant wall said, "Just a few years later, Bill Zuber was throwing onion-sized baseballs at **Yankee Stadium**."

When you grow up in a small town, you aren't entertained. You have to create your own entertainment. I'd listen to Iowa games. I was bigger than most of the kids, and I'd want to play football, but the other kids' mothers wouldn't want them to play football with me. I'd go out in the yard by myself and get started kicking. I'd imagine myself kicking in a big game...the Rose Bowl! Most kids back then had to have a fertile imagination to entertain themselves. The only thing I really had to draw from came from listening to the game on the radio, watching the highlights on the TV news that night, and then reading the *Register* the next morning. There was a half-hour show on the next day, some kind of Iowa football report, and I wouldn't miss any of it.

When I first went to the games, the band was so exciting. When they marched out onto the field, the lines were straight, and they were loud, and they were good. Also, they had the Scottish Highlanders. That's our heritage so that was really special to us. I remember one time sitting in the student section. The band came out on the field early, and most of the students were drunk and raising hell and were not too happy to see the band. But then the **P.A. guy** would say, "Let's meet the "1970 Edition of Your Hawkeye Marching Band." The band would come out on the field and everybody would go nuts. When I was a kid, I liked to watch the small high school marching bands— but the cadence when these guys came out just rocked. When I first started going to the games as a kid, the marching band was all guys, and it was better.

On fall Saturdays, you live and die—every Saturday—with the Iowa Hawkeyes. The whole week is so much better when they win. If they

> **Yankee Stadium is known as "the House that Ruth Built." The school that Babe Ruth attended in his youth, St. Mary's Industrial School for Boys in Baltimore—now called Cardinal Gibbons High School—was known as "the House that Built Ruth."**

> **The public address announcer for the Astros (Colt '45s) in 1962 was Dan Rather. John Forsythe, the actor, was the P.A. announcer for the Brooklyn Dodgers in 1937 and 1938.**

lose, it's not as good. While I've learned to temper that an awful lot as I've gotten older, during the game, I live and die with them. My emotions run the gamut. I run through the highest highs and the lowest lows—a fumble, or an untimely interception. It's *important* to me. It's an important part of who I am. My wife, who is originally from Minnesota, could never, ever quite understand that. It's just part of the fabric of who I am. She didn't have an allegiance to Minnesota so she just doesn't understand it. We grew up in a family where our dad was a Hawkeye fan. He talks about seeing the '39 Iron Men. He went back a way. He just had an intense dislike for Minnesota, just hated them, and he taught that to me.

Bill Bryson, from Des Moines, has written some travel books. In one of his books, I remember him talking about rolling back into Iowa City to see an old friend on a Friday night on a football weekend. He just kind of captured what it's like in downtown Iowa City on the night before a game. Sometimes in Iowa, on a football weekend, we even can get started on a *Thursday* night. It's just a big deal to the whole state. And now, I've grown up…and it still is now…and it always will be!

It's easier to follow the team now than ever. You can get together with a bunch of people no matter where you are. You can go to the Internet and punch up "Hawkeye Marching Band." Hit a couple of keys, and you're listening to "On Iowa." It's so easy to do stuff like that now that we were never able to do before. It just chills me to the bone.

If you don't feel something, going to Iowa City on a crisp, clear, beautiful fall Saturday afternoon when the place is just rocking, and you smell the brats cooking on the grills and hear the band playing, you don't have a pulse, as far as I'm concerned. You're not wired the way I am and you probably never will be. To me, you've got to feel it.

What's the definition of Gross Sports Ignorance?
144 Iowa State Fans...

ROOTIN' FOR THE HAWKS IS LIKE PLAYIN' HOOKY FROM LIFE

Mark Wilson

Life-long Iowa City resident, Mark Wilson, 57, is finally enjoying retirement after a 33-year teaching career. His Hall-of-Fame room contains 205 framed, valuable Hawkeye items. He is an Iowa grad and an Army vet.

As a seventeen-year-old freshman at The University of Iowa in 1964, Rhetoric was a mandatory class all students had to take. To fulfill part of that requirement, speech was an essential part of that course. I'll never forget my only "A" speech that fall semester. It was to be a three-minute speech about a personal experience. I decided to write a speech on how I snuck into Iowa athletic events as a junior high and high school student back in the early sixties.

One of my favorite and most daring attempts was with about 25-30 other boys. To watch the Hawkeyes play football in Iowa Stadium, we would climb the south end zone cyclone fence and perch ourselves on top. At a given call, we would all jump at the same time, mingle with the crowd, and eventually end up on the grassy, hilly area in the southwest or southeast corners of the stadium. Security personnel might catch a few of us and escort us out, but we didn't seem to mind. Ten minutes later, we'd be on our fence perch again, and in due time, we'd be in the stadium watching the game.

Another exciting entry into Iowa Stadium was to use half of a used Knothole ticket that was discarded on the ground. I would firmly pinch the stub with my thumb and forefinger. As I entered the stadium the ticket taker would just rip the half-ticket firmly held in my hand, and, once again, I was in the stadium ready to enjoy the game.

My friends and I would also sneak in with the band as they entered the northwest corner of the stadium. I'd quickly dart in between the tuba players, where there was a little more room, in a crouched position, so I couldn't be easily seen. There was no way that security would interfere, risk getting trampled, and disrupt the band's cadence while they were playing "The Iowa Fight Song." Once again, I was in.

Hiding in the cavernous bowels beneath Iowa Stadium was the most tedious and time-consuming attempt to sneak into an Iowa football game. In order to accomplish that challenge, we had to leave for the stadium 3-4 hours before kickoff. At that time, security had not arrived so it was easy to enter the stadium. We would then journey to the tunnel located in the northwest corner of the stadium. Once inside the murky tunnel, we would find a 16-foot plank, place it against a wall, and shinny up the splintered board to the roof of a concession stand. There we would wait quietly and patiently for hours until the National Anthem was played. Then we would climb down the plank, exit the tunnel, and quickly mingle with the crowd.

Sneaking into the Field House was risky and dangerous, but growing up in a college town as an teenager was always an adventure. My friends and I would always be exploring the campus buildings to create our own fun, thrills, and excitement. On one occasion during our summer vacation, we decided to climb the exterior ladder of the Armory next to the Field House to explore the roof and experience the scenic view of the city and west campus. Once upon the roof, we noticed several large vents, one of which was directly above the wrestling room in the Field House. Since it wasn't much of a drop into the wrestling room, we decided to squeeze through the vent and drop to the mats. During the basketball season, we used this method on several occasions.

Before I get myself into too much trouble, I'll end my Iowa athletic event "sneak-ins" with probably my most adventurous. To sneak into the Field House, my fearless friends and I would also take the underground tunnels beneath Iowa City. We referred to them as the "heat tunnels" because of the heat that was generated from the boiler pipes. One particular route started on Jefferson Street next to Central Junior High. We'd lift a manhole cover and climb down the steps. We'd journey underground traveling west through all of Iowa City, beneath the Iowa dam, up Grand Avenue, and eventually end up, to our surprise, in the Iowa Field House! We then found a small wooden door leading into an office or custodial closet, climbed through the opening, and walked out onto the metal bleachers ready to watch the Hawks play Big Ten basketball. It took hours. It was hot. We were sweaty, cramped, and tired, but it was well worth the effort because I'll never forget the game we saw that one afternoon when Don Nelson and Jerry Lucas battled it out on the court....

When Bob Commings was hired as the head football coach at The University of Iowa in 1974, I was thrilled and excited that a former student-athlete was back on campus taking the reigns of a dismal football program that had gone 0-11 the previous season. My first glimpse of Bob Commings, the player, was in the 1957 Rose Bowl game. I was only ten-years-old at the time and it was my very first Hawkeye game. My family and I took the train to Pasadena and saw the Hawkeyes beat Oregon State 35-19. From that day forward I became a loyal Hawkeye fan.

Coach Commings was a lot like Nile Kinnick in size and stature. He was 5' 9" tall and weighed only 173 pounds his senior season, but he wasn't a halfback like Kinnick, he was a guard, a damn good guard! He was so good that his teammates voted him MVP for the 1956-57 season. To support Coach Commings and his team, generate some personal enthusiasm, and negate some of the pessimism of the Iowa football team, I decided from the very first game to photograph and document everything that was positive about Commings' program at The University of Iowa. I watched every football game and many away games through a 200-millimeter telephoto lens trying to capture a special moment on the field of a player or players making a critical play for his team, whether it was in victory or defeat. I also photographed the fans, the marching band, and the cheerleaders in order to capture the true Hawkeye spirit on game day in Iowa City, Iowa.

After the season was over, I would choose approximately 150-200 of my best slides from the hundreds that I took and put together a slide tray of each football season. I did this for the five years that Commings was the head coach. After Commings' second season, an Iowa booster and neighbor found out that I was photographing everything that was positive about Iowa football. For the next three years, my slides were used at an annual outdoor kick-off party in the fall preceding the first football game of the season. Coach Commings and his staff, as well as other head coaches, assistants and special guests, were in attendance. Two slide trays of the previous season were mounted on a stand in a tree and displayed throughout the evening on the side of a two-story house. Guests seemed to enjoy the close-up action shots of exciting plays and various crowd, band, and cheerleading shots. Commings eventually used these slides on his recruiting trips in the Chicago area.

When Coach Commings' contract was not renewed after the 1978 season, I felt horrible for him and his assistant coaches. I knew how hard he worked to try to turn the program around. The evening that Commings was fired, I decided to go to his home and present him with the two large scrapbooks I compiled consisting of my favorite photographs and articles of everything positive during his five years as head football coach at The University of Iowa. Needless to say, I was very nervous, but I wanted him to have some positive memories of his football program.

When I knocked on the door, sweat was dripping down my arm—and this was in the middle of winter! His son, Bobby Jr., answered the door and I told him that I wanted to give his dad two scrapbooks that I had compiled during his reign as head football coach. Coach Commings finally came down the steps unsteadily and stood on the first step to greet me. I explained what I had for him. He thumbed through page after page in the scrapbook looking at the photos and newspaper articles. The last page in the second scrapbook was the famous "Man in the Arena" speech given by Teddy Roosevelt that my wife printed in Old English that evening. I felt these words really applied to the coach. While reading this speech, I noticed his eyes welling up with tears. He expressed his appreciation by trying to give me a rather firm pat on my shoulder. The only problem was that he missed my shoulder and slapped me on the side of my face. I tried to pretend that it didn't faze me, but boy, were my ears ringing! I will always remember the last words he said to me as I was leaving, "Thanks a helluva lot."

I am a home-grown Iowa fan. Just growing up, being here, seeing these players come to Iowa, perform like they perform, give it their best…there's the work ethic, the Iowa work ethic I see on the floor. Here they are, and I know they've had some darn good coaches, but people like Don Nelson, the Brands boys, Tom and Terry, right down the line with John Johnson, Sam Williams—all these athletes. They've meant so much to me because they've just given it their very best. I love to see a student athlete never give up. In a way, that rubs off on me. That's the way I have been all my life. I'm kind of an over-achiever of sorts. I get a lot of my inspiration from those teams that would just keep trying, never give up. I know they go through losing seasons. Sometimes in life and in jobs, you go through a losing "season" where things aren't going so well. They instill in you some pride and that never-give-up attitude. I guess I've carried that type attitude in whatever I have done with my life. Just keep going. Keep trying. Good things do happen to those who work hard. It has happened to the Iowa football team, as you know, when they started out under Kirk Ferentz with that dismal record, and then the last two years they've won 21 games. If you keep to it and stay with it, good things do happen. That's what these teams have meant to me.

IOWA IOWA IOWA IOWA IOWA IOWA IOWA IOWA IOWA IOWA IOWA IOWA IOWA

Your 1898 Iowa Hawkeyes

A LOAF OF BREAD, A DARK KNIGHT, A CHAPTER OF WINE AND THOU

George Wine

George Wine started his career in the athletic department of Iowa State Teachers' College in Cedar Falls. He moved to The University of Iowa where he served as Sports Information Director from 1971-1999.

Hayden was good to work with. I can't think of a really difficult coach at Iowa. Lute Olson was here for nine years, and he was good to work with. Tom Davis was a sweetheart. Ralph Miller was probably my favorite. He made himself so available, and he was so funny. Ralph Miller was one guy who could insult a member of the media and get away with it, and the media guy would go away feeling good—that was just the way Ralph Miller was. He'd go have a drink with a guy. He always made time for the guys. But then he might tell a guy, "That's the stupidest question…"

At the time Miller left for Oregon State, Evashevski and Nagel were having a feud. That detracted a lot from the 1970 championship season Ralph had. Ralph liked the limelight. Another thing is that Jean, his wife, was just getting more and more tired of Midwest winters. Between the two, when Oregon State came calling, it just seemed like the Nagel-Evashevski thing was never going to end— turned out it did end shortly thereafter, but it was still going on when he left. He told me one time that if we had a good morale situation at Iowa, he probably would have never left……

After losing to Jacksonville in Columbus during the NCAAs in 1970, we were playing Notre Dame back in the days when they were having those third-place games. **Austin Carr** of Notre Dame was

> Of the top twenty individual scoring games in NCAA Tournament history, only one name appears more than once: Austin Carr of Notre Dame. He has three of the top five, and five of the top thirteen.

unstoppable…but a talented Irish team was no match for Iowa. I was sitting on press row at St. John Arena. We were blowing Notre Dame away late in the first half. We had seventy-five points at halftime…75-31. With about two minutes left in the half, the Kentucky team walks in. They were playing Jacksonville in the championship game. They had to walk through the arena to get to the dressing room. **Adolph Rupp** came right by the press row. He looked up at the scoreboard, and he did a real double take. You should have seen that double take he did. When he saw the score, he looked around, and he had to get a seat. He wanted to sit down and watch the last couple of minutes to see what the heck's going on. His team had had really big problems beating Notre Dame, and we were handling them pretty good……

Ronnie Harmon was the best running back I ever saw. We had a team that had so much versatility that we didn't have to run him a lot. But when he got loose with the ball, he made some moves. Every once in a while, I'd just sit there and go, "Wow!" But he wasn't a guy you gave the ball to twenty-five or thirty times a game.

Hayden Fry was really different. He brought his whole staff in when he came, and then he hired McCarney and Alvarez to round it out. He had a terrific staff and most of them had coached together. That was a great advantage, and Hayden knew what he was doing. He didn't have a lot of ups and downs. He realized that you couldn't celebrate too much when you won or get too down when you lost.

He had two big issues, and he conquered both of them. One was the losing attitude—everybody had adjusted to defeat, including me, and we just went around with, "We accept defeat." The fans were still coming and we all thought, "Well, we'll probably win two or three games this year and that's the way it goes." He had to change that attitude in everybody—players, administration, students, fans, contributors, and press. He did a hell of a job doing that. He really did. He's such an upbeat guy, and he convinced his kids, especially,

> **Adolph Rupp, later to be a legendary basketball coach at Kentucky, coached Marshalltown (IA) High School to the 1926 state wrestling title. Rupp did not coach basketball in his one year at Marshalltown.**

that they could win if they would listen to the coaches. He convinced them that the coaches were going to try and do everything they could to help them to win. They started to be competitive and hang in there against good teams—he played Nebraska and Oklahoma very close. He didn't win either game, but he played really tough against both teams. The players recognized he knew what he was doing.

He also had to overcome the facilities…weight rooms, dressing rooms, training rooms…everything was really substandard.

Hayden got some commitments out of Willard Sandy Boyd, the president, who hired him. Boyd would tell you today that Hayden Fry was the only faculty member or coach he ever hired who interviewed him—the president—rather than the president interviewing him. He said, "Hayden came in and interviewed me." He said that Hayden had to get a commitment out of him—and he did it.

The first year or two Hayden was here, he really had to scrounge around and make do with pretty much what he had. He did make some changes. He had to have team meetings, and he didn't have a room big enough to assemble his team and have a meeting. We had to go over next door to the Basic Science Building which had a nice big auditorium.

Hayden now lives in Mesquite, Nevada. **Arnold Palmer** got him involved in that project, and he got in on the ground floor. He has a place there on a golf course, and they can play golf year round. His place here in Iowa City was for sale for a long time, but I think he has sold it. He comes back every once in a while. He and his wife have a lot of kids in Texas so they spend a lot of time there visiting them……

I liked Keith Jackson, **Brent Musberger**, and Dick Vitale. They were all pretty good people. I never got real close to them. I got to be pretty good friends with Bobby Knight. When my first wife was dying, he

Arnold Palmer designed the Bear Creek Golf Club in Denver. Above the urinals in the men's locker room is a picture of Palmer relieving himself against a tree at the club.

Brent Musberger was the home plate umpire when Tim McCarver made his pro baseball debut for Keokuk (IA) in the Midwest League in 1959.

was really kind to her and sent her some nice notes. As I tell people, he wrote her more notes than our own coaches did. He's just that way. It's funny. He's an interesting guy. But, he does not like for people to know that side of him. If you asked him about it, he would just slough it off—might even deny it.

I had a guy, George Dorrington, who was a salesman for our television network, who was dying of cancer. He still was sitting at the scorers' table doing the TV timeouts. Indiana came in, and Dorrington said to me, "You know, George, I've never met **Bob Knight**. I would really like to meet Bob Knight." Knight is so funny, you can hardly see the guy until the game starts. He comes out of the dressing room and strides onto the court the way he does. So I waited back by his dressing room and caught him on the way to the court. I said, "Bob, we've got a guy here at the scoring table who is dying of cancer. He really wants to meet you." He said, "What's his name?" I said, "George Dorrington." He said, "Let's go out and you point him out, and I'll talk to him a little bit."

There were over fifteen thousand people there, and it was just minutes before tip-off. Knight goes over, got introduced to George Dorrington, and they stand there and chit-chat for a while. Dorrington is just beaming. We get a photographer to take their picture. All the coaches were saying, "When is the game going to start?" You never knew where the heck Knight would wind up. I've seen Knight at press conferences where he would just do the dumbest thing, and then the next thing you know, he can charm people and be nice to people.

They used to shoot a gun off because that Field House would get so loud. When I was a student, they started shooting a gun off to make sure the official could hear it 'cause sometimes they couldn't hear that buzzer or horn. Maybe the horn came in after the gun. One time all the students were sitting at the end of the upper balcony there at the Field House. That gun went off and some student had a dead

In the 1962 NCAA semi-final—Ohio State versus Wake Forest—Billy Packer had 17 points while Knight failed to score. It was Knight's last college game, as he did not play in the title game.

chicken he'd brought up there in a sack. The student timed that thing perfectly—he must have thrown it with a second or two left so—the gun goes "BAM" and about a second later, this chicken comes flying down and hits the court. Splat! Imagine what would have happened if Bob Knight was coaching that night.

We opened Carver-Hawkeye in 1983. I would go down for the shoot-arounds, and then I'd take Bob Hamel out to lunch. Bob was the big sportswriter for the Bloomington, Indiana paper. Hamel was a well-known sportswriter in Indiana and Bob Knight's closest friend. We were talking at the shoot-around, and Knight was in a pretty expansive mood. He was just laying all kinds of wonderful things on the arena. He'd not seen the arena before. He said, "I'm glad your architect didn't have his head up his ___ like the guy who built our place."

That night we played, and Iowa won the game—close game. It was a tough loss for Knight. Some member of the Iowa media says, "Coach, what do you think of this arena?" Knight looked at him and said, "What about it?" The guy said, "Well, it's a new arena. What do you think about it?" Knight said, "Seen one, you've seen them all. What the hell's the difference? It looks just like the same damn thing all over the Big Ten, for cryin' out loud." A few hours earlier, he'd just been telling us what a great place it was.

Knight came out to The Lark the night before every game. The Lark was this great restaurant in Tiffin, about 10 miles west of campus. It was Dick Vitale's favorite restaurant in America. Bob always came out with a little entourage, maybe ten people, including Hamel, of course. They go out and have dinner. They get somebody to call **taxis** for them. The taxis show up and they go out to get in the taxis. Everybody is getting into the taxis and one of them leaves. The others are sitting there, and Knight says, "Let's go." They said, "We can't, Bob. Hamel's still in the toilet." Knight said, "Let's go." And they did, and left him there! And, it's not real easy in Iowa City to get from The

> During one off-season, Dave Cowens, the All-Star center for the Boston Celtics, drove a Boston cab for two months as a "life experience." Cowens claimed he took only one customer—an obnoxious Knicks fan—the "long way."

Lark back out to Kinnick at eleven o'clock at night. That's the way that guy is......

Al Coupee was covering the Hawkeyes on the radio and television when Evashevski coached. Al became a good friend of mine when I came back here and got the job as Sports Information Director. He wrote a book about The Iron Men called *One Magic Season*. Coupee used to get The Iron Men back here for a reunion. He was always the instigator and the round-up guy. He was a great storyteller and could just talk for hours about The Iron Men. He loved to tell Nile Kinnick stories. I really miss him and those other guys. I used to go to their parties. One night we were sitting around, and I kept hearing what a great guy Kinnick was. I said, "Oh, come on. Didn't he ever pinch a coed on the butt or spit on the grass or something?" "Oh God no. What the hell. Nile would never...." They were offended that I would even make a joke about that.

This university professor had assembled some letters from Kinnick to his family and friends and some that had been written to Kinnick. He put narrative in between them and suggested that Kinnick might have had sex before he died. I get a phone call from Coupee out in San Diego, and he said, "Did you read what that son-of-a b _ _ _ _ wrote? He said Kinnick had sex. Cripes, we know he never had sex." Coupee was just incensed.

I went to Kinnick's father's funeral. I got to know him quite well. He was a really neat little guy. He wrote me letters. He'd write one full page, single-spaced, and never have a typo or an erasure on it. They were chatty little notes. I've got them saved someplace. He lived in Omaha at 234 S. 89th, which happened to be in my aunt's neighborhood, same street. In about 1990, when he was well in his nineties, he fell down the stairs and died. We leased a plane in Iowa City and a few of us went out to the funeral. At the service, his nephew spoke. For some reason, his nephew decided he had to tell the audience that Mr. Kinnick had married his niece. I knew she was a lot younger than he, and I had met her before the service. Vickie Van Meter was on the plane with us. She was on the staff then. Her husband was related to the Kinnicks. We confronted him and he verified that Mr. Kinnick had lost his wife and a few years later married Nile's cousin.

I've got a good looking niece, about fifty years old, and I tell my wife she'd better watch out. She's available.

Derald Stump wrote one of the many books that have been done about Nile. Derald was an Episcopal priest. He was a chaplain at Penn State. The Kinnicks used to go out to Pennsylvania to visit family. Mr. Kinnick wrote me a note and said, "We're coming through Iowa City on such and such a date. I've never met Hayden Fry, and I would really like to meet him. If you can arrange a meeting, I would really appreciate it." I set it up with Hayden. I wrote back and told Mr. Kinnick that he would be able to meet Hayden. On the hour, he walked in with his wife. I took him to Hayden's office, and Rita said, "He's in a staff meeting, but he said to bring him right in." So we go into the War Room, and the coaches are sitting around the table, and he's got Snyder and Alvarez there. This was in the mid--eighties when Hayden was at his zenith. Hayden jumps right up and introduces Mr. Kinnick to everybody at the table. He said a lot of nice things about Mr. Kinnick and Nile, Jr.—all that Texas B. S. Finally, after he finished, Mr. Kinnick, who was a very small man, looked up at Hayden and said, "Well, Hayden, it's really an honor to meet you after all these years. I'm just glad to say hello to you without those sunglasses on your face." I thought his coaches were going to die.

Gus Shrader of the *Cedar Rapids Gazette* was the guy who, back in the forties, was trying to get the stadium named after Nile Kinnick. Mr. Kinnick stopped it at that time. He didn't think it should be named after one person. So they didn't get it done then since they didn't have Mr. Kinnick's blessing. Then in the early seventies, they started the drive again, thinking we needed something to boost our morale around here because we had those bad teams. This time, Mr. Kinnick gave it his blessing, and we changed the name, and, as they say, the rest is history.

We were playing Oregon State the day we dedicated the stadium name change, and I was talking to the Oregon State radio guy a couple of hours before the game. He said, "What's the story on Nile Kinnick?" I told him all about Nile up to the point of just before Nile died. The Oregon radio guy said, "Hey, would you get him for me at halftime?" I said, "Well, if I do, you're going to have one hell of an interview."

UPON FURTHER REVIEW

When we were kids, we'd drive down to Iowa City from Waterloo and look for a pretty distinguished looking guy. We'd get up ahead of him by four or five persons and would tell the ticket taker, "See that guy back there. That's my dad. He's got the ticket." Back then, there were no turnstiles, so we would just walk in. Sometimes, we'd have to end up sitting on the grass. Now, you even have to have passes to do that.

—JIM WITT, 68, Minneapolis

Two years ago, I went back to the Iowa-Iowa State game and ran into Gary Dolphin downtown. When he heard my name, he said, "I've got to talk to you. I've heard some stories about you." I'm thinking, "Oh boy, where's this guy coming from?" He said, "Come on up and do the second quarter with me in the press box." Iowa was kicking Iowa State all over the field the first half. I remember being in the press box and seeing some women from Iowa State and their gloomy faces. I kept thinking in the back of my mind, "Look at the tradition here. Iowa-Iowa State game, such a big rivalry!" I went and sat in the stands for the second half and all the Hawkeye fans were very happy, very pleased—we're up by 24-7, or whatever. Then, Iowa State came back and won the game. Seeing the range of emotion in that stadium turn from all the Hawk fans almost in shock to the Cyclone fans just going crazy—it was just something you had to be there to experience. I wasn't angry at the Hawkeye fans. I was just analyzing this as a fan. Of course, my love for the Hawkeyes was there, but just seeing this whole thing unfold in front of me and being able to observe it in a sane manner was pretty amazing. Kinnick is really quite a place to watch a game.

—JON LAZAR, 47, Former Iowa star running back

A few friends and I went down for the last home game against Michigan State in 1981, and we didn't have tickets. If Iowa won, and if Ohio State beat Michigan, Iowa would be in the Rose Bowl. This was back in the days before all the ESPN coverage. Somebody up in our part of the stadium had a little TV and was watching the Ohio State-Michigan game. As the game was ending, there were about ten guys standing and huddled around this little TV yelling, "Ohio State is going to beat them!" They counted down at the end—"ten, nine, eight..." It was over, and Ohio State had won. It began to spread around the stadium, and you could watch the crowd as they learned the news. It was like the wave, only slower moving. Then you heard this roar—it just moved around the stadium. It took about a minute, and the place just erupted. Down on the field, Fry didn't know what was happening, and he went over to someone in the stands to ask what was going on. Then, all we had to do was beat Michigan State, which we did easily, 36-7.

I remember being in a bar in downtown Iowa City later that night. It was probably about midnight. The goal posts had gotten torn down. There were girls standing up on the bar dancing, kicking over glasses and bottles. Everyone was into it—it was just out of control. Then, all of a sudden, doors opened and in came a bunch of students yelling and screaming and carrying one of the uprights from the goal post. A perfect day.

—MIKE McGREGOR, 48, Phoenix, AZ

I got caught one time sneaking a keg into Kinnick. They confiscated it and took it out to a security hut on the tennis courts. At halftime, we were going out to Melrose Market to buy some beer. As I walked by the security hut, I looked in, and said to a friend, "You know, I bet I can take that keg back from them." They weren't guarding it very well. I crawled in on my belly, took the keg, rolled it out. I actually got it in a second time and got caught the second time with the same keg inside the stadium—by the same guy who caught me the first time. He physically bumped into me, turned and looked at me and said, "Excuse me." The reason he bumped into me was because I was so big—carrying the keg under a rain poncho. I had borrowed the poncho from a guy there to sneak the keg in. I saw him with the poncho and said, "Can I borrow the poncho?" He said, "No." I said, "Oh please, I need it to sneak this keg in." He said, "Really? You're going to sneak that keg in? Yeah, I'll let you borrow it." Still the second time, they didn't even kick me out. That was then. Nowadays, you'd probably go to jail.

—BRIAN DeCOSTER, Iowa City

Kinnick brings back memories to me of being a child, going there, bundled up in blankets, drinking hot chocolate, trying to stay warm and watching a football game. It's a college football field—not like other places shared with professional sports or concerts. It's big and impressive and historic and ignites a feeling in you of college football. At Kinnick, the crowd seems like they're right on top of the field. There's no running track around the field. Everybody is up, making noise, and enjoying themselves. It's kind of an intimidating atmosphere that just gets your adrenalin going.

I had a friend from my high school days who, when we were in college, had a little too much to drink and went into the stadium, missed the first step trying to go down the steps to the student section, took a tumble, rolled all the way down the steps to the barrier at the bottom row, jumped up, threw his hands in the air, and screamed, yelled, and cheered for the Hawks. He saw a friend of his who was working the netting line at the goal post, pointed to him and waved, and then turned around and walked back up to his seat and sat down without realizing he'd completely shredded his jeans all down the back—basically had flashed everybody in the student section while he was jumping around and cheering and yelling after falling down the stairs.

—SEAN CONNELL, Rochester, Minnesota native

Every year before the season started, my dad would let us pick one game that we could go to. In 1985, I said, "I've got to go to the Michigan game." My stepmom, Ann, his new wife, said, "I think I'd like to go to the Michigan game this year." She's not even a football fan. She ended up going to the game—the game between the two top-ranked teams in the country. I ended up going to the '85 Illinois game. Ten years later, I was talking about it, and she didn't even remember going to the game. It still upsets me to this day. I could have been there—I should have been there. It's come and gone, but there'll never be a game like that again.

—CHUCK JOHNSON, 32, Ankeny, IA

I was working on the *Daily Iowan* when I heard the news that Kinnick had died. Somebody called in with the information, and then it came in over the wire. I guess our thoughts were that he was invincible. He was a guy, 24 years old, who you felt was a man 45, when you talked to him. He was very, very mature. I had interviewed him twice. He was already in law school when I came to Iowa, and you could tell there was an air of greatness about him. It was a tragic moment. I thought, even then, that we'd lost a truly great person. Later on, in retrospect, and in talking to all the people who were associated with him, he's the guy who would have been governor, maybe been a presidential candidate. He was out of the mold of John Kennedy—that kind of a person. He was one of the true great ones. He was a very nice guy. He wasn't big, only about 5' 8". He couldn't run fast. He couldn't jump high. All he could do was win football games. I was the first one to recommend that they name it Kinnick Stadium. I sent a letter to President Hancher. He sent me a nice letter back and said, "Well, we realize how great a person Kinnick was, but many men will die in World War II, and we should wait on this." So, we did. Then in 1972, they finally did name it Kinnick Stadium.

—JIM ZABEL, WHO Radio 1040

My first wife, a very fine lady, was dying of cancer while Nile was in the service. I got letter after letter from him. Now he had many people to write to—a world of friends and family—but when the letters came it was just like a guy walking up to you, putting his arm around your shoulders and saying, "Look old buddy, if nobody else is with you, I am." This is the sort of thing that…it gets you. The day I got the word on Nile…that was no day to want to be around living. But, wherever he is, he's doing a lot of good for someone. I'll say that. And he's somewhere. You wouldn't want to waste a guy like that. The time that he spent here was not wasted. He proved so many things. He wasn't trying to—he just did. He did it all in such a nice way. Nothing he achieved ever rang any bells with him personally. He did it because he was able to do it—it needed to be done and he did it. He proved one thing, that college athletics could be beautiful Everything that can be said that is good about college athletics he was—he didn't represent it—he was it.

—TAIT CUMMINS, on a WMT Radio Commentary, 1974

I met Nile Kinnick in '39. He had been up in the press box doing an interview after the game. I was there with a high-school friend, Bill Shuttleworth, whose father had played at Iowa. Bill was a very good athlete and was following in his father's footsteps. His father introduced

Kinnick to both of us. I don't remember asking him anything. I was just frozen.

Nile's father would occasionally come to Iowa City and would visit around. I got to know him a little bit. He was a professional man, very small of stature, a very proper type of individual. You could tell where Nile got many of his speaking traits. At the time of Nile's death, the news and the papers were full of so many deaths. Young men were being killed by the thousands. The whole aura of the thing was just one tragedy after another. There was mourning going on in many, many, many families. This was a shock, but this was just another fatality of World War II.

—BOB BROOKS, 78, Cedar Rapids

I have a regulation football, and I wrote on it, "To Bruce. To a great athlete, a great guy. Best regards. Nile Kinnick." This was about ten years ago. I show this football to people at parties and they go nuts, not thinking that I wasn't even born when Nile Kinnick was alive… or that I grew up in Maryland. They tell me I ought to have it in a glass case. They go, "Geez, Hopp, you ought to have this thing in a glass case. You shouldn't be handling it and getting it dirty." "Look at this, Mary, 'To Bruce, a great athlete, a great guy, best regards, Nile Kinnick.'" They never figure it out.

A football has four divisions on it. On the opposite side of the "Kinnick" ball, it says, "To the Hopper. A real, real tough, hard-nosed athlete. Best of luck. /signed/ Attila the Hun."…A friend of mine used to say "calling Bob Knight "Bobby" is like calling Attila, the Hun, "Tilly."

—BRUCE HOPP, 46, Cedar Rapids

I remember in 1961, my dad, mom and I drove up from Ottumwa to see Iowa play Wisconsin for Homecoming. It was unbelievable to me. Here I had been this young kid listening on the radio and there I was, eleven years old, walking into that stadium. That was the first major stadium I'd ever seen. The biggest thing I'd seen before that was the high school football field that seats 5,000 people. You walk in there…the place where the Hawkeyes play! I'd been listening on the radio all these years when these guys had been running up and down the field and scoring those touchdowns —this is where it happened. This is where all that noise came from. I was just over-whelmed. It was just incredible.

My mom didn't work. My dad worked at the Hormel meat pack-ing plant. He made three to five thousand dollars a year back then. We had five kids in our family so to go to one Iowa football game a year—that's all we could afford—was a big event. We weren't desti-tute, but we were lower middle class. The Hawkeyes were a really big part of what we did.

—MIKE KIELKOPF, 54, Jacksonville, Florida

When I was younger, the goofiest thing I saw was the black and gold striped bib overalls, very bright paint. They were awful. Unbeliev-able numbers of people wore them to the Iowa games. They brought them back this year. It's part of the throwback deal with Kent State. People want to get something that's a throwback, but these things were hideous. At least, we beat Kent State badly....I saw a guy throw a cold can of beer that hit Bo Schembechler in the head at an Iowa game. That was pretty classless. There used to be a lot of drunken-ness at the games, but now they do more to control that. The bad thing is that some of the college kids are too drunk when they make it into the game.

—DENA SATTLER, Publisher, western Kansas newspaper

In 1964, my brother, who was going to the Iowa medical school, knew the guy in charge of sales at the stadium so he got me a job sell-ing programs and souvenirs. I was able to make $100 to $150 each game. It was a great deal. But in 1965, when we were the pre-season number one pick by *Playboy* magazine, I was all excited—and we end up going 1-9. I didn't have a chance to sell anything—people would throw stuff at me. Here I was looking forward to making my $100 for a Saturday afternoon...I made zero! After the first game, I made nothing. It was just ridiculous. That went by the wayside.

—CHUCK McGREGOR, 57, Phoenix, AZ

Nile Kinnick was my babysitter. My father was an orthopedic sur-geon for the Iron Men. On Friday nights, the team didn't go to motels like they do today. They would put two or three players with different families in town. Most of the time at our house, it was Nile and Bill Green because my folks were just in love with Nile.

I was about a year and a half old. A lot of people don't know, when Nile's plane went down, it was in sight of the carrier, and they saw it sink. They thought he would get out, but what a lot of people don't know is that Nile was a Christian Scientist, and he had a bad shoulder. He would not let my father operate on his shoulder. Dad's thought always was that Nile couldn't get the canopy off the airplane because of his shoulder. That play against Notre Dame that he scored on to win, the play went in and it was supposed to be run to the right, but that was his bad shoulder so when he got in there he told Al Coupee, "We have to run this left because of my bad right shoulder," and he took it in from the left side.

I vaguely remember being in a sack race at City Park with him and Bill Green, who was another of the Iron Men, who ended up working for Maytag. My mother, until the day she died, could not listen to that record, *Hooray for the Hawkeyes*, where Nile gave the speech for the **Heisman**. Eddie Anderson, the coach was my Godfather. He was wonderful. He'd do surgery in the morning and would coach in the afternoon.

—DICK THORNTON, 67, Des Moines

In 1939, the Heisman Trophy winner was Nile Kinnick of Iowa. He is the only Heisman Trophy winner to have his university's football stadium named after him. In 1934, Nile Kinnick was Bob Feller's catcher on an American Legion baseball team.

Name the Northwestern Coach— Win valuable prizes...

NILE KINNICK HEISMAN AWARD ACCEPTANCE SPEECH

"Thank you very, very kindly, Mr. Holcomb. It seems to me that everyone is letting their superlatives run away with them this evening, but none-the-less, I want you to know that I'm mighty, mighty happy to accept this trophy this evening.

Every football player in these United States dreams about winning that trophy and of this fine trip to New York. Every player considers that trophy the acme in recognition of this kind. And the fact that I am actually receiving this trophy tonight almost overwhelms me, and I know that all of those boys who have gone before me must have felt somewhat the same way.

From my own personal viewpoint, I consider my winning this award as, indirectly, a great tribute to the coaching staff at The University of Iowa, headed by Dr. Eddie Anderson, and to my teammates sitting back in Iowa City. A finer man and a better coach never hit these United States, and a finer bunch of boys never graced the gridirons of the Midwest than that Iowa team in 1939. I wish that they might all be with me tonight to receive this trophy. They certainly deserve it.

I want to take this grand opportunity to thank collectively all the sportswriters, and all the sportscasters, and all those who have seen fit to have seen their way clear to cast a ballot in my favor for this trophy. And I also want to take this opportunity to thank Mr. Prince and his committee, the Heisman award committee, and all those connected with the Downtown Athletic Club for this trophy, and for the fine time that they're showing me. And not only for that, but for making this fine and worthy trophy available to the football players of this country.

Finally, if you will permit me, I'd like to make a comment which, in my mind, is indicative, perhaps, of the greater significance of football, and sports emphasis in general in this country, and that is, I thank God I was warring on the gridirons of the Midwest, and not on the battlefields of Europe. I can speak confidently and positively that the players of this country, would much more, much rather struggle and fight to win the Heisman award, than the Croix de Guerre.

Thank you."

Chapter 2

Fandemonium

IF "MR. HERRMANN" COULD LIVE HIS LIFE OVER AGAIN, HE'D LIVE OVER A BAR

Bernie Lowe

Bernie Lowe is a towering figure in Iowa and Arizona insurance circles. Booted out of the University after less than a week on campus as a freshman, he later became co-owner of Voice of the Hawkeyes.

O ver the years, I met a guy who was a Purdue graduate who had a job in Des Moines. We used to work out together at the Y. He was an older gentleman. We became very friendly and decided we were going to go to a Purdue-Iowa game in West Lafayette. He belonged to a Catholic fraternity so we went and met all his friends. We had a wonderful time. We decided we'd do this on a home-and-home basis. The following year—1979—the Purdue guys came back to Iowa and my friend and I met them. The friends from Purdue who had made the trip got drunker'n hell. As we walked into the game I could tell this one guy was going to be a problem. We decided that I was going to introduce him as Mark Herrmann's father. Mark Herrmann was the Purdue quarterback. I introduced him as the father of Mark Herrmann, the Purdue quarterback, from Carmel, Indiana, and a nice guy. He proceeded to get drunker and drunker and became more abusive. Phil Suess was the quarterback for Iowa that game. His father came over and introduced himself to "Mr. Herrmann." The people I sit next to are very nice people, very straitlaced. I wasn't drinking because I was so nervous about having to watch him. I went down at halftime to do something, and when I came back, the guys who sit next to me were about ready to beat "Mr. Herrmann" up. He'd gotten more abusive.

The game was very close and with three or four minutes left in the game, I looked over and he was looking at the field with his hand over his right eye. I asked him what was wrong and he said, "I'm seeing double." Here we are with Iowa going for the winning touchdown. We hadn't beaten Purdue in the last twenty times we played them. Iowa was marching down the field, and he said, "I've got to take a p—." I said, "The game will be over in a minute and a half. Hold still." He said, "I gotta go." I said, "Just sit down." I turned away, and within a second, he'd stood up…he had these double-knit pants on, and he was leaking through his pants. Here it was coming through his pants, hitting the ground. This woman there had a fancy black outfit with fringe on it. She said, "My God, that awful man is urinating on my coat." It was just unbelievable. Finally, the game ended, and some guy came down and said to him, "You're a disgrace to the state of Indiana, to your son, Mark, and to Purdue University." It was really a bad deal. I was driving that day, thank God. We went back to the car, and he immediately passed out. He was totally soaked. I looked down at his shoes, which were black leather, and they had turned white and the toes had turned up—like an elf's shoes. You can only handle a couple of events like that in your life.

Sharm Scheurmann, who was a friend of mine, called me the following Monday and said, "Oh boy, it's all over Iowa City what happened with that guy who was with you." The sad thing is I wasn't drunk. I was kind of an innocent bystander. I was always afraid this would get back to the real Mr. Herrmann, and we'd get some kind of a lawsuit. It died down. Two years later, we went to Iowa City for the Purdue game and "Mr. Herrmann" was with me, but he'd quit drinking by that time. I wore a Long Ranger mask, and I had a diaper bag like mothers carry that has baby powder and diapers in it. They all laughed about it, but that was a pretty bad deal. They still talk about "Mr. Herrmann."

Say what you want about Minnesota…
Frankly, "Losers" comes to mind.

OUTSIDE OF A DOG, A BOOK IS MAN'S BEST FRIEND. INSIDE OF A DOG, IT'S TOO DARK TO READ.

Mike Kielkopf

Mike Kielkopf, 54, a professor at the University of Jacksonville, is one of the most traveled, interesting and creative graduates ever from The University of Iowa. He was raised in Ottumwa, lettered in baseball at Iowa and has taught at universities in South Africa, the Mideast and the Ukraine. Twenty years ago, while a reporter at the Rock Island Argus, *Kielkopf wrote a paperback book called* How 'Bout Them Hawkeye Fans! *It was an intense labor of love, interestingly done and when no publisher expressed an interest, he published it himself. Printed by the Julin Company in Monticello, Iowa, it sold thousands of copies.*

I've always been a Cubs fan and an Iowa fan. Growing up in Ottumwa, I was a very serious part of both fandoms—teams that didn't win—Cubs and Hawkeyes…for all those years. The Iowa people went to Iowa City because they were loyal fans. They just wanted to support the team the best they could. I felt that was a quality that ought to be recognized. That's why I did the book. The players come and go. The coaches come and go. The administrators come and go, but you know very well people have been going to the Red Sox games or the Cubs games or the Hawkeye games for 50 years, and they wouldn't miss it. Those are the people who "are" those teams. It's not the players. It's not good coaches. It's not all the other stuff. It's the people who go sit in the seats and pay the money they don't have to watch a team like the Cubs or the Hawkeyes. Those people deserve some recognition. That's really my bottom line motivation—these people need to be given some credit. A lot of times, they're taken for granted and abused in all kinds of ways by the organizations. There is no team without the people in those seats.

It says on the book: By: Mike Kielkopf and the Hawkeye fans themselves. I didn't just want to do it myself. I didn't just want to give my impressions of what Hawkeye fans are. I wanted them to speak for themselves. There is a lot of my material in there, but, mostly, there is a lot of material from all kinds of people in the book.

So, how was I to get that information from a wide segment of people? I don't know if I did it the best way possible, but what I ended up doing was creating a questionnaire that explained at the top what the project was. I went from Rock Island in the Quad Cities to Iowa City and distributed it at football and basketball games and wrestling meets. I just went there and gave it to people asking them to fill it out and give me their information and mail it back to me. I asked them for pictures—telling them they wouldn't get the pictures back so give me copies instead of originals. If you send me some nice pictures of anything related to the Hawkeyes, we want to put those in the book. We want your favorite memories. We want your favorites: athletes, coaches—all those different things.

It's been long enough ago that I don't remember exact numbers, but I got a significant number of responses. Almost all of them ended up in the book, at least to a certain extent. I remember there's a picture in there of a guy wearing a Hawkeye sweatshirt and cap, leaning against his hot-water heater, which has some kind of a Hawkeye hot-water heater wrap around it. I got pictures of people's personalized license plates. I got pictures of kids' bedrooms decorated in black and gold showing all kinds of handmade stuff. This is what this means to people. This is what they do. They wrap their hot-water heaters in Hawkeye garb. They paint their driveways with a Tiger Hawk. They do all these things because this is a very meaningful part of their life. They spend money and time and the sense of loyalty they feel is very deep-seated. That's the message I was trying to get across, and I wanted them to be able to say it in their words and not for me just to comment on it.

I learned that it is a lot easier to write a book than it is to sell it. Most major publishers are arrogant, lazy, out-of-touch with their customers, liars and cheats; plus, they don't know how to sell. Marketing is the key…it's the whole ballgame.

At that time, Penney's had what they called the Hawk Shop within their stores. I took it to the managers of Penney stores in Iowa, especially some of their big-city stores, Des Moines, Cedar Rapids, etc. I said, "Here, I've got this book. I'd like to place it in your Hawk Shop." I took it down to the Iowa Book and Supply in Iowa City and made a deal with them. I just literally took it myself—put boxes in my car and drove it around to these particular retail outlets. I took out an ad in the Iowa Alumni Magazine and sold a few that way. I could only barely afford a print run of 5,000. We ended up selling between three and four thousand. At that time, "How 'Bout Them Dawgs," was popular and was a cliché that Iowa fans were using—a lot of schools were. I got lots of letters from people who said, "This is great. It's unbelievable that somebody would write this about Iowa fans and include my information in there." I also wrote to some celebrities like Tom Brokaw and Lute Olson, who at that time had just left and gone to Arizona, and to **Hayden Fry**, who was still there. Those people all wrote back and gave comments about their relationship with the Iowa program and their view of the Iowa fans. Those are published in the book.

Brokaw said something like, "I was there in '57-'58. I had to transfer 'cause I was spending too much time watching the Hawkeyes and not enough time studying." I got a nice reply from Lute and Bobbi Olson and from Hayden Fry. Governor Robert Ray, who was governor for so many years, a well-known big Hawkeye fan, answered. I thought it was kind of nice that those people took the time to reply. Those are in the book.

I sold it for $14.95. When you read any kind of book, whether it's a novel or whatever it is, there are many opportunities where you make personal connections with the situations you are reading about. You

> **When Hayden Fry was a high school teacher and coach in west Texas, one of his homeroom students was Roy Orbison.**

go back, and you read about it, and you go, "Oh yeah, I was there when fans waited in the Field House until one o'clock in the morning for the Iowa basketball team to come back after they beat George-town and made the Final Four. I remember that. I hadn't thought about that for a while, but I remember that." So, even though my book is twenty years old, I think people would still enjoy reading about those events......

Having been in those international schools overseas and having kids from more than 50 countries, one of the things I did—I like to have a very lively classroom—I put up about a hundred quotes, some of my favorite quotes, some about literature, some about writing, some just about life in general. I call that my "open textbook," and would use those on a daily basis. I put up my American flag, and I put up my Iowa flag. Every once in a while, we might be talking about democ-racy or personal liberties or whatever, and I'd point to the Iowa flag and say, "Look at that and tell me what that motto is." It's right there on the flag—'Our liberties we prize and our rights we will maintain.' That's what we're talking about when we talk about American democ-racy and about the state of Iowa, in particular. That's what we're talking about. Do you understand that? That's a very clear state-ment—'Our liberties we prize, and our rights we *will*'—not, will try or maybe—'maintain.' That's a tremendous motto. I've been sad-dened by some of the things I've seen and heard and know about in terms of the changes that have come about in Iowa in the last few years where I don't think that motto is being lived up to.

After a while, the students start to understand what people from Iowa are like. It's the old "Iowa stubborn" thing where they understand that part. They understand that whenever I tell them something, I mean it. I don't feed them a bunch of baloney. They leave with a whole different impression of Iowa and the Midwest and, maybe, the United States than what they came in with. I try to just do it that way—just be who I am. If they like it, fine, and if they don't, then that's fine, too, but they know they're going to hear what I have to say. I would take the globe down and set it on the table. I said, "Let's look at this. Where is it that people are living pretty well. We've got the United States and Canada. Mexico, maybe? Central America—I don't know about that. South America—I don't think so. Asia, China, Russia, Eastern Europe. So you end up with Western Europe, which is much smaller than most people think, The United States, Canada, Australia, Japan—okay. You look at the rest of the world. Africa, South America, Asia, Eastern Europe—what do you have? Most people in those places are living in the same conditions that people lived in a thousand years ago" A lot of us don't understand that. They don't really stop and think about that. They never really stop and look at that globe and say, "Where would I want to be? Where are all those people who are doing so much better than we are? Where are they?" Well, they aren't there.

My folks are just people who are honest, hard-working people. If they had not grown up at the time they did, they could be college presidents and CEO's or whatever they wanted to be. My dad went into the Air Force in World War II. He had gone through eighth grade. They gave him the IQ test, and he scored 132. I'm sitting here in a university office today because he went to war and gave me a chance to do that. He's more than I am. He's never done anything with his career other than working in a factory. He's a helluva man.

Iowans understand that people have intrinsic value. It doesn't matter if they're a university professor or if they're a meat packing plant worker, they deserve your respect. Working hard counts. Being honest means something. You give your word—you live by that. There is no option. That's Iowa!

When Joe Paterno takes his glasses off, does his nose come off, too?

ROCK, CHALK, IOWA HAWK

Dena Sattler

Dena Sattler is the editor/publisher of the Garden City Telegram, *in Garden City, Kansas. Dena has attended the first two Iowa Fan Fests. She was raised in Burlington, and graduated from Iowa in 1984.*

As a kid going to the games, Iowa had twenty consecutive losing seasons. In those days, you would cheer loudly *for a first down!* Believe me, scoring was a bonus! The first downs were a cause for celebration.

I lived in Ottawa, Kansas when I heard Iowa was having a Fan Fest. It sounded to me a lot like the annual Cubs convention. My dad and I had gone to those, and just had a terrific time. The Iowa Fan Fest was a "meet and greet" with players and coaches. It gave you a behind-the-scenes look at how the football program worked. I was pretty excited, but my husband was a little reluctant—he's not quite the Iowa fan that I am. His father hadn't started dragging him, when he was eight years old, to the games like mine did. We went to the first Fan Fest in downtown Iowa City. The first night it was pretty informal. A good number of players were there just meeting with fans, having conversations, taking time to sign autographs.

We got to meet Dallas Clark. We were impressed with what a genuine, down-to-earth guy he was. We met Fred Russell and Robert Gallery, which is an impressive first meeting for anybody. The guy's just a mountain, but a really nice guy. We met a number of people and got to talk to them so it was fun to watch them play after that.

Every fan received an Orange Bowl football that you could get signed. I brought a lot of my own things. I took some game programs and had the players who appeared on the game programs sign those. I keep them here in a curio cabinet in my home. I have a sports room where I have loads of Hawkeye and other memorabilia. If it weren't for the Fan Fest, I wouldn't have an opportunity to have most of those memories.

The second Fan Fest was in Cedar Rapids at the Collins Plaza. They did that to actually emulate what they do on a game weekend. They took you through the routine—the discussions they would have with players, the pre-game talks. The players were not quite as accessible as at the first Fan Fest. Maybe it was because there were more people. They didn't give you as much opportunity to talk to them as they did the first year.

My husband and I go to all the home games—a 22-hour round trip. When I was a kid, my dad and I went to a number of road games. Here we're really out of the way for any of Iowa's away games, but we don't miss the Hawks on TV. Iowa sports have been, for us, an escape. Like the Cubs, there are a lot of Iowa fans everywhere. We had so many losing seasons that it's so good now that you have to take it all in. After all the bad games I sat through…and I sat through a lot…it's not hard to drive eleven hours one-way to go to a game now. There's just something special about football Saturdays in Kinnick Stadium.

Wisconsin:
First in Beer,
First in Cheese,
Last in the Big Ten.

HE'S JUST A REGULAR GUY WHO SOMETIMES WEARS A CAPE

Joe Sample

In November 1994, Iowa student, Joe Sample, went with some friends and their fathers to the Iowa-Minnesota game at the Metrodome. That night he was on ESPN.

I decided to make a costume. It was basically a gorilla outfit without the mask. Then I had a big yellow flag with the "I" on it and used it as a cape. I went to the game in that outfit, plus had some Hawkeye logos painted on my face.

We were there with my buddy's dad, Mike Betz, who is a big-time banker and his lawyer friend, Richard Heitman—both from Minnesota. The lawyer and the bank guy said, "Hey, why don't you jump down and run out on the field?" You can drink in that stadium so we were doing some heavy drinking. During the fourth quarter, with about seven minutes left in the game, I jumped down from the end zone and a couple of security guards came down and tried to get me. They missed me, and I kept running, and another guy dived and missed me. Right through the middle of the game, I ran end zone to end zone, with a security guard chasing me the whole way. The crowd was just roaring as I'm going—cheering me on. People on the sidelines were moving their hands to "go...go...go!"

It was crazy. I just got caught up in the moment—being on stage in front of seventy thousand people. It was loud. I could hear everything going on. As I ran down the field, the crowd just kept getting louder and louder. There were more Iowa fans there than there were Minnesota fans.

I did a little Heisman pose when I got to the end zone. Then, about seven security guys came in on me and they took me away. It was on ESPN SportsCenter show that night. Kenny Mayne said, "He's at the twenty. He's at the ten. Iowa Batman in for a touchdown." I had run about a hundred and ten yards, and I was dead tired by the time I got to the end zone.

The security guys were pretty friendly. They took me back to a back room and let me watch the game from there. My buddy's dad called the police and came down and picked me up. The police gave me a disorderly conduct ticket—I had to pay a hundred dollar fine.

Then after the weekend, I went back to Iowa City, and woke up on Monday morning, and there I was—on the front page of the newspaper—the security guard and me running across the twenty-yard line, stride for stride. It was pretty cool; I was an instant celebrity.

I always liked to go to The Airliner when I was in college. I got to know Randy Larson, the then-owner, pretty well. I was in there early one night, and there was going to be an Iowa-Northwestern basketball game later that evening. Randy Larson said, "Why don't you get that gorilla suit on and go to the game?" I'm like, "I don't know." Well, he passed a hat around the bar to get money and collected a little over three hundred bucks if I would do it. I went and got my gorilla suit on, and came back to The Airliner. Randy held the money for me, and let me drink a little bit for free there in the bar. He had gotten me tickets to the game. I was right on the first row. I was high-fiving Herky, talking to everybody and having a good time. I had a buddy of mine go to the other end of the court when there were about seven minutes left in the game. Mon'ter Glasper was getting ready to inbound the ball, and I ran onto the court holding a little mini-basketball. By this time, Glasper had inbounded the basketball. I collided with him. I lost my ball, and the Northwestern guy gets it at about half court. I said, "Give me the ball." I grab at it. I ran down and jumped on the Northwestern player's back and got the ball. There were mixed reactions from the crowd on that one. Security escorted us out of the arena, and gave us disorderly conduct tickets—a hundred and ten dollar ticket. Randy had someone there with bail money. They paid my fine and everything. They booked me, and I was out within five-ten minutes. Randy took me back to The Airliner. Newspapers found out I was there. They called and did phone interviews with Randy and me. I don't know if Randy did it to get some free advertisement or what. After that my buddies and I, still in the gorilla suit, went out and went to each bar and everybody at the bars was buying us drinks. I got the three hundred dollars and ended up not having to pay a cent for the bail or the ticket or for the drinks.

It was just some stupid stunt a dumb young college kid did back in '94 that got turned into something huge. That was it—I haven't done it again. I've been interviewed about it since then, and told them, "You never know. You might see the gorilla again someday."

IOWA IOWA IOWA IOWA IOWA IOWA IOWA IOWA IOWA IOWA IOWA IOWA IOWA

Michael Crow with a Hawkeye banner in Al Asad, Iraq.

GREAT SCOT
GREAT HAWK

Dr. Lyell Hogg

*Lyell Hogg is an oral surgeon in Clear Lake, Iowa. He and his child bride, Susan, have been married for a dozen years. Hogg grew up in southwest **Scotland** and is an alumnus of Iowa.*

I've been an Iowa Hawkeye fan since 1992. I had grown up in the United Kingdom and didn't know anything about Iowa, had never even heard of it until I met my wife, Susan. She was an exchange student studying at the University of Glasgow. I started dental school there, met her, and one thing led to another. I ended up transferring and finishing my dental degree at Iowa.

A friend of mine in dental school took me to a football game in October of '92. Iowa was hosting Ohio State. It was pouring down rain, and Iowa was getting their tails kicked. It was amazing to me that there were seventy thousand people sitting there watching this happen in the pouring rain. It was something completely foreign to me. At the same time, being at the game was just so great…there is absolutely nothing like being at an Iowa football game. The atmosphere in Iowa City prior to the game, being at the game—it's just one of the most exciting things I had ever done. From that second, I just kind of caught the bug. I didn't know much about football, so I educated myself. I watched a lot of games on TV. It just disappointed the heck out of my wife. She thought she was marrying this nice, wholesome Scottish boy and she wouldn't have to deal with that entire American sports-fanatic thing—and look at what I've become.

> **Until the late 1950s, the British Open was played on Wednesday, Thursday and Friday. Saturday was set aside for a possible playoff. It was illegal to play golf on Sunday in Scotland.**

She went to Iowa State University, for which I forgive her. There was a turning point that occurred only a few years ago. Iowa State was playing Nebraska in Ames, and we were watching the end of it on TV. It was when Iowa State beat Nebraska, and she turned to me and said, "You know what? Those Iowa State fans are going to be insufferable now." I'm like, "Okay. Now I know that you're an Iowa Hawkeye fan."

Being an Iowa Hawkeye fan is kind of like being in a secret club. Every year, like all Iowa fans in general, I follow the Hawks, and walk around with this chip on my shoulder because no one ever thinks that much of Iowa. It's just farm country, and we're a bunch of hicks. Especially the last few years, it's just been an amazing experience to be a part of the Iowa fandom to follow the Hawks and be so proud of the football team. It's kind of like this brotherhood, this secret-club bit. You just have a link whenever you meet another Hawkeye fan, you understand what it's like to be nuts about the Hawks.

Coming to Iowa for the first time, the big thing to me was how darn flat this place is, how straight the roads are. That surprised me, growing up in Scotland where you can't see more than half a mile ahead of you because there's either a curve in the road or a hill in the way. In Iowa, you can see forever. I guess I've got a little bit of a skewed perspective because my wife and her family lived in Cedar Rapids, which is a big town. There you don't get this feeling like you're out in the country. Driving into Iowa City, it's a modern city. You hear recruiting stories about kids who are coming from other states to look at the University. They have heard that we all walk around with overalls and bibs on and a piece of straw in our mouth and all of us work in the fields all day. Then they get here and find it's this modern civilized place where you can actually have a fun time.

One of my hobbies is to put together highlight videos after each win. I post that on a website for other people to see. I've been contacted by various parents of current players and have gotten an e-mail relationship going with some of them. When I was down at Fan Fest this year, I actually met Matt Roth's mom and mentioned some videos that Matt was in. They love that kind of stuff so I introduced myself to Matt and told him who I was. He's three times the size of me. He said, "You're Scothawk! Are you kidding me?" I got a very similar reaction just before the Outback Bowl last year. One of the assistant coaches had contacted me through the website. Apparently it's a daily ritual for some of the coaches and players to get onto the website and watch the videos. He asked me if I would mail copies of the videos I have because they wanted to show them to players and they might show them to recruits. I thought that was awesome. At Fan Fest this year, I had a chance to meet several coaches, Coach O'Keefe and Norm Parker, who were just as nice as could be about the fact that I do this. Anything I do through the website, I always try to do in as positive a manner for the Hawks as possible. It's been neat to meet some of those people just through what I do as a hobby.

I've had no education or training on how to do these videos or websites. Actually, it came about as a fluke. I got a new Macintosh laptop, and I was just fussing around with it one day. I had a new video camera and somehow figured out that I could import video into my hard drive. The Apple Macintosh is known as *the* machine for dealing with digital media and digital content. There was a discussion on HawkeyeReport on one of the boards, about how people were complaining that most of the highlight videos they see are just really generic and never have any good music. I wondered to myself if I could do something like that. Tim Dwight is one of my all-time favorite Iowa Hawkeye football players. I took a short excerpt, and put it to music. Then I put some basic graphics and titles on it and, presto. It just grew from there.

It was a lot of fun for me to put it together and I got a great reaction when I posted it on HawkeyeReport. The fans went nuts, and it just fed on itself from there. I don't even want to tell you how much money I've spent on computer equipment. I've just taken the time to educate myself and buy books and DVDs and learn how to use the software and upgrade the software as I go. It does take a lot of time to do, but it's a lot of fun. I have a patient wife, thank God.

The easiest way to get to the website is to do a Google search for Scothawk. Or you can ask on HawkeyeReport and people there will direct you to it.

My website isn't commercial, and I don't charge any money for it whatsoever. As far as distributing it, I don't do that either. I spend a lot of my money doing this. With the music copyright laws, that is definitely a concern to me. I get a lot of people who contact me through the site asking me to sell the DVDs and videos to them. I'm not interested in doing that. I make a good living in my professional career, and I'm not here to make money doing that.

It's a lot of fun that there are so many websites about Iowa sports. It has its pluses and its minuses. The pluses are that it brings everybody together. You could live in California or on the other side of the world, and you're able to check up on the Hawks every day. Not more than a few hours goes by every day, even at work, that I don't get on HawkeyeReport and check on recruiting or just see what's going on. You almost form a relationship with some of those people you've never even met. It's kind of weird.

But, at the same time, it has a negative, in that you can have people who tend to type and write whatever they want and have no consequence for it. I know for a fact that players and coaches and recruits and families of those people look at those sites. If Iowa is trying to recruit a certain guy, and he reads negative stuff about him coming out of the mouths of Iowa fans, then that can have a negative impact on recruiting. For the most part, I think it's positive and is a good way for people to express their opinions and frustrations and delights and whatever.

I have an elaborate home theater system, upgraded to include two extra sound channels on the immediate left and right of the viewing area. It makes watching football just rock. On the road games, there are usually a lot of people in the basement watching the Hawks on the big screen. Then we usually have other Big Ten games going on the other two screens at the same time. It's a lot of fun. When we built the basement, I made sure to put in a beer-tapper and popcorn machine so it's a fun place to be on a Saturday afternoon. If you can't be in Kinnick, it's *just about* as much fun—but not quite.

The devotion and intense interest just shows a lot about people who are involved with Iowa athletics and the University as a whole. All you have to do is look at the likes of Robert Gallery, Dallas Clark,

Tim Dwight—these are the guys you want to emulate, even in your professional life because they came from very working class, rural backgrounds—maybe not Dwight, but both Clark and Gallery did. They're all about work ethic, working hard, applying yourself, doing more than you ever thought you could. That just speaks to the heart of what Iowans are about. They remind me a lot of the type of people I grew up with in Scotland. Scotland is also a very rural, farm-oriented society. You deal with down-to-earth people who are not going to look down their noses at you, who are going to give you a pound of flesh every single day and go home happy about it. That's what makes you proud to be part of this state and part of the University.

In Scotland, people are involved with **soccer** teams and rugby teams, but it's not on the same visceral level that Iowa fans seem to be on with their sports teams.

My biggest wish for Iowa would have to be an Iowa football national championship. If that were to happen, I don't even think I would make it through the game. I don't know if I'd make it to kickoff. The amount of sheer stress that it would put upon a Hawkeye Nation, as a whole, I don't know if many fans would be able to take it. If we got to the national title game, it would be a dream come true—unreal. I'd need to take a defibrillator along with me, especially if we won.

> **More U. S. kids play soccer today than any organized sport, including youth football. The reason so many kids play soccer is so they don't have to watch it.**

THE REASON NORTHWESTERN HAS TWO DIRECTIONS IN THEIR NAME? THEY DON'T KNOW IF THEY'RE COMING OR GOING.

SO SAY YOU ONE, SO SAY YOU ALL

A few years ago, a bunch of guys from Cedar Rapids were going up to Camp Randall Stadium in Madison, Wisconsin for the Iowa-Wisconsin game. Wesley Ralston was driving. Right after they crossed over the bridge in Dubuque into Wisconsin territory, Wesley turns to Jimmy Jones, in the front seat, and says, "Jimmy, I sure wish I had my console TV with us today." Jimmy says, "Console TV? We're going to an Iowa football game. What the heck would you want your console TV for?" Wes says, "Well, if I had my console TV with us, we'd have our tickets. Right now they're setting on top of that TV back home in Cedar Rapids."

—BRUCE HOPP, 46, Cedar Rapids

I always envisioned myself being a Hawkeye growing up and being an Iowa basketball player. I can remember the 1980 season when Iowa went to the Final Four. I was fourteen years old at the time, and was playing junior high basketball. I had all the moves of Ronnie Lester and Kevin Boyle and had Vince Brookins' shot. I must have played those different guys in my driveway a million times. The football team at that time had just started to come back. I can remember running like Ronnie Harmon, hitting like Larry Station and thought about being those guys, too. If you're interested in Iowa, and you go to a game at Kinnick, as a kid, it's hard not to dream about being one of those guys.

—TOM KAKERT, Iowa Grad, Writer

I went to school with Nile Kinnick. I worked at the Memorial Union—worked my butt off to get my degree, and I'm ever so proud of my degree at Iowa. With the training table there, the athletes all came so I met him there. Then, later, I was in Business Organization, Corporation Finance, Labor Economics, Money and Banking classes with Nile Kinnick. I often jest that he got the "As" and I got the "Cs." He was a brilliant guy. My formative years, 1926 to 1936, I lived in North Liberty which had a population of 161. Now about 7,200 people are there. I went to University High School from 1932 to '36; The University of Iowa from '36 to '40. Now, everyone wants to know Kinnick. He was a marvelous, wonderful person, very modest.

I was in the Army in Ottumwa, Iowa when I heard Nile Kinnick had been killed. It was a shock. You just couldn't believe it. He was an invincible person. Why him? In 1943, when he was killed, there were things happening every day—bad news every day. Nile's father was a great guy. He didn't want anybody to glamorize Nile because there were so many in that era who were paying the price. I guess my favorite Hawkeye memory is the win over Notre Dame on November 11, 1939, in Iowa City, where a Cinderella team came and gelled and did the impossible to beat these big giants. That was a really big thing.

I remember the south end of the stadium, especially when rabbits used to be there and occasionally during the game, one would run out. Even more exciting was for a dog to chase that rabbit. That would happen, but not too often. When I was a kid, Knothole was ten cents. In the deep Depression, when money didn't mean much—what am I saying—it meant a lot. In grade school, you could go to an Iowa game for ten cents; whereas, in high school it was twenty-five cents. That was for a few years. Following the Hawkeyes is a full-time job. This morning I sent four tickets to the widow of a dear friend, Paul Grange from Waterloo. He died recently and won't enjoy them, but his family will. Following all the Iowa Hawkeye teams has brought tremendous enjoyment. As a matter of fact, maybe I spent too much of my time following and worrying and feeling pressure, etc. I really couldn't do much about it. Now, all along, I'm just a spectator. It meant a great deal to me. You talk about the Johnny-come-lately fan; well, I'm just the opposite. My wife is a good Iowa fan. She echoes most everything I say. We go to the games together. She's a great fan. I met her in typing class, and I decided she was just my type.

—CHARLIE SMITH, 86, Iowa City

There had been three different stations with their broadcast teams broadcasting Iowa sports when it was decided to go with one outlet. I grew up listening to those guys so I knew there was a lot of pressure. I tried not to dwell on who I was replacing, other than just trying to do a good job. I came into that booth with twenty-six or twenty-seven years of experience so it wasn't like I had never done an Iowa game.

I'd done Northwestern for six years prior to that, so I'd done the Big Ten for many years. I'd done a thousand high school games. From a technical standpoint, there wasn't really any pressure from me to do that first game but if you think about who you're replacing, certainly you're a little on edge, not so much that they're not supporting me, because they all did, as well as Podolak and Hansen, but how would the listener react? Here's a guy from Cascade, Iowa, for crying out loud, and for the most part, they hadn't heard me do games. It took some time and I daresay that after seven-eight seasons, I still have people I need to win over who will always be a Jim Zabel, Ron Gonder, or Bob Brooks fan. Well, you know what? So will I. I understand that.

I feel like I have a huge advantage in growing up in the state, understanding how radio and the Iowa fan are intertwined, how they depend on each other. I think I had a good understanding of that coming into this job, and I've always tried to carry that with me. At the same time, I've tried to combine some of the talents of the three guys that went before me—Zabel with his love and his passion for Iowa athletics. He didn't care if people called him a homer. Gonder, with his not only excellent play-by-play call, but his down-home humor. I am a firm believer that you've got to have fun while you're on the air. It's a game. It's not a battle in Afghanistan or Baghdad. Then you have the consummate professional in Bob Brooks, who always did it by the book. What you see is what you got with Brooksy. He never deviated off center court. He always had a very professional, responsible play-by-play call. Brooksy had his sayings, but he never got too gushy or humorous on the air. He always felt that he was there to do the game, and a lot of people agreed with him because he's covering Iowa to this day to the tune of sixty years. I respect Ron Gonder as much as anybody because when he turned sixty-five, he just upped and walked away. He doesn't miss it one bit. He and his lovely wife, Pat, travel. They go to Alaska and host a lot of tours and trips. He doesn't miss it one bit. And yet Zabel and Brooksy wouldn't be without an Iowa football game in the fall. They're always there, if not in person, in spirit, listening, and they're still actively involved in the broadcast side. So I always tried to combine the talents of those three into my broadcasts, and have we done that perfect broadcast? Certainly not. We keep striving for it.

—GARY DOLPHIN, Voice of the Hawkeyes

We were tailgating at the Magic Bus. It was Homecoming. Rick Derringer was playing on top of the Magic Bus, which was quite a feat for Brian, the owner of the bus, to pull off—to get a guy like that to play there. I had to go home to meet my parents for a little birthday dinner, and it was a long walk back to my apartment. My buddy, Crazy Tom, came up and said, "Don't worry about it. I got us a ride." We hopped in this KNRA-Radio van and started back to my place. About halfway back to my apartment, the car phone rings. It turns out that the people, the local radio station who own the van, want it back. I'm almost home so Crazy Tom drops me off and takes off in the van. I assumed he was taking it back. The word was that they found it at a bar that night. About a year later, I was at the same tailgater. The same DJ who was always leaving his keys in his vans and getting them locked in his van was there. I told him about this story where I'd been at a party and needed a ride home and a buddy of mine grabbed the van and took me. He was pretty upset about that, and he told me he didn't like me very much. The radio station got a hell of a lot of good publicity out of that, I would say. It was all over the news and all over everything. That's why you probably wouldn't want to use my name. At the time, I was pretty much oblivious.

—ANDY PONGRACZ, Iowa City
(Not his real name. His real name is Aaron Whalen)

Twenty years ago, my wife and I had four season tickets to Iowa football games—before our divorce. It was a fair divorce. She got the inside of the house. I got the outside…plus the luggage. In the process of the divorce, I didn't get my four tickets—my wife kept them. My wife had possession of all four of the tickets so I didn't have any tickets for the Michigan home game on a beautiful fall day in Iowa City. I go down and stand on the corner in front of the stadium at Melrose and hold up my index finger, indicating I needed one ticket. Here comes a vehicle by, and I happened to be looking the opposite way. The driver honks his horn.

I turn around, and he almost runs over my toe. It's MY brand new van with my friend, Kenny Mostaert, driving it with my wife and her friends in there. And I've got my index finger up for a ticket. My wife looks out the window and shows me a different finger...and flashes the four tickets with her other hand.

I'm standing there with my finger up for one ticket, and Mostaert, my best buddy, is driving MY van. We had always gone down to the games together. There's Kenny and his wife and my wife and a few other neighbors. So there go MY season tickets, MY new van, MY best friend, MY wife and the farm! She was the only child, and her folks owned the farm, so I lost it all. Kenny Mostaert told me I was the only guy he knew who won the "Iowa Lottery" and gave it back.

...and Mom thought my life wouldn't work out.

—TOM CORRICK, Superintendent of the Bennett (Iowa) School District, native of Elma, Iowa

Our fan following is unbelievable. I had the theory that I was the "fan at the game." I got excited. I represented the fan. Some of the newer broadcasters who have come along are kind of what I call "computer heads." They have all the stats, but they leave the human element out of it. Football coaches are involved in X's and O's. Athletic directors are involved in programs. The fans are involved in the emotion—and so was I. I was an emotional broadcaster.

—JIM ZABEL, WHO

Tom Arnold usually comes back for one of our big games every year. We always have him on the air. He's a unique guy, a different character. He's fidgety, always jumping around, can't sit in one spot for longer than two minutes. His television show has been wildly successful. He always seems to land on his feet. There's not a bigger public persona out there in terms of being an Iowa fan than Tom Arnold. Right after Robert Gallery won the Outland Trophy, he took a couple of autographed Hawkeye jerseys to Arnold on his Fox show. Tom had the Hawkeye helmet in the center of the table. It's fun to look at the other guys—the John Salleys of the world, Chris Rose and some of those guys—and watch their reaction to Arnold's passion for the Tiger Hawk. It certainly gets Iowa millions of dollars worth of free publicity throughout the year. It's fun having Tom out there as a beacon for Hawkeye athletics.

—GARY DOLPHIN, Hawkeye announcer

I think the Hawkeye fans are as loyal as any group of people in the country. There was no doubt in my mind that our people were the greatest fans. A lot of people say that, but we always have statistics to back it up. The relationship between the fans and the players is second to none. You see what happens when we get in a bowl game. We take over other states. Our people are awesome. We are the "pro" team in the state. On football Saturdays, the entire state gets together for a big family reunion so to speak.

I grew up in Iowa, so close to the University, and so people were able to start following my career at a very young age. You get a relationship with people just through your playing days in high school. Then all of a sudden, you're playing in Carver-Hawkeye Arena. It grows from that. I tell people that if I had a chance to do it all over again, I'd go to the same school without thinking twice. It was a great opportunity—a dream come true from the time I was a kid. It all comes down to it being a nice feeling to look into the stands and see people you knew and had connections with. Right now, the relationship is still wonderful. It's so nice to stop and talk to the people on the street.

—JESS SETTLES, Former Hawkeye Basketball Star

David Cook, my very best non-football friend at Iowa, died today. He lived in Fallbrook, California. When you would go to away games, the Iowa students would hold hands and make a tunnel as you came out of the locker room before the game. My senior year, when we went to Minnesota, it stated in the paper that the students would not be allowed on the field by the tunnel. No more. Before the game, they had all these Boy Scouts, 50 on each side, there at the tunnel. As we were running through, there was David Cook right in the middle of those Boy Scouts holding hands with them. We both graduated at the same time. The day after we graduated, he showed up in this old convertible and said, "I'm going to California. Do you want to go?" I would love to have gone, but my dad was dying of cancer at the time. David Cook came up every fall for the last seven or eight years and would go to two Iowa football games. He *was* a Hawkeye fan!

—LOU MATYKIEWICZ, Coal Valley, Illinois. Iowa Letterman '52, '53 and '54.

In the Quad Cities, the biggest Iowa fan would be Wayne Wood. He's involved with the booster club and now I think he's with the national I-Club. There was a guy named Tommy Thompson, a real estate guy, up here, and they got me going to the I-Club. They asked me to emcee a few times. Those guys would drive at 4:30 in the morning to the Johnson County I-Club breakfast where Hayden would come and talk. They'd tape it, and drive it back to the Quad Cities. Back then, they had their I-Club meetings over at Velie's in Moline. They'd play the tape there for a noon luncheon. Those guys did that for years and still do it. Wayne goes to every away game no matter where it is. He's probably the biggest, gung-ho Iowa fan I know. He makes a great Bloody Mary soup before the games!

—THOM CORNELIS, sports anchor, KWQC-TV

The old Field House was a great place to see games. When Iowa went to the Final Four in 1980, Dan Gable's team had just won a national championship. On Sunday night of that weekend, there was a huge pep rally in the Field House for them. It held twelve or thirteen thousand people, and it was completely filled. Dan Gable and the wrestling team came in with the band and cheerleaders, and people were all screaming. Then, about midnight, the basketball team walked in after their game, and the Field House was still packed. I remember Lute Olson saying, "Don't you guys know it's after midnight on a Sunday night?" The crowd went crazy again.

I want the old Field House back because Carver-Hawkeye is just a sterile place to play. You don't get a very good sound level down at the floor in Carver-Hawkeye. When I was a freshman in medical school, I got season tickets, and was in the last row—the top row. I could yell and nobody would hear you. In the old Field House, you were on top of each other. One nice thing about the old Field House is that above the wooden bleachers, they had metal bleachers. You had to stand up because, in the winter, people would be coming in wearing boots. Their boots were right next to your butt. The snow from their boots would melt and get your butt wet. You'd end up standing up so you wouldn't get your bottom wet, so that was good. Then you could cheer better. When the students would be gone, you could buy general admission student tickets and you could sit wherever you wanted to in the student section.

—CHUCK McGREGOR, 57, Manson, Iowa native

When I was a kid, for my birthday, my folks would take me to one Hawkeye football game a year. Back then my dad listened to KGLO, Mason City, which had their own announcer, Ken Kew, who ended up being the mayor of Mason City. That was back in the days when Iowa had twelve radio stations…and they all did play-by-play. I'd be hanging around my dad at the radio. He'd get all excited about the Hawks. In 1957, when they played in the Rose Bowl, we had to drive to a friend's house, about five or six miles north of town, because we couldn't get the NBC affiliate. I remember driving out to their farm high on a hill, and they could just barely get the Rose Bowl. It was all snowy. That was my first recollection of being a Hawk fan. That was when I was about six years old. The first time I walked into Iowa Stadium almost took my breath away. I was a little kid, about eight, from a small town in Iowa. To this day, when that fight song plays before a football game, I get chills! During the '72 season, Alex Agase was the coach for Northwestern. As one of the student managers, I was running the game ball in and out to the field, keeping it dry. I'm on the Northwestern sideline. Iowa scored, and I'm there cheering. Coach Agase comes down to me and says, "I want you to knock that off." I said, "I'm just a good Hawk fan." He says, "You're going to be a dead Hawk fan if you don't get away from me." That's exactly what he told me. It scared me enough that I moved—down and away about fifteen yards—but I kept cheering!

—MARK JENNINGS, Iowa Foundation, from downtown Hanlontown, Iowa

IOWA IOWA IOWA IOWA IOWA IOWA IOWA IOWA IOWA IOWA IOWA IOWA IOWA

Jim Bain can't be on the $25,000 Pyramid because he doesn't have a clue.

Chapter 3

Put Me In Coach

It Was a Ball

RANDY DUNCAN IS A LAWYER. WHY DID YOU THINK HE WAS A STOCKBROKER? "I HEARD HE HANDLED JUNK BLONDS!"

Randy Duncan

Randy Duncan was all-everything at Roosevelt High in Des Moines before becoming a consensus All-American quarterback at Iowa. He was second in the Heisman voting and was the first overall choice in the 1959 NFL draft. He spurned the Green Bay Packers with their rookie coach, Vince Lombardi, and signed with the AFL for their inaugural season. Forest Evashevski calls Duncan the most improved, most pleasant surprise of all his Iowa players. Duncan was picked College Player-of-the-Year by three organizations in 1958, but many older, randy Iowans remember him for an incident at the end of his sophomore season.

When I was a sophomore, there was a reporter—I don't know where he was from—calling up all the ball players. "What do you want for New Year's Day when you go to California for the Rose Bowl?" All of them were saying, "A victory over Oregon State." I wanted a victory over Oregon State, but I said, "Hey, I want a date with Jayne Mansfield."

Somebody in the Los Angeles area picked it up off an Iowa story, and they must have gotten in touch with her before the Big Ten banquet they had every year. The banquet was in Los Angeles, and Bob Hope was the emcee. I remember Bob Hope said, "The first time I heard the name Forest Evashevski, I thought it was a park in Russia."

There we are at the banquet, and all of a sudden Hope introduces Jayne Mansfield. She said, "I want to see one of the Iowa football players, and his name is Randy Duncan." Oh man, I got right up there. I grabbed her and gave her a great big smooch. It was great! She was really put together. There's a picture somewhere. I had both hands on both her buns. All my teammates are yelling at me—I became a hero overnight to my teammates. The place was going wild. She didn't say anything, just went along with the gag.

When I went to Iowa it was mid-year, and they just put me on the hamburger squad where I played defense for the whole spring semester. That would have been normally my senior year in high school. Freshmen weren't eligible to play so I just played on the hamburger squad all year. Another quarterback was Olen Treadway, an all-state quarterback from Oklahoma. We had a lot of good players, Bob Jeter, Willie Fleming, a great football player who only played here one year then played in Canada for twelve, and Alex Karras, great player.

A lot of players went to Solon to drink so we wouldn't be downtown—we'd be invisible. I never heard of anybody getting caught because back in those days, they didn't enforce the twenty-one year-old rule.

I played football in Canada, and there were a lot of Iowa guys up there: Kenny Ploen, Calvin Jones, Ray Jauch, Willie Fleming. They paid better money then than the NFL. Then, I was with the Dallas Texans for a year. The next year, the Dallas Texans became the Kansas City Chiefs. Hank Stram was the coach. It was okay, but I always thought I should have been starting, and Stram didn't. They were starting a guy named Cotton Davidson from Baylor. After that, I went to night school at Southern Methodist and got my law degree and have been practicing law ever since as a trial lawyer.

If I had to do it all over again, I'd probably do it just the same. You know, I think you should never look back—no regrets, no fear of the future. Every now and then, people with long memories bring up the Jayne Mansfield thing.

When we played **Indiana** in Bloomington in 1957, it hadn't rained down there in Monroe County for three months. We go out to warm

> **Indiana University ranks twelfth in winning percentage in Big Ten football history...behind the University of Chicago.**

up, and the field is a quagmire—mud all over the place. We came back in the locker room and Evashevski had smoke coming out of his ears, "I've never had a coach water a field on me." He just ranted and raved. We go out and just killed Indiana. After the game, we're flying home and Bob Flora, an assistant coach, sat next to me. He said, "This game really reminds me of a game a few years ago when Notre Dame came to Iowa City. Evashevski got all the coaches up at midnight to go out to the Iowa Stadium, turn on the hoses and flood the fields so we could slow down the fast Notre Dame running backs."

Randy Duncan and Jayne Mansfield

EXPERIENCE IS WHAT YOU GET WHEN YOU DON'T GET WHAT YOU WANT.

Jon Lazar

Jon Lazar was an All-Everything star at South Tama High School and was the Hawkeyes' blue-chip recruit in 1975. For three years he led the Hawks in rushing and twice in receiving. The former fullback and '78 captain lived in Indianapolis for 17 years and is currently a vice-president with Reman Technologies in North Carolina.

As a young kid, it's all new to you. Kinnick was so big and so enormous that you look at it with a totally different perspective than you do now, but it's still electrifying regardless of how you look at it. My older brother said to me, "See that player down there. I was in a wedding with him last year." I was thinking, "Boy, that's really a big deal." Never would I have thought that in ten to fifteen years I was going to be playing on that field—walking out onto that stadium and being in front of those thousands of fans and representing The University of Iowa. It's something that would never have crossed my mind. It was kind of like a dream and a fairy tale, all in one.

To me, the best part about being a Hawkeye fan for so many years is that you just live the game—walking into Kinnick Stadium or even years back when they used to have the old Field House, you could just feel that electricity going through the stadium at those times. Now when you go back to Kinnick, it's the same way. You're excited. You start walking toward the stadium. You can smell the cut grass and the tailgate parties going and hear the band playing—the whole excitement is so electrifying—it just seemed to, and still does, put the chill down my spine every time I go back to a game. I think a lot of Hawkeye fans relate to that because that's the way they feel when they go back to these games.

As a young player, when you're being recruited by Iowa, you see and feel the electricity in that stadium. You know that you're going to have the opportunity to go play in that stadium. You walk out on that field, and those fans are just going crazy. You're playing not only in a beautiful stadium, but you're playing against some of the best teams in the country. When you walk out onto that field and hear the support of the fans, and even back in the days when we played, we still had a lot of people coming to the games, and we weren't winning ten games or 11 games. That alone tells about the true Hawkeye fans.

I left the year before Hayden Fry came so there was that wish that I could have played for him. The teams back in the seventies weren't doing as much redshirting as the teams do today. Your freshman year today, you're usually going to be a redshirt, which is going to give you that extra year to mature. A team that was doing it back then was Nebraska. They were doing a lot of the redshirting, and that was when they had a lot of the great teams. They had that whole program down to where you didn't play **varsity** when you were a freshman. I played varsity when I was a freshman, but only played about five home games where I ran down with the kick-off team and lost a whole year of eligibility. If you really think about it, a redshirt would have been really great, and that would have put me there playing one year under Hayden Fry.

I remember the first time I signed an autograph for a fan. It seemed like such a neat thing. I'm sure it was pretty messy. It was the kind of thing you accepted with the territory because people knew who I was coming out of high school. It was really neat to be able to do that and see some little kid get a big smile on his face. That was gratifying.

When I try to show my kids my scrapbook and say, "Hey, that's your dad," it's like, "Yeah, okay." But, our family is pretty active in sports, and we'll sit down and watch hockey and other sports. Once I take my kids back to an Iowa game, they're going to be hooked. Once they see the stadium and walk in and see the excitement, the band— there's a lot of different things to watch there in the stadium. Our

"Varsity" is the British short form for the word "university."

band's great. The cheerleaders are always doing something funny. There are always little things going on out on the field that make it remarkable to be there.

As a father, I think it would be great if my son would grow up to play football at Iowa. You don't realize, when you're going through it as a player, how proud your father is of you. I would be very blessed to have my children do well. My daughter's going to be athletic. She's got some talent. You just don't know. I'll give my son a kicking tee and tell him to stay off offense and defense and be safe!

From seventh grade through my senior year at Iowa, my mom made scrapbooks for me. She did the games. She did pictures. She did everything. It was pretty amazing to me just to go through them and look and get a feel for what was going on from your perspective today. I even had some tapes on Beta from the Bob Commings' shows.

When I was a senior, there was a freshman linebacker named Todd Simonsen. We went to Indiana for a game and our rooms were in a horseshoe shape. There was a little courtyard, and I could see across into Coach Solomon's room and would see players go in and out of the room. I had Coach's voice down pretty pat so I called Todd Simonsen's room. I said, "Bring your playbook and come to my room 'cause we're going to have a meeting. I'm going to put you on special teams tomorrow." So, this freshman gets all excited, grabs his playbook and comes running out of his room, which I could see from my room. I could see him running all the way around this courtyard and coming up to Coach Solomon's door. He knocks on the door, and Coach Solomon opens the door. Todd walks right on in and plops himself down. The coach said, "What are you doing here?" Todd said, "You called me up and told me to come over here because you were going to put me on some special teams for tomorrow." Coach said, "I never called you." Simonsen is going to kill me when he reads this!

Iowa turns out pros... Miami turns out cons...

THE WORLD WAS DIFFERENT WHEN LOU PLAYED. FOR ONE THING, IT WAS FLAT.

Lou Matykiewicz

Lou Matykiewicz was a hard-nosed, all-round athlete in south suburban Chicago a half century ago. The big galoot graduated Blue Island High School in 1951 and headed for the great unknown—Iowa City, Iowa. Matykiewicz is enjoying his retirement in Coal Valley, Illinois.

Bump Elliot recruited me because he had the Chicago area. Richard Rumke, an attorney in downtown Chicago, an Iowa grad, took four of us to Iowa City. Before that visit, I had never—never—thought about Iowa. Our coaches at Blue Island High School were anti-Illinois. I don't know any reason why, but they hated Illinois. The trip was very impressive to me. That was over fifty years ago, and the practice fields and locker rooms weren't anywhere near what they have now, but they were a heck of a lot better than our high school's were. There weren't any lockers, but there were steel cages about six feet high and about three feet wide where you could hang your things and leave your equipment after practice and games. When you had two-a-days, the electric fans were blowing. When you came back the second day, everything was dry. You walk in and you have clean socks, clean underwear, clean jock—all laid out in your locker. I was impressed with that—but any high school kid would be impressed back then. Going to Iowa changed everything about my life. I was the first in our family to even consider going to college. It opened up a whole new avenue for me.

In '52, as a sophomore, it was two-platoon—in and out—everybody in and out. I played defense. The following spring, they switch it to one-platoon. If you came out in that quarter, you could not go back in during that quarter. I had played quarterback in high school, and Jerry Reichow was the Iowa quarterback, but he couldn't tackle your grandma, so I did most of the starting.

Tait Cummings' son, Cameron, and I roomed together for two years. Cam wasn't a starter but lettered for two or three years. I would spend time with his dad, Tait, and he would try to pronounce my name…he never did get it right. We'd drink chocolate milk and eat graham crackers. Tait would speak at a lot of banquets. He was so popular in the eastern part of the state. Tait would give Cam and I speaking engagements. We'd go out and get fifty bucks for them. I remember speaking at the Anamosa Reformatory. The coach at Anamosa High School at that time was Larry Lawrence's dad.

Evy had a tower built. It was about twenty feet high. During practice, he'd climb up a ladder, and he'd stay up there. He had a bullhorn. He could see both the offense and the defense and see what was going on. Practice would start at three o'clock, but everybody had to be out there by two-thirty to run formations and do specialty practices. The coaches weren't out there one afternoon, and Cam got up on the tower. He got the bullhorn and said, "This is your God speaking"—imitating Evy. And, of course, Evy and the other coaches happened to walk on the field a little early that day. Evy said, "Cam, you'd better be able to fly down from that tower—if you're God. You'd better not climb down."

We were up at Minnesota my senior year, and we got beat 22-20. We punted, and I'm covering the outside, and the kicker is coming right across the field, right to where I think I'm gonna really lay him out. I get about six inches from him, and he gets hit from the back, and his head snaps in my face. Nobody wore facemasks then. It busted my nose all over. We're trying to stop the clock 'cause I'm hurt. But one of *our* players was faking an injury, and the trainers ran right by me—there with blood all over my face—to the guy who was faking an injury. I've got a picture of me, which was in *Sports Illustrated*, walking off the field after that game. We were the visiting team, so we had white jerseys on, and my jersey and my face were covered with blood.

George "Binky" Broeder was our fullback. We had another fullback named Roger Wiegmann, who was really good, also. Binky was the coach's favorite. Roger was good, and he was always bitching, "I'm better. I should be playing more." We encouraged Roger to go see Evy and tell him that he definitely should be playing. So he did. Roger goes in there, and we're all waiting outside the door. We don't know what's happening. Roger comes back out. We all said, "What happened?" Roger said, "I told Evy I'm gonna try harder." That was the end of it.

The '53 team had a reunion last year, and it was great. Nine years ago, I had hip replacement, and it was the best thing I ever did. I feel great, everything's great. Don Chelf, a tackle, had a hip put in, and he could hardly walk at the reunion. He said it just didn't work out for him. We had drinks served, and more than a handful had to say, "No, no, no. I'm a recovering alcoholic." Dusty Rice was there. He retired as a Major out of the Army and then went to work for Wal-Mart in Bentonville, Arkansas. He has a couple of children in Cincinnati and he's living there now. Dusty was probably one of the finest halfbacks ever in the Big Ten until he got hurt. Both his ankles and his knee were all banged up. Jerry Hilgenberg looked real good…but we were all older than we've ever been before!

IOWA IOWA IOWA IOWA IOWA IOWA IOWA IOWA IOWA IOWA IOWA IOWA IOWA

The Answer is Jesus! What is the question? The question is: What is the name of Felipe Alou's brother?

IF THERE WAS A SPONGE THAT CLEANED UP BROKEN DREAMS, WOOLWORTHS WOULD STILL BE IN BUSINESS

Jay Bickford

Jay Bickford was on the Iowa football team from 1995 to 1999, four years under Hayden Fry and one year under Kirk Ferentz, playing as a defensive lineman the first two years and offensive left guard the last three. Originally from Poughkeepsie, about an hour north of New York City, he is a teacher at Mid-Prairie Middle School in Kalona, Iowa. He is a Ph.D. student at The University of Iowa. He was an Academic All-Big-Ten in 1998 and 1999.

I've been an Iowa Hawkeye fan since December of '94 when I came on my recruiting visit. I never thought I'd come to Iowa. I had other visits lined up; you could take five. I figured I'd come to Iowa and see what it looked like. I wanted to see corn. I was joking with my friends, telling them that I'd bring them back corn because we had all these misconceptions of just a complete redneck environment Iowa was going to be. I came here, and once I got on campus and started walking around, the people absolutely amazed me. It was amazing how nice the people were—they opened doors for me, they'd give you a little nod when they were walking down the street, strangers would just strike up a conversation with you. It just blew me away. The first night I was here I knew that I would come to school here. I just felt so at home, even though my family was a thousand miles away, and I knew nobody other than the coaches. I just fell in love with the place. I'm an Iowan now. I'm not leaving Iowa. I married an Iowa girl.

My wife is a huge Hawkeye fan, and she likes the memorabilia as much as I do. I have a letter from Coach Ferentz after I graduated

81

telling me how sorry he was that I was injured my senior year and giving me some compliments. I have the gloves that I wore when I played, my old helmet. When Iowa won the Big Ten championship, Ferentz, the classy guy that he is, mailed everybody who had been on his first two Iowa teams—that hadn't experienced much success—a rock. Our mantra the first few years was 'break the rock.' The idea that if you just keep pounding on a rock day after day, it may look like nothing's changing, but eventually the rock is going to shatter. We all got pieces of that—pretty neat stuff.

I just love going back and thinking about my first game here. It was against Northern Iowa in '95. It was a sold-out game. Everyone was so loud. When we jogged out on the field the first time, I thought I was going to fall over. I joke with my friends back home when I was telling them about it, "You know, it's not like you just got prickles when you're standing on the sideline, and someone scores or when there's a big play. Your hairs don't just stand up end. The fat on your sides jiggles." Right now I weigh about 240, but at one point, I was around 300 pounds. I was a Twinkie away from 300. I'm 6' 3".

The Iowa crowds were very inspiring. There were certain games where it seemed like the fans just willed you to play well. I remember in '96 against Michigan State, they jumped out to a 17-0 lead. We were playing bad and just kept turning the ball over and over and over. At this point, I was glued to the sideline, 'cause I was behind so many other players. The fans wouldn't stop screaming their heads off. I remember being down 17-0 and was wondering, "When is everyone's going to pack it in." They just kept cheering and cheering and cheering, and it was just amazing watching that comeback. Then, when we finally won, jogging off the field, I remember thinking to myself, "If anyone didn't quit today, it was the fans." Like Purdue in '97 it was a similar situation where we started out playing dreadfully. They jumped up on us, and the fans brought us back in. Then, I remember specifically in '98 against Michigan, it was rainy and terribly wet. The year before, we had choked up a big lead. Those stands were packed. The field was ugly. It was so muddy out there. The fans did not pack it in, they were cheering so hard for us. We almost pulled it out. We only lost by three. I was so disappointed after that game.

I was injured at Penn State when Courtney Brown, first-round pick of the Browns, landed on the back of my ankle and tore my Achilles and sprained my ankle in a couple of different areas. I was irate because I knew as soon as I hit the ground that it was over…that I wouldn't be able to play anymore, and that I would spend the rest of the year on crutches. When I was walking off the field, I was beside myself. In the locker room, I took a shower and when I went back out onto the field, it was the middle of the third quarter. Fans started clapping for me. By the time I got to our sideline, the students were giving me a standing ovation. It was very meaningful.

At that point, I still had illusions that we were going to go to a bowl game in '99, Kirk's first year, my last. You're so focused that you truly believe that you can will yourself to victory. I never thought that we would lose, and I just truly, truly believed that we were going to turn it around because our practices were getting so good, and we were really seeing improvement. If you compare the first couple of games and the last couple of games, we were so much more competitive.

The first year I ever played football was in third grade and then, in '99, after I was injured, I knew that would be my last year. I knew that if I didn't have a shot at the NFL that I was just going to walk away with my pride. But the last night, before we played Minnesota, because I was injured, I knew I wasn't going to see a down of action. While we were in the meetings, it just hit me that this was it—that in just 24 hours I wouldn't be a football player any more. I couldn't stop crying. I wasn't sitting there blubbering, but I just kept tearing up. I was so sad. I didn't want to cry in front of everybody, but I couldn't stop. It's like when you find out that your grandfather died. After meetings that night—it was about nine o'clock, and we were in Cedar Rapids—I walked out to the fire escape stairs and just sat there on the stairwell for about an hour blubbering like a little baby because I was so sad that it was ending. I was so disappointed that we would have such a losing season. I was so disappointed, not so much

> The 1942 Rose Bowl game between Oregon State and Duke was played in Durham, North Carolina because of fears that the Rose Bowl in Pasadena could be attacked like Pearl Harbor was three weeks earlier.

for me from a selfish perspective like "man, I wish we were playing for the **Rose Bowl**," or "man, I wish I was NFL-bound," but it was just as much for the fans. It was embarrassing walking off the field losing, getting our butts kicked in some of the games. I was so disappointed knowing that my class and the guys who were with me and the guys who dropped off and quit the program from my class and the classes in front of and behind me really left the program in a lousy state. I assume it's the American dream for parents to want their kids to do better than they did. It's the same thing when it comes to your recruiting class. You don't want to be the class that screwed it up. No matter how hard I worked and no matter how well I played, I was an offensive lineman on probably the youngest offensive line ever. It was me and three freshmen and a sophomore starting. It was tough. There in that stairwell, I just could not stop crying thinking that it was over. I was so sad. But, the bottom line is, though—life goes on.

But, those five years were a special, special five years of my life. I would never trade them.

IOWA IOWA IOWA IOWA IOWA IOWA IOWA IOWA IOWA IOWA IOWA IOWA IOWA

THE MARGIN OF ERROR IN A COLLEGE FOOTBALL POLL IS PLUS OR MINUS 100%

HOOPS, THERE IT IS!

Jess Settles

Jess Settles of Winfield, Iowa is considered by many experts to be the greatest basketball player in the history of Iowa prep sports. After a stellar career for the Hawkeyes, his pro prospects—once bright—were cut short by recurring back problems.

I've been an Iowa Hawkeye fan since I was just a couple of years old. In looking back through old photo albums, my mom and dad had me wearing Hawkeye gear before I could walk. Just growing up half an hour from Iowa Stadium, it was obviously the team to root for, and they were the guys I looked up to.

With Iowa, I just grabbed the opportunity and embraced that platform as a player. The reason it was so easy to do is that the Iowa people are such great people. Most of us in the state of Iowa have small-town roots. It's just a great family of people—tremendous neighbors. It's very neat on game day or game night when everybody gets together and roots for the same cause. It's a special deal.

It's amazing some of the letters you get. Probably the most special ones are when you get a letter from somebody and they say they've named their kid after you. That's very humbling. Another one I'll never forget—probably a third or fourth grade kid from Des Moines sent me a letter inviting me to his birthday party. I actually called him on that night. It's a great privilege to do it. I remember when I was a young kid I looked up to B. J. Armstrong and Roy Marble and Eddie Horton and Jeff Moe, Chuck Long, Ronnie Harmon, Larry Station. I was the same kid outside of Kinnick Stadium with my Magic Marker just dreaming of someday getting an autograph from a player or getting to shake their hand. To go from standing outside that arena to actually being on the field, on the court a few years later, I totally understand what that's like. That was a time in your life where it's a tremendous honor and a fun time to be around young Hawkeye fans. It really rubs off.

I probably love uniforms more than anything else as far as keeping stuff. People ask me what my best memory is and I usually tell them that if you remember when you were playing in high school, your mom has to wash your uniform. We played at Winfield and had a red and white uniform, and it seemed like a lot of times the white ones ended up turning pink by the end of the season. You have a pair of socks and one pair of shoes. When you play at The University of Iowa, my greatest memory coming in, in my freshman year, the first official game ever at Iowa, you come in and here's this bright gold, brand new uniform all pressed and folded, laying in your locker. Just the dream of your life, as a young Hawkeye fan growing up in the state, is to play for the Hawkeyes. Everybody wants to do it, and here you are. You realize, "I'm standing in the doggone locker room here and my dreams are coming true." To be able to put on that uniform was a very special moment. I remember that moment about as well as any game I played in. To be able to slip on that fresh, pressed, bright gold…. It looked like the sun was shining off of it. There's something about that uniform.

Game day is a representation of what goes on in our communities in the state of Iowa. We're still a state that values family. So many of us still have grandparents involved in our lives. People know their neighbors. We rely on each other. It's still a farming community state. The games are just a representation of who we are as people. For me, personally, my grandparents and parents were fans of the Hawkeyes long before I had an opportunity to play there. Nothing's changed after that. It's wonderful to have the support of the people in your community and your family members.

I remember being in the stands for the #1 Iowa-#2 Michigan football game…the Rob Houghtlin kick. My dad rushed out on the field and was jumping up on Mike Flagg's back. It's pretty cool to see your dad rushing the field, jumping on the players. That was a pretty sweet moment.

When I was in fourth grade, we had to write one of those "What do you want to be when you grow up?" Mine was that I wanted to win the Heisman Trophy and play football for the Iowa Hawkeyes. We were football people long before I got into the basketball games.

As far as being in Kinnick itself watching games, I like to be in the north end zone where it angles near the northwest part of it, almost near the student section. You're not directly in the end zone there. I like that spot. I like listening to the Iowa games on the radio. I have so many great memories of being in the farm truck or being on the tractor listening to games. Maybe that's just something about growing up in Iowa.

When I was a kid, the man for me was Chuck Long. In my opinion, as a fan growing up, he was the greatest player who ever played at Iowa. Hayden Fry and Chuck Long are the two guys who took our program to the next level. I loved Dan Gable. I grew up watching Steve Carfino and Brad Lohaus, all those guys.

I've always thought that the Iowa fans were tremendous and fair fans for the players. If you're a player, regardless of how good you are, or aren't, if you will lay it on the line for the people of Iowa, they'll respect you and be behind you regardless of wins and losses. Obviously when you're a coach, it's a little tougher. You've got to win. Iowa fans are very supportive of their coaches. They're the most famous people in the state. The expectations are very high at Iowa, but I also think they're very realistic. Iowa fans are usually pretty forgiving and treat their coaches with respect. As far as Dr. Tom is concerned, I think Dr. Tom is more popular in the state of Iowa now that he's gone than he even was when he was here. I don't know one person who has anything bad to say about him. He was a tremendous coach for me. I loved playing for him. Some people thought it was time for him to move on, and he handled it very professionally under very trying circumstances. His legacy will be that most Iowa fans had a lot of respect for him. As far as how the program is going right now, I think Iowa fans have realistic expectations for their teams. They feel like the teams the last few years have not played up to their potential. There's a remnant of fans out there right now who have really lost interest in the basketball program, but nothing that a few wins won't cure.

I would love to be sitting in some dome somewhere during the Final Four weekend and watching a player with an Iowa uniform get up and cut down that net. When I came into The University of Iowa, as a player, that was my dream. I really felt that was my destiny, so to speak, as a player. I was not able to get that done, but would be so thrilled to be sitting at a Final Four watching us cut down the nets. I would love to see that happen. I know that somewhere around the state of Iowa, there's some little kid practicing right now who has the same dream and hopefully will make it a reality. That's my Iowa wish list.

IOWA IOWA IOWA IOWA IOWA IOWA IOWA IOWA IOWA IOWA IOWA IOWA IOWA

The Hawk Bus at the basketball arena.

PLAYIN' FAVORITES

The weekend Kennedy died, we were playing Notre Dame. That was my senior year. We stayed in a motel the night before the game out in Mt. Vernon. We all got up Saturday morning and were wondering if the game would be played, but hadn't heard anything. We were actually getting our ankles taped when word came down that the game was called off. They cut the tape off, put us on the bus, and drove us back to Iowa City. It was a somber time, and everybody was real concerned. We didn't know all the details at that time. There was a lot of concern and tears. The bus dropped us off at The Airliner. Many of my teammates needed liquid fortification against the unknown.

That day was to be Mike Reilly Day. The fans from Dubuque had three buses coming down to Iowa City. They were going to honor me, and I was going to ride the bus home with them, and there was a dinner planned that night in Dubuque. I always kid them and say, "Well, what ever happened to that car you were going to give me?"

—MIKE REILLY, 62, Dubuque, Iowa, ex-Chicago Bear

Bob Commings was coaching in 1977. There was a high school All-American football player named John Harty from Sioux City. My wife, Bob, and I flew up to Sioux City to visit him. We walked in the house. John Harty was the biggest guy I've ever seen in my life, and he was sitting there in a stuffed chair. I said to myself, "We've got to get this guy. He looks too good." He came to Iowa—signed on the steps of the State Capitol. Bob Ray was there. Bob Commings was there. It was a real important signing. I don't know what Bob had promised him before, but he said, "Everything I've said to you will come true if you come to Iowa." He came to Iowa and was a good football player who later signed with the 49-ers.

—EARL MURPHY, Iowa City, retired clothier

> The Oakland A's colors are green and gold because their late owner, Charles O. Finley, grew up in La Porte, Indiana and loved Notre Dame...when he bought the Kansas City A's, he changed their uniforms to the Notre Dame colors. The Green Bay Packers also adopted Notre Dame colors because Curly Lambeau played at Notre Dame.

In that 1986 Rose Bowl game, Ronnie Harmon had three fumbles in the first half—the first being at the goal line on our first possession. He hadn't fumbled all year—he just simply was not a fumbler. Fry said they took a long, hard look at those tapes, and we even had the FBI come in and talk to our coaches because there were rumors going around. Hayden was concerned enough that he really investigated it in-house as much as he could. After his in-house investigation, and looking at the tapes, and talking to Ronnie head-to-head, he just thinks what happens was—UCLA did a terrific scouting job on us for that game. They did two things. They figured out Harmon liked to swing the ball when he ran. And they figured out that Larry Station often overran the play when they cut back against the grain. In that game, UCLA had a running back we'd never heard of, Eric Ball, who gained 227 yards on us. They just kept blocking Station out of the play when he just cut back against the grain—that, and the fact that UCLA's running game was so good that day. Because they saw that weakness, they just knocked the ball loose from Harmon in the first half.

Harmon was a really private kid, quiet. When he was at Iowa, I never really got to know him. I knew him better after he left Iowa. He had a really good pro career. He's coaching now somewhere. He was hurt by all the questions, but he came back, and I think it all blew over.

—*GEORGE WINE*, former Iowa SID

Kyle McCann was much maligned throughout the 2001 season, not only by the fans, but by the press. I've become fairly objective so I've never jumped on any the-guy's-gotta-go bandwagon or anything like that. I was always pretty fair with everybody. I take the middle of the road…unless it was so obvious that you could get away with hammering somebody or maybe giving them a little extra kudos along the way. But, McCann played really well in that Alamo Bowl. We were down in the post-game room, and McCann was going to come out for an interview. It dragged on forever. As we had been walking in from the field, I walked in with him. The guy was 6' 5" and had an Afro so it made him look like he was 6' 9". He had his helmet perched up on top of his head so now he looked like he was about 7' 4". I said, "Hey Kyle." He said, "Hey." I said, "Well, is this about the best you've ever felt in an Iowa uniform?" He looks down at me and says,

"Oh yeah," and he just walks in to the locker room. I'm waiting for him after all the interviews are done, and everybody else is in there, and he's making us wait *on purpose*. He walked into the room and looked at everybody in there and said, something to the effect of, "You can all put that in your pipe and smoke it," as far as his performance on the field that day. He knew he did a good job. He knew he kept that team in contention for that bowl win, and it was his payback—his payback to the media and everybody to make them wait and then come in there and be cocky during the interview process. And you know what? He deserved it. He deserved every second that he made everybody wait for him to come in that day. There's too much pressure put on some of the college athletes to perform. These guys are good, or they wouldn't be there. To Kyle McCann, he took the criticism, he took the heat, he took everything that everybody could throw at him and he persevered. He did it his way. He kept his head held high.

—**MIKE ZIERATH**, Writer, *Planet Hawkeye*

My dad started taking me to games when I was eight years old, driving from Des Moines to Iowa City and back. He'd be talking to me about the game, "Here's the program. See if you can memorize the names and numbers, and I'll give you a quarter." That was back in '48 or '49. Bill Reichart was my favorite player. My dad had worked his way through college working in Reich's Café, in Iowa City, run by Bills parents. Bill was a little baby then. When Bill became a college player at Iowa, my dad had that connection so we always went down to "watch Bill play."

I was really attracted to a couple of things about Arena Football because it's basically single-platoon football. That's what I grew up on—having to play both offense and defense. I played because I was versatile enough to play both. We had guys who were probably better than me who could only do one or the other, but they couldn't do both. They would have such a gaping weakness that a more versatile athlete could play both ways. I always thought when we changed the single platoon to two-platoon football, which happened shortly after I finished playing, you began to get this offensive team and defensive team practicing separately. It's almost like having two different teams—two different coaching staffs. I didn't like it, didn't like the change. Somebody was always blaming somebody else. I thought single-platoon football was the way to go.

Nowadays, you've got coaching staffs of 12 to 15 people in the big-time, where we had a coaching staff of six. The whole thing has changed. I think it's a better game to play both ways. It requires a better athlete. Of course, they did it because they felt like they had to compete with the specialization of the pros.

—GARY FLETCHER, Des Moines, ex-Hawk player, coach and color analyst

Tim Dwight would be my favorite all-time Iowa player. To watch him on TV was one thing, but to see that man in person…. Tim Dwight was wide open on almost every play, but we didn't have a quarterback to get him the ball on every play. When he went to return a punt—look out. He returned a punt against Michigan right at the end of the half. I had learned my lesson a couple of weeks earlier—they would let you leave Kinnick at halftime and go out to tailgate and then come back in for the second half, but after 9/11, you can't do that anymore. We'd always leave three—four minutes before the half ended to beat the crowd. I'd missed a great play a couple of weeks earlier by doing that so I didn't leave. Michigan had to punt to Tim Dwight, and we were down by about seventeen or twenty. Dwight jukes right, and he jukes left, he runs down the field, jukes right and goes clear around the end, then comes back across the field—scores a touchdown with about thirty seconds left. It was an incredible run. If I hadn't learned my lesson earlier, I would have been out of the Stadium and would have missed it.

One time I took my wife's seventeen-year-old twin nieces over to a game. We were in the parking lot afterward and out walks Tim Dwight. My nieces thought he was such a doll. We told them to go talk to him, but they wouldn't. I went over and talked to Dwight and told him there were a couple of twin high school girls over here who would just love to meet him. He walked over to where they were and introduced himself to them. I just thought that was such a cool thing for somebody of that caliber.

—PANAMA FARLOW, Osceola, Iowa

Playing football with the guys was a very humbling experience when you realize how highly regarded these players are, and you realize what wonderful people they are, too, not like some of these NFL jerks out there who are rude, terrible people, but a guy like Tim Dwight, probably the hardest worker I'd ever been around. The kids just worshipped him. I just think, "Man, if my kid ever grows up to be as good a person as he is, let alone a football player."

In the eyes of the players, Tim Dwight was probably the most respected. There were some guys who were really good players, and on Mondays and Tuesdays they wouldn't practice because they were so banged up. I can't ever remember him missing practice. He had a hamstring pull before the Sun Bowl in '97 and he did miss a couple of days, but other than that, it was like he was playing in the Super Bowl every day, whether it was the day before the biggest game of the year or the last day of spring ball when you're in half pads before the spring game. He was absolutely the hardest worker I've ever been around.

JAY BICKFORD, Hawkeye Player, '98-'99

I'm proud to say that of all the young men and women, mostly men, that I worked around, I never met one I really didn't like. They were all different, different backgrounds, and everything else, but they were all very well behaved. Everyone was terrified of Tyrone Dye, yet he was one of the nicest young men I've ever known. He was a very tall, big, black guy. When he came in, he was almost illiterate, and the coaches got him in school. The cops were even terrified of him. He wouldn't have harmed any of them. He played football from 1972 to 1975. He stayed in school and received his Masters degree. He used to play a game with me, learning a new word each day. He'd come in every day and tell me the new word. I always insisted that every freshman who came in had to have a pocket dictionary. A lot of them had never had a dictionary at home. Tyrone would look up a word and come tearing in and ask me if he was pronouncing it correctly. I think I'm most proud of him—he's one of the best success stories I can think of. He didn't go on to big professional sports. He's still around here in Iowa.

—HELEN HOHLE, 82, Retired from Iowa Athletic Library

 We were at a home game when I was ten or eleven years old. My buddies and I played midget football, and we were all Iowa fans. We were sitting way up high on the fifty-yard line. There was this real big guy in front of us. My father started talking to him. His name was Matt Petrzelka, and he was an offensive tackle for Iowa. He was injured, had a pinched nerve, and wasn't down with the team. I remember during the game people were booing the fullback when he was running 'cause they didn't think he was running that hard. The game ended and Matt turned to me and my friend and said, "Hey, do you guys want to go in the locker room with me?" Our eyes lit up like saucers, and we said, "Yeah, sure." He took us down to the locker room. He went inside, and then he came out and got us and took us in. I can remember it like yesterday. Bob Commings locked himself in the office and wouldn't come out. One thing that struck me the most was I remember the fullback was in there. I was staring at him while he was taking his shoe off and remembered how the crowd had booed him every time he touched the ball. When he took his shoe off, it was full of blood. Since that day, I have never booed a home team player.

—KEVIN McCOY, Allen, Texas, Bettendorf Native

Jim Willet, a kid from my hometown, played for Iowa back in the mid-fifties and went to the '57 Rose Bowl. I don't think he played very much. He was so much older than I, that I didn't really know him, but just to see him was so awe-inspiring. One year, my brother, Chuck, got me a football, and Jim Willet signed it......The town of Manson didn't have a café, but there were a couple of taverns where you could go in and get a bowl of chili. I was in my early twenties, and was sitting in there, and this guy came in who was BIG. He was probably twenty years older than I, but he still looked so tough. I remember someone saying, "That's Sherwyn Thorson." He was from Ft. Dodge, about twenty miles away. I think he was first team, All-Big-10 guard, and the NCAA heavyweight wrestling champion.

—MIKE McGREGOR, 48, Manson, Iowa

IOWA IOWA IOWA IOWA IOWA IOWA IOWA IOWA IOWA IOWA IOWA IOWA IOWA

Chapter 4

A Coach is a Teacher With a Death Wish

There's More To Coaching Than Ignoring Your Best Players

Mr. Evashevski

THE FOREST WHO LED IOWA OUT OF THE WOODS

Forest Evashevski

Forest Evashevski may be the most important figure in the history of Hawkeye football. When he arrived from Washington State in 1952, the Hawks had enjoyed only two winning seasons since the 1930s. Evashevski had initially gained fame as the blocking back at the University of Michigan who paved the way for Tom Harmon. Harmon won the Heisman Trophy in 1940. Evy and his wife, Ruth, have enjoyed the good life in beautiful Petoskey, Michigan for the last 34 years.

I was at Washington State, which is three hundred miles away from the center of population, and when you've been playing Cal and Southern Cal and Stanford, it's a pretty tough thing. I was real glad to get the Iowa job. I'd spent a year in Iowa at Iowa Pre-flight in the Navy. I liked Iowa City, and I liked the state of Iowa so that's why I wanted to take the job. Paul Brechler was the athletic director then.

I can't get out of my mind, the first season I was there in Iowa City, how low Iowa athletics was. In 1952, I came to Iowa from Washington State where I coached in the Pacific Coast Conference. Iowa was right at the decadence of its football program. One of the big things that helped turn it around was that in 1952 Ohio State had a great football team. They came to Iowa City, and Iowa beat them 8-0—a missed extra point and a safety. That really got our football program started.

Ricky Nelson and John DeLorean married daughters of Tom Harmon.

That was our first real big win at Iowa, and I tell you, it got the Iowa fans back active again. It was the start of a successful reign there.

The first year I was there, I recruited Binky Broeder, from St. Louis. He started his first game as a sophomore and played three years. He was the first one we recruited who was well-sought after. The great one we got was Willie Fleming from Detroit. The second year we got Kenny Ploen from Clinton, Iowa. At that time, Kenny wasn't the most sought-after player although he became one of our best football players.

We hit a gold mine in Steubenville, Ohio, Dean Martin's home town. I didn't have a connection to Steubenville. I got a letter from someone telling me he had followed me during my college days at Michigan, and he wished me well as a coach. He named the Steubenville team as a great team and said, "They have a great football player here by the name of Calvin Jones." I checked, and he was. He was sought after by everybody. Really, in order to get Calvin, we made a pitch for Frank Gilliam and Eddie Vincent, and all three of them came. That was a real find because Eddie Vincent and Gilliam both did a great job for us, too.

In that famous '53 game, Notre Dame had used all their time outs. They couldn't stop the clock unless someone was injured, so they faked an injury of one of the Notre Dame players. On the bench, we realized what they had done, but there wasn't much we could do about it. After the game, Coach Frank Leahy shook my hand and congratulated me saying something about a fine team or something like that. It was a brief exchange. I certainly didn't carry on any pleasant conversation with him. It was a disappointment to have had that happen.

That first year I was at Iowa, and most of '53, there wasn't a sellout for a game. In '54 we did have some sellouts and from that time on the fans have always supported the Hawks. That allowed us to get more Iowa kids interested in football because up to that time, they went to Drake or Iowa State or Illinois, Nebraska. We hadn't had our picks, but from that time on, we did. That was the real start of it.

The thing I was very pleased with at Iowa was the contact with the Iowa fans. It was very good. When you win, it's easy to have a good crowd behind you, but when you lose—I've been at stadiums where they threw apples at you and expressed their displeasure in many ways. At Iowa, I always thought we had a great rooting section of fans—very wholesome. I can't ever remember a crowd becoming obnoxious during a football game.

If I had to name a recruit who most surprised us, it would be Randy Duncan. Randy Duncan had a reputation, but frankly we didn't think he was that hot a prospect. He was an Iowa boy from Des Moines-Roosevelt so we went after him. He really turned out to be a great field general and a fine passer. Randy came along and was a fine quarterback. He didn't have speed. We couldn't run him like we did Kenny Ploen or Jerry Reichow. He was a good ball handler and made the deception work on our offense and also was a fine passer—not that he was a long passer, but the thing Randy did—he didn't throw the interception. He was smart, a real heady player. Gene Veit from Clinton was a pretty good passer and a great ball handler. The only thing with him was that he didn't have the speed to run the ball.

Going to the Rose Bowl for the first time was a great experience. When Jayne Mansfield kissed Randy Duncan, that was a great time. I just couldn't get over all the hype that went with it. It was tough to coach a football team and get ready for a game. They had so many activities going on, and our practices were interrupted by flashbulbs from picture-takers. We had very little privacy. Of course that was my fault—I opened the practices up to the press. It was tough because I thought we were going to throw our game plan to the winds and everybody was enjoying the hype of Hollywood. One of the coaches said, "Evy, the best thing to do is when you get out there, take the first two or three days and let your kids do all the exploring they want. Let them visit the movie sets and Hollywood and get it out of their system. You'll find that then your team is coachable. It turned out just that way. They had a lot of fun the first couple of days out there and then they got down and prepared for the contest. Whoever was the one who told me that was real accurate because that was exactly what happened. Oregon State had the opposite. They held the kids in and scrimmaged them, and by the time the game rolled around, they weren't ready to play.

I'd say the toughest to coach against was Benny Oosterbaan at Michigan. I didn't mind coaching against Woody Hayes at all. I knew him well and had seen him through a lot of turmoil. He and I had a lot of exchanges but really we were pretty good friends. Woody was terrible on the football field. He would charge out and do all kinds of things, but he had another side to him. I never knew Woody to make an illegal offer to any athlete. We recruited against each other because we went into Ohio, but never once did Woody ever break a rule recruiting, and I would have been aware of it if he had. We were after the same kids, many times.

Ralph Miller and I were close friends. One time Frosty, my son, played in a golf tournament in Portland and Ralph asked him down to visit Oregon State. Frosty had known him when Ralph was at Iowa. Frosty thought Oregon State was just great. He liked the country. When he got his law degree, he moved out there and practiced law.

Tom Harmon and I have stayed close over the years, and in fact, he was best man at my wedding. I talk to Mark Harmon frequently. I wanted Mark to go to Iowa, but there was no way he was going to come there. Tom Harmon helped me get one recruit, Charley Lee. Tom talked to a few others, but it was almost impossible to get a kid to come to Iowa when Southern Cal was after them. They didn't want to play in the snow and bad weather. All your good backs wanted a dry ball and a dry field.

Playing **Notre Dame** was good 'cause it sold out and was a good money game. It was a good recruiting tool because a lot of kids would like to play against Notre Dame. And, it was an incentive for your kids to get up for that game. I think we always had an advantage because our kids could fire up for Notre Dame, and I'm not so sure Notre Dame could fire up for Iowa. It was a good game on our schedule, and too bad that it ended. The series with Notre Dame ended. We wanted to keep it going, but Notre Dame had a conflict. I think the other thing was that we were getting a little too strong. The weekend

> **At Notre Dame, 1956 Heisman Trophy winner Paul Hornung played halfback, fullback, and quarterback; punted, kicked-off, kicked field goals; ran back punts and kickoffs; and was a starting safety. Against Iowa that year, he ran a quarterback sneak 80 yards.**

Kennedy was shot, it was my feeling that we should play the game, but we didn't get to. I had met Kennedy and later when my wife met him, he asked, "Any relation to Forest?" Ruth's dad, Prentice Brown, was a senator in Washington and that's how she happened to meet Kennedy. In retrospect, that tie we had with Notre Dame earlier actually helped our program. It brought a lot of attention to the game and brought us a lot of publicity. Back in those days, we needed it because it was tough to recruit at Iowa. As we went along, we found that each year it became a little easier.

I think Coach Ferentz has done a great job. I haven't been to a *game* in Iowa City in years—I've just been to Iowa City. I've got quite a few friends who I hear from quite often.

We got into a pretty hot battle with Indiana for Alex Karras, out of Gary, Indiana. I think if Purdue had gone after Karras as hard as Indiana did, we might not have gotten him. There was a high school coach there in Indiana who really helped us get Alex. Alex was fine on the football field, and we never had any problem with him. It was after he had played in the NFL that Alex got a little off base, I thought.

I can't remember any of our players getting into trouble. A few of the players we had there were headed for trouble, but we saved them. I think I could still coach today—but they wouldn't have earrings and a few things like that. What they would wear in their own home or outside the program, that would be up to them, but not anybody who was going to school and was a member of the football team. I don't think you have to tolerate that. All the years I ever coached, including my first year at Hamilton College, the kids always made their own rules—that's the way I did it.

Looking back, I'm very glad I went to Iowa. I had job offers from Indiana and Iowa at the same time. I had spent a year in Iowa when I was in the Navy at Iowa Pre-flight. I liked Iowa City and liked the people in Iowa, and that was why I went. Iowans are pretty tough to beat, as people. Ruth and I were so happy there and glad that we were able to raise our children there. We'll always have a lot of love for Iowa in our hearts.

QUICK HITS AND INTERESTING BITS

I think Hayden Fry would probably be my favorite Hawkeye coach because he really turned the program around and changed the whole mentality of the football program. There was that old Oklahoma story when they went down there and almost beat Oklahoma, and he said, "If I see one guy smiling on this bus, I'll knock your head off." That was the mentality Iowa had—"Well, we almost beat them, and we're happy with that." He changed it from that to where you expect to win.

—**KEVIN McCOY**, Allen, Texas; Bettendorf Native

Kirk Ferentz, Barry Alvarez and I went to the Shrine game every year at the UNI-Dome. They had the outstanding high school players in Iowa. One year, about the second quarter, Barry got the program and said, "Who's number so and so?" I said, "His name is Bryce Paup." Alvarez said, "We just missed the best football player in Iowa. He's one of the best football players I've ever seen." They kept noticing what a good player he was. He said, "That boy is going to be an All-American at UNI. You mark my word. And, he's going to sign for a lot of money." Bryce Paup went to UNI, and he signed to go with the Buffalo Bills and made a lot of money. He was one of the first Northern Iowa players to ever get a major contract.

Every time I would see Barry Alvarez after that, instead of saying, "Hi," he would say, "Bryce Paup." I say, "Bryce Paup." And that's how we would greet. We went into Chicago for a media day one time. They have about eleven booths, all the same size. There are two football players in each of them. My wife and I went in one year, and as we are walking in, Barry Alvarez was getting interviewed by some TV station. He was standing up there and, during this interview, he looked over and sees me, and he raises his hand and said to me, "Bryce Paup." I must have been about 50 feet away from him. Barry is a hell of a nice guy.

—**EARL MURPHY**, 80, Iowa City

Mike Price and I were on the staff as assistant coaches the first year with Warren Powers at Washington State. When Mike decided he was going to Alabama, I left a message on his phone: "Before you take this job, check with me, but I want you to know that I'm going to try to talk you out of taking it." He didn't call back, and then the next thing I know he's going to Alabama. Ego—how can you turn down Alabama? It was never a fit. The thing is, he walked away from history. I said, "Why would you leave Washington State? They're going to name buildings after you in Pullman. Fields and stadiums will be named after you if you stay here and retire here, but if you leave, they're not going to name anything after you." I was born and raised 90 miles from Tuscaloosa. My sister and brother-in-law live there, and he is a retired minister. What Mike didn't know anything about— he didn't understand the religious culture of the Deep South. It doesn't matter. They can all go to the country clubs and drink, but don't go to the bars and drink. You just have to know where you can and can't be "non-Baptist."

I left another message after he took the job and said, "Look if you've got a couple of hours, give me a call, and I'll tell you how to adjust and how to survive in the South. Mike, you really need some input here." He called back and left a message, "I got your voice mail. I'll get back to you as soon as I catch my breath." He never called. So now, a few months later, he goes to Pensacola, Florida, which he doesn't understand. In the first place, he shouldn't have gone to a girlie bar to start with. That offended the Baptists and the Methodist and the Episcopalians and everybody else. They can't deal with that there. He didn't know the difference between Pensacola, Florida and L.A. It's like L.A. is to **Pullman**.

The passion of SEC football is so great that everybody knows who everybody is. When he went in that bar, everybody in that bar knew who he was. Everybody was on their cell phone within two minutes calling their buddies.

> **Pullman, home of Washington State University, has a population of twenty-five thousand. Martin Stadium, the home stadium for the Washington State Cougars holds thirty-eight thousand...In the late 1950s, the Cougars had a home game during a blizzard. The paid attendance was 1. The Athletic Department gave that paying fan a lifetime pass to Washington State football games.**

In Iowa, there are a lot of people who truly do pull for Iowa when they're not playing Iowa State, and vice versa. That does not happen in the South. If you're in Alabama, and a 'Bama fan, your best day is when Alabama wins and Auburn loses. There is no better day in your life than when that happens. That's just the way they are. It's just cut-and-dried. Those teams don't like one another—period. Since time began, the people who support the teams of the Southeastern Conference think they invented football, and you're never going to convince them they're wrong.

—**JIM WALDEN**, Mississippi native, Ames resident

I moved to Hannibal in fifth grade from Keokuk. Hannibal didn't have a kids' wrestling program. I asked if I could practice with the middle school team and, thankfully, they allowed that. They had an athletic banquet one time that I was invited to attend. Dan Gable was the featured speaker. That was about twenty years ago and was right in the middle of his heyday. I'm sure he gave his standard speech that he gives at all athletic banquets, but, more importantly, afterward I got to shake his hand and talk with him a little bit. Probably the biggest impact he had on me was a couple of years later. I was a freshman in high school and wrote him a letter. I asked him, never thinking that he'd reply, for some advice. I told him a little bit about my previous experience that year and my accomplishments and my shortfalls. Lo and behold, a short time later, he wrote back a letter—not just a one-paragraph letter. It was three pages long, detailing out the different steps that he would take if he were in my place. From that day, I just thought that he was such a great man—to do something like that for a high school kid who'd written him a letter. Here, he takes time out of his busy schedule to make such a detailed response to my questions. That was just a big impact on me as far as respect for him. I still have that letter and that's my most treasured thing I have regarding Iowa athletics.

—**KEVIN FOWLER,** 31, Hannibal, Missouri

All things being equal, I think Ferentz is about the classiest person I've ever been around. To be able to stand steel-jawed with everyone criticizing him being hired and Iowa not taking Bobby Stoops. To deal with the lack of a full cupboard his first couple of years, and to really see improvements from the beginning to the end of each year—he is a wonderful, wonderful person, and a wonderful, wonderful coach. He deserves all the accolades that he gets. I was very disappointed that before the 2001 season, when Jon Beutjer left and went to Illinois, everyone started calling for Ferentz' head. There was all this business over the Internet and all these op-ed pieces about him. He just really shrugged it all off. To be able to deal with everything he's dealt with, even though he's getting all these praises now, he's still got to be thinking in the back of his mind, "You people were booing me at the Michigan game in 2001." He's a wonderful person, and if I could have played five years under one person, it would be Ferentz. Part of that also is that he was an offensive line coach, and he was a very offensive-line minded person; whereas, Fry was definitely a quarterbacks and receivers coach.

Fry knew everybody's name, whether it was a first-year walk-on or Tim Dwight. He'd come and talk to you. It was no "prince and pauper" type thing. It's just that there were definitely some "princes" when he came, but there weren't any "paupers." He went out of his way to make sure everybody was a member of the team.

When we left **Northwestern** in '95, when they had that special Rose Bowl year—we had beaten them about twenty years in a row—Fry must have been real disappointed when we lost to those guys. I remember the next day when we were in a meeting, he said something like, "Even the sun shines on the ugly dog's ass every once in a while."

—JAY BICKFORD, Hawkeye Player, '99-'99

In the eighties, at an Iowa football game, I was down in the corner of the south end zone talking to some friends, when I sensed there was somebody right next to me; whereas, when I walked over there, there

> Former Northwestern running back and TV color analyst, Mike Adamle, was the last NFL running back who wore a number lower than "20"...his number was "1"

was no one there. I turned around and right next to me, just inches away, was John Mackovic, the Illinois football coach. Behind him was the entire Illinois squad getting ready to charge onto the field. What I remember was how small Mackovic looked and, particularly, how pale he looked. He looked like he had white makeup on—almost looked like a mime. I was thinking, "I cannot believe this guy's the coach of a major college football team."

—DICK FOX, 62, Falmouth, Massachusetts

To me, all the coaches were nuts. Hayden Fry was the funniest one. When he first came, he used to try to scare me. He'd have friends come up from Texas and he had them bring up an armadillo and he turned it loose in my office. Of course, I screamed bloody murder. I told Hayden that I almost wet my pants. Then Jay Robinson, assistant wrestling coach, adopted some wild horses and supposedly put them in my name. Some people who identified themselves as 'federal people' called me and told me I had to go pick them up. I was terrified about this because my husband would have been furious for being responsible for picking up wild horses—we lived in town. Of course that was a joke. There were two businessmen here in town who came up to the office one day and started laughing at me. They, supposedly, had been the 'federal people' who had called. It was just a fun place to work and to play. We were serious but we had a lot of fun.

It's fun to see the athletes after they leave school—to see them mature and grow. One of the wrestlers, who is now a head wrestling coach, won a national championship and was stoned at the time. Another one was drunk when he wrestled. They were just young people.

Hayden Fry was divorcing his wife when he first came up here and he brought his girlfriend with him to the spring football game. The secretaries and people who worked in the building would all go to watch him. They decided people needed to stay at work so they would have it on a Saturday. We had the Per Mar Security people, and they're wacky, too. They put up a big barricade, and they weren't going to let Hayden bring his girlfriend in. Here, he's the head football coach for the spring football game. Hayden came over and talked to me and I told Per Mar to let her in. They didn't know who he was. I think that's why he and I become friends. After he married his girlfriend, we never socialized with them. We used to have parties and luncheons and he and I would tease one another, but I was never in his home. In wrestling, we used to have parties all the time—continuously. They were pretty wild. They used to go steal pigs and have pig roasts. They would have skydivers who would dive naked, just typical ornery people.

I didn't like Lute Olson. I thought he was an arrogant person. It used to drive me nuts the way he would pull his pants up and smooth his hair back. He reminds me of our present basketball coach. The wrestlers didn't like him. When we were in the Field House, the wrestling department had a sauna in the basement and one time they locked Lute in there. He always hated wrestlers after that, and I don't blame him. I don't think he was in there too long, but it was enough that he raised hell about it.

—HELEN HOHLE, 82, Retired from Athletic Department

As a coach, Bob Commings really taught a lot of lessons. We learned a lot of lessons about how to face adversity in our careers from him. We were playing against a lot of great teams, and we weren't always coming out on the winning side, but during that time, you're not going to quit. You're going to face adversity. After the game, you're going to face the fact that you didn't have that good a game and that the fans are going to ridicule you or whatever. A lot of those lessons that Coach Commings taught to me stick with me today. I can only relate to being under Commings' tutelage and learning from him. It's a matter of who you play under as to what lessons you take with you.

—JON LAZAR, '79, Leading rusher three years

I think Kirk Ferentz is great. What's really amazing about this is that I had seen one night on ESPN Classic the story of Nile Kinnick. I was glued to the screen through the whole show, and they were talking about his days at Iowa and how he got out of school and talked about how he could have been President of the United States. I wrote Kirk Ferentz a letter and said, "After playing at Iowa in Kinnick Stadium, and being a captain, and going out on the field when they flipped the coin that has Kinnick's head on one side and a tail on the other side, I really got to thinking about all of it. I wish I had known about the tradition of Iowa and the history of Kinnick when I was a young player. You should show your players this tape. I think it's very important for Iowa history in sports and football." He wrote me back and said, "We're on the same page. We're going to show it to the team this week."

A couple of years ago they had something in the Iowa City paper about "Where Are They Now?" One week, it featured me. Kirk read that and wrote me a letter telling me to stop by his office if I was ever in Iowa City. I think for a coach in his position, with all the responsibilities and all the things he has to do, to reach back and reach out to some of the old players is unique in itself. That shows a lot of character. Beyond what he's doing with the team, which we all know is very good, he's doing other things that are beyond the call of duty.

—JON LAZAR, Iowa Captain, 1978

We used to laugh at the Illinois people after the Deon Thomas scandal. I said, "We do things a little differently in Iowa. We give cars to our coaches where you give cars to your players." Johnny Winnie, the tennis coach at Iowa for a number of years, used to go to these Big Ten tennis meetings. They'd ask him, "John, how come you get a new car every year." He said, "I don't get a new car every year. I get a new car every four months." I'd switch them every four months—just give them another one. Greg Lansing, assistant basketball coach, and Steve Houghton, the tennis coach have two of our cars now. It's been a good program. It's good for the coaches. Right after I gave the car to Lansing, I was at a function. Steve Alford walked over to me and said, "You're taking way too good care of my coach." I said, "What's wrong?" He said, "He's got a nicer vehicle than I do."

When we furnish cars to the university, they give us a receipt showing that we spent however many dollars at the University. We use that as a write-off. We get no tickets, just use it as a donation.

At Iowa State, it's somewhat different. They give two free basketball tickets and two free football tickets for the cars. The dealers are allowed to purchase however many more they want. Iowa State actually takes all their car dealers to one away football game every year, by plane, and puts them up for two nights. We've all talked about that, and I say, "Maybe that's why we didn't have to drop baseball, guy, did you ever think of that?"

—PAUL STUELAND, Stueland Auto Center, Tipton, Iowa...participates in coaches-car program—Iowa Athletic Department

The year Dan Gable went to the Olympics, Kurdelmeier decided he wanted to hire Dan Gable. Roy Carver and John Marks were the recruiters. The first time I saw Dan, he had skin blemishes all over his face and was so shy he couldn't look at you. Now, I guess if I would admire anybody, it would be Dan Gable because he's a good speaker to this day. It was interesting to watch Dan develop, to watch his everyday life, to see how he developed and carried himself—to watch him mature.

Bob Bowlsby was doing an internship under Harry Ostrander. Bowlsby had put some beer in a Coke machine. I happened to hit it, and I emptied out all of his six-packs and took it back to the wrestling room. Gary Kurdelmeier and I were drinking it when Bowlsby came in to ask us if we knew anything about it. We just laughed at him. He told us it was his beer.... We were at a party after a wrestling meet one time, and it was the first time I knew any of the wrestlers smoked dope. I got mad at all of them and left, walking home, and it was middle of winter.

—HELEN HOHLE, retired, Iowa Wresting Department

People will probably put me to death for saying this, but I really liked Tom Davis. I enjoy Kirk Ferentz and everybody adores Hayden Fry, for all the obvious reasons. You can keep the Bobby Bowdens of the world, and the Steve Spurriers of the world, who have been very successful, but at what price? I believe Tom Davis was a successful coach at Iowa, and I was actually sorry at the way he was dealt with there. A lot of people might disagree with the system of basketball that he taught and the fact that they'd never been to the Final Four and never won a championship, but there's something to be said for having the kind of guy lead your program, that, if you're going to send your kid to that program, is he going to turn out to be a man afterward? Is he going to have the values of being a sportsman, of learning about life and being the right kind of person and winning the proper way? That, to me, is important. Winning at all costs is not the kind of athletic department that I would want to follow. Those guys just exude class, integrity, respect and are humble about it.

—LYELL HOGG, 33, Season Ticket holder

Let me tell you how hard it is—Bill Snyder has done the most phenomenal job. He is *the* number one coach on my list of all time. What he has done at Kansas State far exceeds any coach—**Bear Bryant** would be the next most prolific coach in my lifetime. It would be Bill Snyder, then Bear Bryant to me—in my lifetime—of coaches that I've seen do things. Even when Bear went to Kentucky, Texas A&M and Alabama, they were not as bad as Kansas State was bad. That's why Bill gets the nod. And, yet, he's only won one conference championship. With all Bill Snyder's done and the glory he's brought Kansas State, he has still only managed one conference championship. Trying to beat the powers in the Big 12 conference is not unlike trying to beat Ohio State and Michigan…it is very, very difficult. I would love to see somebody…sometime…take Iowa State to a conference football championship for these people. One time. Just once. So our fans could experience that. I watched the gleam in their eyes when they won the basketball titles.

—JIM WALDEN, former Iowa State head football coach

In my mind, Hayden Fry is my favorite coach. People, especially newer fans, do not know the depths of despair that Iowa football was in before he came. It was one of the worst programs in the country consistently making the Playboy Worst Twenty! It was a broken program for years. For him to be able to come in and take the team to the Rose Bowl in his third year is just nothing short of miraculous.

I wouldn't want to take anything away from what Ferentz has done because he's built a fantastic program, and he inherited a shambles himself. But Fry paved the way. Fry made it possible for all that to happen—the Bowl exposures, a much more national interest in Iowa football, TV exposure that never would have come otherwise. And, he stayed there when we know he had opportunities to go to go to greener pastures.

It was great for Fry to be able to bring the Iowa program to the point where it could play powerhouses like Nebraska—not only play them but take them on head to head and win. Like Muhammad Ali said, "He shocked the world on that day." Iowa finished the 1980 season with a big, big win against Michigan State. They won 41-0. So I was very optimistic going into '81, but I don't know if anyone

> **In the TV show "B.J. and the Bear," Bear was a chimpanzee named after Bear Bryant.**

else was. The idea that we could even be in a close game with Nebraska was not even something we would consider. The fact that we would actually beat them—mind numbing! And then, the next week, losing at Iowa State, it looked like it was just a fluke. Then coming back the week after that and beating UCLA and then taking Michigan down a couple of weeks later—he did it. He built the defense. You look at the names on that defense and you know he had a lot of talent, some great, great defensive players.

—CHARLIE HENNEMAN, Charlottesville, Virginia

I pride myself on getting along with coaches. I'm very empathetic toward coaches. I know a lot of them are hard-nosed. A lot of them are very difficult to get along with, like Bobby Knight. Most coaches I did get along with because I did understand them. I understand that their job, I don't care what they're being paid, is a job where every-body is looking over their shoulder. If you win, you're the greatest guy in the world. If you lost, you're the worst guy in the world. There are more highs than lows. It's not like being a doctor or a dentist or a lawyer where you win or lose cases and things like that. You've got a hundred thousand people looking at you when you do it as a coach. Some of them have had kind of rough edges to them going back to the early days when you had the Bernie Biermans and the Woody Hayes—they were tough guys. If you understood them, and gave them a good shot, they'd give you a good interview.

—JIM ZABEL

I was on the selection committee when we hired Kirk Ferentz. Of course, we got blasted for not hiring Bob Stoops. I told people right on through the whole time Ferentz was a quality guy and a good coach with a good staff and to hang with them. I've had a number of people come up to me and remind me that I said things like that. Of course, part of my job was to be positive, but I actually did believe it. Kirk is smart as hell and very organized. Some of us who got to know the assistant coaches found out how they were and how dedicated they were, very good with the kids. That first year you could talk to the kids who were playing for them, and they could tell you how good these coaches were. Even that first year, these guys were impressed with the coaches.

—MARK JENNINGS, Iowa Foundation

When Hayden Fry held his first press conference, I can remember thinking, "What the hell are we getting ourselves into?" He was starting to use all that Texas drawl, and all those stories…he was a marvelous ambassador for the game. What he did at Iowa was amazing. That first year we realized he could be successful by the people he was attracting around him, the way he went about his operations, the way he was organized. It as obvious that he was going to get players. Besides his great football mind, he attracted outstanding people around him, much the same as Ferentz is doing today.

—**BOB BROOKS**, KMRY, Cedar Rapids

During and after that 1999 first season, I really liked Kirk Ferentz' demeanor. He had a thought. He stuck with it. In his speeches in December, after his first year, even after going 1-10, he was still saying the same things and had the same tone as in August before the season began. He never changed his mindset. There was never a sign of any apology. Never a sign of any concept that we've got the wrong people. He never acknowledged that he had to be sick to his gullet listening to how they didn't hire Bobby Stoops. There was never an acknowledgment that he was even aware of that. That sold me on the guy. I knew he had something—had substance and would transfer that to his players. He stayed the course with not only what he wanted to do, but stayed the course with all those people he brought there when everybody was saying he didn't have a very good offensive coordinator…and everybody was bad. He never changed. He didn't argue with anybody—he just kept going.

When he beat Penn State in overtime there his second year, I knew he'd turned the corner. I said, "It's all downhill for him now. He's really gonna go." You can go back to that game as being the turning point of Kirk Ferentz' career: One—they were playing *at* Penn State. Two, they were playing—*and beating* a legend. Three— you don't have a very good football team and yet your team who has been getting the daylights kicked out of it has never lost faith in what your coaches are teaching. That's what told me. They had enough presence to go into "mighty Penn State"—in any circumstance, it's not easy to win there, let alone a team that is struggling for any type of identity, to win some ball games, and to still believe in their coaches enough that not only could you sneak in and win a ball game you were not supposed to win, but you took them to overtime, and then did it!

—JIM WALDEN, Ex-Pac 10 and Big 12 head coach

You find out a guy's character and their coaching ability when they're not winning. Most people don't understand that. If you can see through the losses, and you find out how a guy handles losing, what do his players think about him when you're losing, and so we found out who Kirk Ferentz was the first few years at Iowa. Now he's getting rewarded for who he's always been. The great thing, as a former player, that I've noticed about him is that if you come into The University of Iowa as a player on the football team, and you have any type of work ethic at all, you're gonna leave four years later a lot better. If you come in here as a hard working kid, you're going to leave as a good player. If you come in here as a good player, you're going to leave as a great player. If you come in as a great player, well then you're going to leave as a first-round draft pick. The foundation of his program, in my opinion, has been player development. I don't see anybody in the country right now doing it better. The other thing was that when you talk to the guys who were here when we were losing all the time, they always believed in him even through the losses. That really says a lot about him. He's just a tremendous person. I had an event with him a few months ago, and he's a great guy. He seems like the type of guy who could be anybody's neighbor in Iowa. Those are the type of coaches we like the best.

—JESS SETTLES, ex-Iowa basketball star

IOWA IOWA IOWA IOWA IOWA IOWA IOWA IOWA IOWA IOWA IOWA IOWA IOWA

When watching Penn State, do you root for the defense or the prosecution?

Chapter 5

Turn Your Radio On

I've Never Met Jim Zabel, But I've Known Him All My Life

CHEVY CHASE ONCE HOSTED THE OSCARS, HENDRIX ONCE OPENED FOR THE MONKEES, JIM ZABEL ONCE RACED JESSE OWENS... THERE ARE SOME THINGS YOU JUST CAN'T MAKE UP!

Jim Zabel

Jim Zabel is Iowa Hawkeye sports. He recently completed his 60th year at WHO, Des Moines. Zabel is semi-retired at his home in Scottsdale, Arizona.

I was born and raised in Davenport and was a big Hawkeye fan. My dad used to take me to the games. Even though Iowa lost most of the games back then, I still became a Hawkeye. I graduated from Davenport High School in 1939. I took a year off, and hitchhiked to Mexico. All my friends went to Iowa so I went there, too. I became a Sigma Chi and became editor of the *Daily Iowan* and graduated in three and a half years.

When I was eight or ten years old, my dad and I started going to games. We would take a train to the game. For a young kid, it was big time—it was thrilling. Iowa didn't win most of those games. You can look at their record. Minnesota would come down and crucify them. But, they had standout guys like Joe Laws, Dick Crayne—I saw that 103 yard punt—The Ebony Eel, Ozzie Simmons. Those guys just became indelible in a young guy's mind, and they were heroes to me. There weren't too many other young kids on the train—mostly older guys all smoking cigars and drinking beer. At the games, we would get pretty good seats, thirty or forty-yard line. Then, the stadium held 52,000—now it holds 72,000. The end zones were open and had shrubbery, grass and trees growing there. It had a different look to it then than it does now. The press box, which I later worked in, was right on top of the West stands, just attached to it, as opposed to the one they have now. The one they have now has been there fifty years, and they are going to tear that one down.

Davenport High School was the biggest school in the state. We had 3,600 kids in school at that time. I graduated in 1939 and was only 17 years old, a young graduate. I had won the state indoor championship in the quarter-mile and was captain of the track team. In June my coach, Jesse Day, called me and said, "Jim, how would you like to run an exhibition race over at Douglas Park in Rock Island tomorrow night before the baseball game?" I was kind of a cocky kid, and I said, "Well, coach, I've beaten everybody in this area." He said, "Well, you haven't beaten this guy." I said, "Who is it?" He said, "Jesse Owens."

I just about fell over. Owens, at that time, held every single world record from the 50-yard dash to the 220-yard dash, the low hurdles and the broad jump. He was the Olympic champion, and he was coming to town to run an exhibition race. He was trying to make some money following the great performances in the 1936 Olympic Games. I got over to Douglas Park. We were going to run the exhibition race down the third-base line. Owens came over and put his arm around me and said, "Hey kid. I'd like to help you in this race." I said, "Believe me, I'm going to need some help." Owens was just electrifying to me. It was like a Little League kid being introduced to **Mickey Mantle**. He said, "Well, I'll tell you what I'll do. I'll give you a lead of 16-yards in the race." It was a hundred-yard dash. I thought for a moment and said, "Well, I appreciate that, Mr. Owens, but that wouldn't be honest or sportsmanlike for me to accept." So we compromised on twelve yards.

There's something about running at night—something about the night air that makes you feel you're invincible. I got down in my crouch. We dug two holes in the ground because we didn't have any starting blocks. The starting gun went off. I took out of there and for an amazing distance, I led the great Jesse Owens. I think it was about three yards. All of a sudden, I felt a breeze go by me. Owens ran the

> **If Mickey Mantle's strikeouts and walks were combined, he would have played the equivalent of seven years without hitting the ball.**

hundred that night in 9.8 seconds—.4 of a second off his world record. I got to know him very well. I interviewed him a number of times when he was Grand Marshal of the Drake Relays. In fact, when I was down here at Scottsdale one time, I covered his funeral. He was a big hero to me—one of the all-time greats.

Right at that time, my parents had moved to Aurora, Illinois. I was involved in an auto accident and got my leg banged up and even though I was offered a scholarship at Iowa, I couldn't take it because I had leg problems. After all that, I had a very weak ankle. My track days were over so I concentrated on writing and broadcasting.

In high school, we did a weekly show on WOC-Radio, which I was on. I took part in dramatic art and elocution and debate. I also wrote for the student newspaper so I felt I had talents along those lines. When I got to Iowa, I started working on the paper and eventually got to be editor-in-chief of the *Daily Iowan*. I wrote a very popular column and did shows on WSUI. All that gave me a tremendous interest in radio—before the days of television. When I graduated from Iowa in 1943—war-time years—I was classified 1-B, due to my leg injury. I had three job offers, all in New York City: from *Life* magazine, *Look* magazine and the *New York Herald Tribune*—all big-time offers. My draft board said they wanted me to stick closer to home because they were going to start taking 1-B classifieds. I got a job in Chicago writing scripts for a CBS show called "America in the Air." I was 21 years old, and was a scriptwriter in Chicago.

Jack Shelley, of WHO came through Chicago looking for people to work in the news department. In the spring of 1944, he offered me a job as a writer and a broadcaster. I went to WHO-Des Moines on May 18, 1944. I have now been at WHO for over 60 years. My only broadcast experience had been at WSUI at University of Iowa. I had interviewed Shelley a couple of times, and he knew my background. One year I was voted, "Young Newspaper Man of the Year." I had won the Sigma Delta Chi award.

The jobs kept getting better and better. In 1949, I was offered the job of sports directorship. I had done the Drake Relays one year, and they liked the job I did. During the way, we weren't doing much sports.

Ronald Reagan had left WHO in 1937. He came back a couple of times, and I got to interview him. He was great. I'll never forget an interview I did with him in 1950 when he came through town. He'd made a movie with Piper Laurie. He was coming down Walnut Street and our offices were at 914 Walnut. They had a parade for him. Our general manager said, "Get him out of the car. Get him in here and do an interview with him." I got him in the building. We sat down to do a live interview on the air. We talked about this and about that. He was so glib that he could remember everything—contrary to the disease that finally claimed him—every player, every game, every score. We talked and talked and talked. Finally, after 45 minutes, I said, "Well, Dutch, I guess we'd better terminate the interview. We've talked so long the station may want to hire you back, and I'll be out of a job." He said, "Jim, you stay out of Hollywood…I'll stay out of Des Moines." Over the years, I interviewed him eighteen times. I interviewed him at the White House right after he'd been shot. I interviewed him during the presidential race. Interviewed him when he was a movie star. Interviewed him when he was governor. A friend of mine used to joke that the reason that Reagan didn't get killed when he got shot was because he thought the whole thing was a movie.

Back in the forties, there was no exclusivity. We had three stations in Des Moines broadcasting, originating Iowa games. Iowa had a total of 22 originations at that time, Cedar Rapids, Davenport, Sioux City—all of them sent their own announcers down.

There were so many in the press box that we were practically falling all over one another, and some guys were even sitting out in the stands doing the game. That was a different time—it was when Iowa was actually looking for people to promote the games and broadcast the games, as opposed to now.

I'd done a little play-by-play of track and field 'cause I did the Drake Relays one year. I helped out on some high school games on WSUI. I'd never really done play-by-play. I came out cold turkey and did it. I managed to do it well enough. Then as I continued to do it, I gradually got better and better and developed my own style.

That first game was scary. I was nervous. One game in 1949 that I vividly recall was against Oregon. This was my first year of broadcasting. Iowa was trailing 31-10 going into the fourth quarter. Everybody was leaving the stadium. All of a sudden, Bill Reichardt runs a kickoff back 100 yards and Bob Longley runs a punt back 90-yards for a touchdown. Iowa won the game 54-31. That's when I first discovered the power of radio, the power of WHO, and the success of being a broadcaster. Everybody on Monday said, "What a great game you called!" They were all listening on their car radios. They couldn't believe Iowa came back and won that game. That was a game, among many, that just stuck in my mind.

Eddie Anderson was the coach in those days. He was a tough coach—out of the mold of coaches of that era, Evashevski, Bernie Bierman, Woody Hayes—tough guys. He had coached Iowa for four years in the late '30s, left for service, came back and coached again.

Leonard Raffensberger, the coach before Evashevski, was a nice guy, but he was in over his head. He coached two years there. He had been a high-school coach in Waterloo and was at Iowa as the freshman coach. Paul Brechler, the athletic director, traveled around and was looking for a new head coach and Raff was a popular guy, but to jump from high school to college….

My baptism by fire was in 1950. We went to Columbus, Ohio. Raff was the coach, and we played Ohio State when Wes Fesler was coach. They had a national championship team there. The score, at the end of three minutes, was 21-0. The score at the end of the half was 55-0. They beat Iowa 83-21 that day.

The A.D., Paul Brechler, and some of his cohorts made a national tour. They were looking for a coach to replace Raffensberger. They hired Forest Evashevski, who was a young, very successful coach at Washington State at that time. He was a legend at the University of Michigan. He was tough, smart, a great coach. He was a tough guy to get along with, but he was a terrific coach. He came in and Iowa hadn't won much for fifty years. He just stomped around the state, made something like 72 speeches in 30 days. I was at a lot of them and got to know him very well. I did all of his shows. I called all of his games. I revere the memory of him, but I can sympathize with people who had to work with him 'cause he was a tough guy, he really was, but coaches were that way in those days.

You could tell, from the beginning that he could turn the program around. He knew what he wanted to do. He had a game plan. He had to recruit—had to get players in there. He was very innovative, a coaching genius. In 1952, he didn't have any talent at all. Ohio State came to town. In one week, Iowa went from the single-wing to the split-T. Iowa completely surprised Woody Hayes and won that game 8-0. It was one of the all-time great Iowa victories. I was amazed. I thought, "I can't believe this is happening." All of a sudden, he went on to legendary greatness—went to the Rose Bowl in 1956 and 1958. I thought the '58 team was maybe the greatest team in Iowa history—one of the great Big Ten teams of all time. Bernie Bierman called it the best offensive team he'd ever seen. That was Willie Fleming, Randy Duncan, Bobby Jeter and those guys.

I still razz Randy Duncan about being kissed by Jayne Mansfield. I'll never forget it—Bob Hope comes in there at the Biltmore Bowl, which is a stage and theater-type arrangement, in the Biltmore Hotel in Los Angeles. He was the emcee, and he said, "Well, here she is, boys—38-24-36-Hike, Jayne Mansfield." Randy comes up and kissed her, and Hope says, "Don't make a meal out of it, Liver Lips."

In 1953, in South Bend, Indiana that was quite a game. They recorded that one and still play it around the country—the Fainting Irish game. Iowa came in there very much underrated. I thought they were a better team that what they were showing. They just weren't winning games. Notre Dame, rated #1, was fighting Oklahoma for the top ranking in the country. Iowa took a 7-0 lead. Notre Dame came back to tie it. Iowa took a 14-7 lead. Notre Dame, in the closing moments, with the Fainting Irish, a Notre Dame player grabbed his knee and fell down to stop the clock. You could tell it was a fake—and we said so on the broadcast. Vee Green, the former Drake coach, was my color man. He said, "Jim, I think there's something phony about that down there." I said, "Well, he grabbed his knee, but it looks like he's acting." It turned out he was, but nevertheless, Ralph Guglielmi was the quarterback, and he passes to Dan Shannon in the end zone and they scored the touchdown because they got the extra time. They really came from behind to tie Iowa 14-14. But, the fakery in that game cost Frank Leahy his job, I think. It was even printed in the paper that Notre Dame was faking the knee injury. Notre Dame had an untarnished reputation, and they couldn't stand the scandal of the whole thing. A while later, Leahy resigned.

Thirty minutes after that game, people were so stunned, they were still sitting in the stands. They couldn't believe it. Here was Iowa coming out of nowhere, tying the great Notre Dame team, taking them right down to the wire. They tied one for the Gipper.

In 1956 we beat Minnesota 7-0, beat Ohio State 6-0, but I really thought the game that put Iowa in the Rose Bowl was played early in the season at West Lafayette, Indiana against Purdue. Iowa took a 21-0 lead. Purdue came back and missed an extra point. Iowa won that game 21-20. Lenny Dawson was the Purdue quarterback in a game that went literally down to the wire. I think that was the most important game for Evy that season. Back then it was fantastic to go to the Rose Bowl game. Now, out of 10 teams in the conference, seven or eight of them will go to **bowl games**. Then, only one team went to a bowl game, and it was the Rose Bowl. That was like a trip to Mars. You couldn't imagine that Iowa could go. You could imagine that Ohio State or Michigan could go 'cause they always did, but not Iowa. All of a sudden, here we were, beating Ohio State 6-0 when Jim Gibbons caught that pass and all of a sudden we were in the Rose Bowl. Just incredible! I made the trip and did the game, and it was fantastic.

There were a lot of bad-weather games in the state of Iowa, and all over the Midwest—you just get used to it. I remember October 8, 1957—the snow-bowl game—we were playing Northwestern at Evanston, and eight inches of snow fell. They tried to blade the field, but it was a grass field so they took all the grass off. It became a

> When Clemson University plays in a bowl game, most of their fans pay their bills with $2 bills to show their economic impact…and increase their chances of a future invitation.

"mud bowl," an absolute "mud bowl." Randy Duncan finally completed a pass to Kevin Furlong and we won the game 6-0.

Evy was forced out in 1960 when they gave him a choice of being either athletic director or football coach. One season, he could be both, which he was in 1960, and then he had to make a choice. I always thought that was a very dumb move on the part of the athletic board. They were scared to death of Evy, scared of his power. He made the choice of being athletic director instead of being coach. He should have stayed on as coach. First of all, they should have let him be both coach and athletic director—yet he was forced out.

They were afraid of him. He was powerful. He was a guy who just dominated things. The board in control of athletics, at that time, was made up of people who were afraid of their own shadows, and they were afraid of Evashevski. They made the pretense that they did not want a man to have that much power to be athletic director and coach. It was a bad, very costly decision.

Then there was the Jerry Burns era. He was a brilliant coach, but I don't think he really had a great chance at Iowa to prove himself. He later went on in the pros, both at Green Bay and at Minnesota, to prove what a great coach he was. He was a terrific guy.

In 1963, when Kennedy was killed, that was shocking. I was at home. Iowa officials had a big debate as to whether or not they were even going to play the game. They canceled the game. In 1958 I had interviewed Kennedy at a Notre Dame game when he was in the press box. They asked me if I'd like to interview him, and I said, "Yeah." Senator Kennedy came up and Iowa was leading in the game 25-0 at halftime. I said, "Well, Senator, what do you think of the game?" He said, "Well, I'm pulling for Iowa and praying for Notre Dame."

In 1965, the 1-9 year, a whole bunch of things happened. Not enough talent, not enough recruiting, dissension on the team. That may have been the player revolt, too. With the "war" going on in the athletic department and with the team, a lot of things happened behind the scenes. Did they have enough talent? Did they have enough power? There was a tug-of-war going on between Evy and Nagel—no question about that. Nagel was a good offensive coach, but he didn't have much defense. There was a lot of skullduggery and pressure and pulling and pushing and different factions that wanted Evashevski back as coach.

If you go by statistics, the most important game ever played for Iowa was the Michigan game in 1985 when Iowa was #1 in the nation, and Michigan was #2. Iowa beat Michigan in Iowa City. To me, the most dramatic game ever played was November 14, 1987 in Columbus, Ohio, when Hartlieb passed to Cook with six seconds to go and Iowa beat Ohio State 29-27. It was always difficult to try to beat Ohio State in Columbus. In 1981, Iowa beat Nebraska, UCLA and Michigan under Hayden Fry, who'd only been there three years, and went to the Rose Bowl. They beat Michigan 9-7 on three field goals by Tommy Nichol. Those two games played at Ann Arbor, Michigan in 1981, and at Columbus, Ohio in 1987 were the most memorable.

As far as opposing players go, Archie Griffin at Ohio State was awful good—the best opponent's player I ever saw. And there have been some great Big Ten quarterbacks over the years. Evy was my color man for a number of years. He was terrific. Randy Duncan was my color man for a while. Bill Reichardt was my color man. Vee Green was my color man. Then Ed Podolak was my color man for about 15 years. Vee Green played as a center at **Illinois** on Red Grange's team. He was a good host, did not have the greatest material, but he was a great talker and could spin a lot of tales, so he was very good. Evy was terrific because he could talk forever about the days of Tom Harmon, and of the great Michigan games. He was such a great football analyst, with a mind like a steel trap. He was a football genius. Podolak was absolutely terrific, and he's still going strong. Podolak was a great all-around player himself, and he knows the modern game of football. He knows the passing game. He had a great mind for football. I think he's the best color man around.

I knew about Hayden Fry when he was coaching down in Texas, and the job he did at SMU and at North Texas. He was kind of a legend

> **The Chicago Bears wear blue and orange because those are the colors that team founder George Halas wore when he played for the University of Illinois.**

down there—then, all of a sudden, he was hired as coach of Iowa. There were some questions marks. Could a guy from Texas come up and do the job that needed to be done. I wasn't sure anybody could turn Iowa around at that point. But Hayden came in 1979 and, within three years, Iowa was in the Rose Bowl—1981. He came in and brought a great coaching staff with him—look at his coaching staff. Bill Snyder, Bobby Stoops, Kirk Ferentz, Barry Alvarez—these were the guys he had on his staff. I'm not so sure that wasn't the greatest coaching staff of all time. Here's how tough the Big Ten Conference is: a few years ago, Barry Alvarez took Wisconsin to the Rose Bowl and was named National Coach of the Year. Meanwhile, the same season, the Ohio State fans wanted to run Coach John Cooper out of town…yet each team had a 10-1-1 record.

At the time Hayden Fry was coming in, it wasn't a matter of it being Hayden Fry. It was, "Can anybody come in and turn this program around? Could they recruit?" There was a lot of bitterness and a lot of factionalism. There were "Evy people" still. There were "Nagel people." There were "Jerry Burns people." I wasn't sure anybody could come in and turn that program around because of the trouble behind the scenes. Hayden got in there, and he made all the right moves. He talked to Evy for two hours before he even took the job and got Evy on his side. He got a great coaching staff together. He knew how to recruit. Those three elements brought them together.

One of my standard lines I used in the early days of Hayden Fry, when I did an I-Club Function was "Thank God for Hayden Fry. He finally brought a football team that lives up to my play-by-play." I love Hayden Fry. He's incredible. I just love to talk to him. To this day, we talk probably once every two months on the phone. He loves where he is in Nevada. He wanted to get away from the football scene. He still makes a lot of speeches. I didn't think anybody could resurrect Kansas State. That has to be an amazing job down there. Hayden Fry at Iowa and Bill Snyder at Kansas State—two best coaching jobs of the past twenty-five years.

Stoops was a good kid, a smart kid, a sharp kid. I just knew him as a young guy when he was a graduate assistant and when he was a player. You could tell he was headed someplace because he had a good head on his shoulders. I'm not at all surprised by how well he's done. I was one of Bob Stoops' fans and thought he would be the coach at Iowa. At one time, he wanted the job. I'm not saying it didn't turn out good the way it did because I'm not sure we could have a better coach than Kirk Ferentz. It has really turned out well for everybody. Kirk is a heck of a guy, a great coach. Kirk is a great line coach. When Hayden has those great teams in the early 1980s, don't forget that Kirk Ferentz was the line coach on those teams. I think it turned out well, but at the time there was a lot of furor behind the scenes because a lot of people thought Bobby Stoops should have the job.

After his first year, nobody thought Ferentz could turn it all around. You thought, "Well, he's a nice guy. He's a good line coach." But, he did—as soon as he could get his recruits in there. Ferentz and the team had looked good, even in losing some games, but when they started to win some games, and when you looked at the quality of talent he was getting, particularly the offensive lines and the linebackers, you knew good things were going to happen. That has been his strength. This year, for instance, he's got a good offensive line coming in, and he probably has the best linebackers in the country. He's gonna win some games this year—he's gonna win a lot of games this year—that 44-7 ASU debacle aside. He's got a total program going, where he knows how to evaluate material. I like him as a guy because he doesn't get carried away with a victory. He doesn't get down in the dumps with a loss. He's very consistent with his personality. He's terrific. He's proven himself to be much better than most people thought he could be.

I owe everything to the Iowa fans, WHO and The University of Iowa. I'm grateful and thankful.

HE'S GOT PEP IN HIS STEP AND GLIDE IN HIS STRIDE.

Bob Brooks

When most sports fans in eastern Iowa think of sports, they think of Bob Brooks. He has been doing Iowa play-by-play since 1943. The always likeable, always friendly Brooks still plies his trade at KMRY in Cedar Rapids.

The reason I got into this business was because I was an Iowa fan, and my folks were Iowa fans. In 1938, I went to my first Iowa game. Iowa played Colgate and lost 14-0. I was 13 years old and just about as impressionable as you can get. My parents had season tickets but, in the throes of the depression, you had to be very careful about what you spent your money on. I would ride down with them because I joined the Knothole Section. For the year, it cost a quarter—the whole season—four home games.

I was at a game in 1939, which set up the Iowa season, which is never mentioned. It was the first conference game—Iowa played Indiana. Iowa at that time was drawing so few people that as soon as you got in the end zone seat, you jumped out of that section and went into the stands because there wasn't anybody else around. It was a high-scoring game for that time. Both teams marched up and down the field. The fans could just follow them by constantly changing seats. When Iowa went to the south end of the field, the people just moved down to the south end of the field. When Indiana went to the north end of the field, everybody moved and went to the north end. Iowa won the game 32-29. Had they not won that particular game, the Iron Men would have never existed.

What happened later on would have not been as heroic and headline-friendly as what it was. Kinnick undoubtedly never would have won the Heisman Trophy had they not won that game. During that year, Iowa lost at Michigan 27-7, and they played a tie with North-western. In between, there were these two weeks when the beat Notre Dame and Minnesota back-to-back. That created the legend of the Iron Men.

Back then, people dressed up to go to the games. The field was lined differently. There were no numbers. The goal lines were different. There weren't any double stripes or boundaries or hash marks. Iowa had a marching band and cheerleaders then, too. Iowa had a group of men they called the Scottish Highlanders who played the bagpipes and drums and wore kilts and Scottish attire. Early in the sixties, they did away with the Scottish Highlanders.

I attended Iowa and majored in journalism. By 1943, WSUI, the uni-versity station, didn't have anybody who could announce anything from the male gender side. I was willing to do it as an intern so I got on in the summer and filled in whenever I could and just went on from there. WSUI broadcast the games in those days, and that was part of your student development. Consequently, I had experience broadcasting games so I free-lanced a few high school games. In '44, I spotted for the broadcasts at WMT at Cedar Rapids. Pat Patterson was WMT's play-by-play man at that time.

College was accelerated in those days. If you were going to stay in college and not be drafted, although I wasn't a draftable age until the war was over, you had to go to summer school—go to school all year. So I got out of school in three and a half years.

In those early days, in the press box, there would be an engineer and a couple of spotters there with me. We'd get people to come up to the press box for half-time interviews. Everything then was done live. After WSUI, I came aboard with KCRG radio in Cedar Rapids in August of 1948. They were starting to do the Iowa games, and I immediately began doing the play-by-play. In those days, we didn't have color guys. My most memorable play would be Kenny Ploen's touchdown pass to Jim Gibbons that beat Ohio State and put Iowa in the Rose Bowl.

In 1956, Iowa went to the Rose Bowl. We had three United propel-ler-driven planes to take everybody out there. We had a big send-off at the Cedar Rapids airport. Everybody got a cardboard key to the city, and the band was there, and they had balloons. The team and the official party couldn't get on the planes because of the fog and rain there at the airport. The pilots had to fly the three aircraft over to Moline, and we had to bus over there to take off for Pasadena. I can remember going to the Huntington-Sheraton Hotel in Pasadena. It was late at night when we got there. Jim Zabel and I stood in the courtyard and looked up. I said, "Jim, did you ever think in your wildest imagination that Iowa would ever be in the Rose Bowl?" He turned, and just shook his head. That was both our feelings. We never thought that would happen.

I told Jim Zabel the only reason he ever got to buy that palatial palace out in Scottsdale was because I had paid for all of his meals. He said, "Listen, you helped."

Things go in cycles. When you're in the parameters of Iowa, and what you have to deal with in regard to recruiting and resources and everything. I think it's bound to be a cyclical thing. You don't want that down cycle to last so long. There is a good side to that, too. I've told a lot of people this. I really believe the same thing happened in Iowa basketball. You can go along and go from this coach to that coach to success. The days of being down and not winning make you appreciate the good days even more.

I would think that in their devotion and in every facet of backing, Iowa fans would be the envy of most teams. Iowa football and basketball is my life, as well as Cedar Rapids' high school athletics.

Mac Lewis suffered from
Anorexia Ponderosa

A WHALE OF AN ANNOUNCER

Gary Dolphin

Gary Dolphin is the radio voice of the Hawkeyes. A native of Cascade, Iowa, he handles all play-by-play action of both Iowa football and men's basketball. Dolphin also hosts the Kirk Ferentz and Steve Alford coaches' shows. In 2001, he was named Iowa Sportscaster of the Year. Dolphin is in his 32nd year of broadcasting, including six years at Northwestern.

I grew up in Cascade, a little town about sixty miles northwest of Iowa City. My mom and dad were season ticket holders for a lot of years, and mom still is. We went to a lot of football and basketball games beginning in the early sixties. I've been a lifelong Hawkeye fan. I like all Iowa sports and enjoyed going down and sitting in the old Field House, as well as Carver, and obviously Kinnick Stadium, which is a very special place. And here thirty-five years later, to be picked as the Voice of the Hawkeyes is like a dream come true. I had the chance to do Iowa football and basketball in the seventies for six years when we had a bunch of radio stations that would pay 'rights' fees and do the games. I have spent the better part of thirty years in this business covering the Hawks. It's been a real joy and a real treat for me.

The other thing that makes Iowa kind of a focal point is that with Iowa and Iowa State you have two quality institutions within the same borders that are members of two of the power conferences. That's a rarity, with Iowa State in the Big 12 and Iowa in the Big Ten. That's unique and draws more attention to the state as well.

Having never played the game at a high level—I just wasn't talented enough—to be asked that first time to sign an autograph is kind of awkward and odd. It still feels awkward today when some young kid comes up, ten, twelve years old, and wants my autograph next to

Kirk's or Steve's. I've gotten over the point of saying to them, "Gee, whiz! You want *my autograph?*" Their typical response would be, "Absolutely. We listen to you every Saturday." It humbles one to know that not only do you have a lot of people out there listening or hanging on your every word, but that they're passionate about attending the game and bringing their Walkman or headset along. I can't tell you how many times I've run into farmers at I-Club outings who tell me they can't get to the games in September and October because it's harvest time so they have Dolphin and Podolak on the radio in the cab of their tractor or truck or at the feed mill or when running up and down I-80. It's very rewarding. It's very humbling. It does point out the true passion Iowans have for their football and basketball.

Carver was built in 1983, and it's a great building to watch a game in because of the unobstructed sight lines. For 15,500 people, there really isn't a bad seat in the house. It was way ahead of its time when Lute Olson started the groundswell for a new arena. But, having said that, I really miss the Field House because it was so loud in there. Coaches to this day whether it be Johnny Orr or guys who played in the building like Rudy Tomjanovich and Don Nelson, they always felt the Field House was something special. That old iron, steel and brick building really held the noise in, and, of course, some great Iowa teams played in there back to Bucky O'Connor's days and the Final Four teams of the fifties. I love both buildings, but I'm kind of a history buff so I would say I enjoyed watching a game in the Field House a little bit more. But I do think Carver's one of the finest buildings in college basketball.

There is a blind, young guy in Mason City named Joel. I met him at University Hospital a few years ago. He's just a passionate Hawkeye fan and lives by the radio. We are his eyes and his sound for Hawkeye football and basketball. I hear from Joel all the time and see him when we go to Mason City for the North Iowa I-Club. There's another young man in Oskaloosa named Tyler who is a passionate Hawk fan—loves Hawkeye wrestling. He's been battling a rare form of cancer for several years. He wanted in the worst way to wrestle for Iowa. This affliction has, of course, set him back. He's been to Duke University Hospital Cancer Research Center and all over the country trying to fight this rare form of cancer. A lot of people didn't give him a nickel's chance of beating it, and here he is beating it. He tells me that part of his attitude adjustments and looking at life positively is loving the Hawkeyes—whether it be wrestling, football or basketball. Those are heartwarming stories and there are a bunch of them like that.

There's a guy in Ottumwa whose basement walls, from one side to the other, are plugged with Hawkeye memorabilia. Every program from every game, from every bowl game, every pin from Homecoming parades for the last fifty years. He even got Hayden Fry to come down and look at it one time, and Hayden was amazed at the amount of Hawk stuff this guy has in his basement. We did a feature on it for Coach Ferentz' TV show a few years back.

If there's one thing that Kirk Ferentz has proven in his six years at Iowa, it is that special teams—and he said this when he first came in here—will win anywhere from two to three to four games a year. I'll be doggoned if that hasn't played out true at The University of Iowa. It's incredible to me, field-position wise, if you can stick the guy back deep in his own red zone on a kick or a punt, and you have a very good defense, the field position is "it" in football. It takes all the pieces of the puzzle to fit together. Football's so unique a game in that you've got a hundred and twenty players, you've got ten coaches, and everyone is responsible for their area. It's unique to me how it always seems to come down to special teams in the end. All the other components are important, but special teams will decide a game one to four times a year.

My favorite memory as a Hawkeye fan, would have to be the first Iowa basketball game I ever attended. My dad took my brother and me, in '62. Don Nelson was everything to Iowa basketball at the time. It was Don Nelson Night and was his final game in the Field House as a Hawk. Iowa was playing **Wisconsin**, and Nelson scored thirty-five points. I was on top of the world. I got to see the great Don

Arnold Schwarzenegger graduated from the University of Wisconsin in 1979.

Nelson, the All-American, play his final game inside the Field House as a Hawk. That memory will last forever.

As a broadcaster, I'd be remiss if I didn't give you one favorite memory for football and one for basketball. Basketball has to be Steve Alford's first game as coach, beating Connecticut, the defending national champions in Madison Square Garden in November that first year at the Coaches Against Cancer Classic. Just being inside Madison Square Garden for the first time was such a thrill. Second, to beat Jim Calhoun who had most of the components coming back from that championship team, other than Rick Hamilton, it was really a thrill to win that game. For football, it would be hard to top the Outback Bowl. To me, when Kirk's program really turned around, it was the double overtime victory at Penn State in his second year. They finished 3-9 that year, but they almost beat a very good Wisconsin team the week before. They go to Happy Valley. They're on a big losing streak and they knock off Penn State in double overtime. They come back home the next week and beat a very good Northwestern team, costing them a shot at the Rose Bowl. That Penn State game in Happy Valley in double overtime would be the marquee game for me because you could just see the program turn at that moment. The next year they won the Alamo Bowl and beat a very good **Texas Tech** team. Then they had the wonderful year with eleven wins and the Orange Bowl, and now to the Outback Bowl. The bell cow for the program would have to be that double overtime win at Penn State in Kirk's second year.

> **Texas Tech's basketball arena, the United Spirit Center in Lubbock, is on Indiana Avenue. Texas Tech's nickname is the Red Raiders. The nickname of Bob Knight's Orrville, Ohio high school was the Red Raiders.**

The formula for the BCS Bowls is actually a recipe for chili.

THE QUAD-CITIES IS TWICE
AS GOOD AS THE TWIN CITIES.

Thom Cornelis

Thom Cornelis has been the sports anchor at KWQC-TV in Davenport so long that his shoes have gone out of style seven times. A graduate of Alleman High School in Rock Island and Western Illinois University, Cornelis has covered the Hawks for over a quarter of a century.

All the stations in the Quad Cities cover Iowa fairly well because of its closeness. I was the first basketball TV play-by-play guy for Iowa basketball back in '78. We put together a bunch of stations, and we originated from WQAD in Moline. We did the Iowa-Illinois game at the old Field House. Bump Elliott, the A.D. at the time was very leery about having TV cover the game. He didn't allow us to put a camera on the floor because we were blocking fans' views. The game was so well received that he came right back to us and said, "You want to do the Purdue game next month?" They put it out for bids, and I did it for about three years. Then I did radio for KSTT for Iowa football for seven years. At first, I was doing color with John Cloughessey. When he left for WFAN in New York, I took over and had various color guys—Rob Fick, the old quarterback who is now a big realtor in Davenport; Eddie Podolak for a year, and now he's still doing it with the *big boys*…various ones.

When we played basketball once at Wichita State, I knew I had arrived. Back then, Kansas was a dry state, and the only way you could get a drink after a game was to be a member of a club. For some reason, I had an Elks Club pass for Wichita. When Zabel found out I had a card, I was his friend for life. And, of course, I paid for them, too.

Iowa was playing Michigan State when word came down into the stands that Ohio State had beaten Michigan. That clinched the **Rose Bowl** for Iowa. The buzz coming down from the press box was kind of like an audio wave going around the stadium. All of a sudden, roses popped out everywhere. Fans rushed the field. I actually was, literally, carried out. I was standing at mid-field with the cameraman. Their enthusiasm picked us both up, and my feet did not touch the ground until we were past the end zone. That made me realize what could happen in a soccer riot. The crush of the crowd trying to get to the players, and the players trying to get their locker room—it was just amazing.

When I first saw Hayden, I thought, "This guy can sell snow to Eskimos." I just knew it, and he knew it, and we got to be friends through the years. We'd know just coming in every Tuesday for the press conference that he was going to use someone as a whipping boy. Every now and then, it would be somebody in the media. It was usually before a game Iowa was expected to win…when he needed to get the players revved up. He wanted to get the players focused on it. Then he'd wink at me and say, "You knew that was coming, didn't you, Tommy?" I'd say, "Yeah. Nothing personal."

Kirk Ferentz was so much more low-key than Hayden. Hayden was such a salesman and up-front and a promoter. Ferentz is low-key, down-home. It was tough to get to know him at first, but he was so honest with you, and you knew he was never conning you. Everybody knew exactly where they stood—players, media and everybody. The cupboard was a little bare when he came over. He's such a nice guy that we all said, "Gee, I hope he makes it." Slowly, but surely, you saw all the principles he believed in. He stuck to his guns and fought through that first season, 1-10. Then, they got up to 4-5. Then, they turned it around and have been going great guns ever since.

I think the only job Ferentz would leave Iowa for, being a Pittsburgh native, would be if the Steelers job opens up. I think Ferentz is at least committed to getting his son through college. That's another two-three years.

> **The Rose Bowl Parade originally had nothing to do with the Rose Bowl football game. It was a celebration in Pasadena for the ripening of the oranges.**

PHOENIX IS KNOWN AS "THE VALLEY OF THE SUN." IN SUMMER, IT SHOULD BE KNOWN AS "THE SURFACE OF THE SUN."

Al McCoy

Williams, Iowa native, Al McCoy, is nearing legendary status among NBA play-by-play announcers. Now in his 33rd year with the Phoenix Suns, McCoy is arguably the most popular sports figure in Arizona. After graduating from Drake in 1954, McCoy received a graduate assistantship at The University of Iowa. He also did some teaching in Iowa City and worked at KXIC, the only commercial station in town at that time. His first job was at KJFJ in Webster City followed by WHO and KWDM in Des Moines. The one thing that he remembers most vividly about games at the old Field House is how cold it was even with a huge crowd.

A lot of people are surprised at my answer when they ask me, "When did you see your first NBA game?" I tell them, "I saw my first NBA game in Iowa in 1949 when the Waterloo ProHawks were in the NBA." I was in high school then and went to Waterloo several times to see the ProHawks play in the Hippodrome. They won 19 games that year. Johnny Orr was with them part of that season and played some games. People are always surprised when I say, "Oh, I saw my first NBA game in Waterloo, Iowa." "What was there?" "Waterloo was in the NBA." That always gets a few chuckles.

As a kid growing up, one of the first Iowa basketball teams I remember had Dick Ives, Dave Danner, and Herb and Clayton Wilkinson. The coach was Pops Harrison. Interestingly enough, the first time I ever saw a guy who could dunk the basketball was at Iowa State. I played basketball in high school, and our coach took us down to see Iowa State play. The guy, Gaylord Anderson, was only about 6' 4".

He didn't play a lot but he could dunk the basketball. People used to come for the warm-ups just to see him dunk. He was the only one on the team who could dunk it.

I grew up on a farm. My whole lifestyle was sports and radio. In my high school, there were probably a hundred, with about fifteen in my graduating class. You did everything. You played basketball, baseball—whatever was in season. Radio was really important, and that's how I got interested in broadcasting. I listened to all the Cubs games and the Cardinals and everything else—all the fights with Don Dunphy and Bill Stern, who was probably the biggest national name at that time. They certainly all were tremendous influences on me.

The year I was at Iowa, I lived at 310 Golf View Avenue—on the same street was Bucky O'Connor, the basketball coach, and Forest Evashevski, the football coach. All the time I was in school, I was working at radio stations. I got the graduate assistantship at Iowa because they had a lot of TV courses. TV was in its infancy. The only television station was Channel 5, WOI-TV in Ames, at that time. After that, I had a brief stop in Chicago, a brief stop in Buffalo, New York, and then came out here to Phoenix in 1958.

I think more sports announcers come from small towns because maybe you're more sports oriented and maybe have a closer feel for the game—and radio, of course, was a big part of it. The only things we had to do at that time were to play sports and to listen to sports. In the summertime, we listened to the Cubs games and we played baseball. In the wintertime, you listened to basketball games and then you'd go throw baskets some place. High school sports were and are so important, and everybody knows sports. When I started with the Suns, I used to say, "More people in Williams, Iowa knew what was going on with the Suns and the NBA than the people in Phoenix did."

I still keep in contact with my basketball coach who is still living in Boone, Chuck Lovin. He loves to tell the story that people used to ask him when I was in high school, "How come you played Al McCoy so much in the games?" He said, "Well, when he's on the bench, he's always pretending he's broadcasting the game, and he's so bad, I'd rather have him playing in it than to sit there and listen to him." That's a true story.

THE ROAD TO THE HALL OF FAME WENT THROUGH MT. VERNON AND IOWA CITY.

Harry Kalas

*Former WSUI sportscaster, Harry Kalas, was enshrined in Baseball's Hall of Fame in Cooperstown in 2003. He has been "God" for 33 years as the Voice of the Philadelphia **Phillies**. He also replaced the legendary John Facenda for NFL Films. Urban myth held that Kalas worked at a gas station in Mt. Vernon, Iowa, while going to Cornell College...and a regular customer—in those days of full service only—said, "With that voice, you have to become a broadcaster"...whereupon Kalas transferred to The University of Iowa and majored in communications. "Not so!" says Kalas.*

I graduated from Naperville High School in west suburban Chicago fifty years ago. My dad was a minister so just by virtue of being a "P.K."—preacher's kid, I got a partial scholarship to Cornell College in Mt. Vernon, Iowa. I was there for one year and got into a little trouble. They asked me not to come back. Cornell was a church-affiliated school, and unfortunately, in those years, I was inclined to have a beer or two. I got great encouragement while at Cornell from a blind speech professor, Walter Stromer. I knew that I wanted to be a sportscaster, even in high school, and he really encouraged me to do it.

I was working at radio station, KPIG, in Cedar Rapids during the summer. Those were the actual call letters of the station. I wanted to

> P. K. Wrigley and Milton Hershey were bitter business rivals. When Wrigley bought the Chicago Cubs, Hershey tried to buy the Philadelphia Phillies...and sell chocolate gum. Hershey failed in both efforts.

continue my college education and it was suggested that I go to Iowa University because they had a good communications school. That's how I ended up there.

Going to Iowa City was one of the best moves I ever made. I pledged Phi Delta Beta, and Randy Duncan was also a member. I got involved at the campus station, WSUI, and got great experience there doing all the Hawkeye sports. Every sports event the Hawkeyes were involved in, we were out there with microphones making fools of ourselves. But, what great experience! Randy Duncan was a big guy there. Being in the same fraternity, he really helped me a lot as far as Hawkeye football players and the teams they were playing. I did baseball and basketball games for the campus station. You didn't have all the information about the players you would like to have, so it was just feeling your way through the game and trying to call the game.

I just got in the mail that they're having an Airliner reunion. I worked at the Airliner when I was in school, washing pots and pans. It was good because after I finished my work, I was one of those "at the bar." It was the hot spot on campus.

IOWA IOWA IOWA IOWA IOWA IOWA IOWA IOWA IOWA IOWA IOWA IOWA IOWA

Northwestern thinks it's like golf—low score wins...

I SAW IT ON THE RADIO

Frosty Mitchell's broadcasting style was "All right, it's third down and six, the center, his name is Jack Smith, hikes the ball, Jack was the third chair flute in the high school band." He throws in stuff like that, that meant absolutely nothing, and that was his style. Zabel's was scream, scream, scream. Frosty gave little tidbits of information on a player that meant absolutely nothing. "His dad works for the landfill back in…." He'd do his homework and have family history and on a football Saturday he'd have all this information—even on the opposing team. "His dad, the dairy farmer, up in Wisconsin, they…." That to me was heartland, backward country, and down-home stuff. Part of it, too, was it was small-town Iowa, and he had a small-town station. It was absolutely great.

—**DAVE GALLAGHER**, Grinnell, Iowa native

I first started listening to Iowa football with Jim Zabel. I always loved listening to Ed Podolak there with him. When they first switched over to having Gary Dolphin and only one network, to tell you the truth, I hated it, absolutely hated it. But over the past few years, I've actually grown to like Dolphin. I've had a chance to meet him a couple of times. It was just a case of people were used to listening to Iowa football in a certain way. Just as people became attached to Hayden, people became attached to the likes of Jim Zabel and Bob Brooks and Ron Gonder. Those guys were the voices of Iowa football. It was a big change for a lot of people, but now I look at it as a good change.

—**LYELL HOGG**, Clear Lake, Iowa

Jim Zabel and I did Iowa Barnstormers Arena Football games for a while. When he and I went to dinner after a game, we would just split the tab. After we had eaten a hamburger, or something like that, I threw my share—$15—on the table. About ten minutes later, the owner of the team we were playing and John, our head coach, came in. The owner picked up the tab for our dinner, and Jim never gave me back my money. When I asked about it, he said, "Oh I left it on the table for a tip." Right.

Jim was always trying to get this Iowa heavyweight wrestler, Mocco, on the air, saying he was such a great wrestler. The rest of us said we didn't want him on. Well, Mocco dropped out of school and didn't compete at Iowa because he wanted to pursue his Olympic ambitions. He goes out to Colorado Springs and does that whole thing and gets beat—he doesn't make the Olympic wrestling team. Word gets out that Mocco is impressed with John Smith, the wrestling coach at Okie State. So, don't look now, but he transfers. He leaves Iowa, and he transfers to Oklahoma State. When that all came out, I called Jim and said, "Did you hear about Mocco?" "No." "Mocco is going to leave Iowa and go to Okie State." He said, in a really sad tone, "Oh, okay." The ultimate Hawkeye...er...well... block him out...gone. Last summer, Iowa State had a good football player here named Berryman, who got into trouble. He confronted a kid on the campus and beat him up and took a couple of bucks out of his pocket. Bad scene. I tell Jim about it, and he said, "Well, do you want to get somebody on to talk about it?" I said, "Well, if we do, let's get somebody on to talk about Berryman, and then we'll get somebody on to talk about Mocco." There's this stone silence on the other end. He said, "Well, in that case, maybe we don't have to talk about it."

I tell everybody that I'm on the phone two hours a week on Sunday with a really, truly living legend. To the people of this state, like him or not, and, believe me, a lot of the Iowa Staters don't like Jim Zabel because he's so "Hawkeye," but regardless of that, he is a deep-feeling, sensitive, "love-Iowa" legend. Make no bones about it; the man's got a heart of gold. He's a tremendous human being. He's got a gift of gab and a memory, at 82 years of age, that you would kill for when you were 60—or 50, for that matter. The overall feeling I have about Jim Zabel is that I've been allowed to spend seven years with a legend—with a true legend in his business. He's been a sports broadcaster for 60 years, and I've been honored by that. I don't think we get enough time to spend time with legends. Who would not have liked to have spent the same amount of time with **Howard Cosell**, or

When former ESPN and current NFL Channel anchor Rich Eisen was in college, his stand-up comedy routine included reading "Letters to Penthouse" using Howard Cosell's voice.

pick anybody you know of as a legend in your life and say, "I got to spend seven years with this guy."

Zabel brings so much to the table. You can tease him. He has a great sense of humor, unbelievable sense of humor. To me, it has been an honor, even with his idiosyncrasies of interrupting. My idea was that I joined his world—he didn't join mine. So, as far as I'm concerned, he does very little wrong. The stories he has shared with me have damn near made me cry my eyes out from laughter. I miss him in the studio because when we can see each other, we have great chemistry. I'm just selfish, partly because I know he'll tell me a story and crack a joke. We traveled together for three years. We'd do Saturday Night Barnstormers and then we'd do the "Two Guys Named Jim Show" the next night. It has been a joy for me. I think that's why I'm still in Iowa. People ask me why I'm still here, I think it's because I just like hanging out with Zabel.

—JIM WALDEN, partner of Jim Zabel on "Two Guys Named Jim" show

When we were growing up, my mom listened to the Musical Scoreboard on KGRN, a Grinnell radio station, with her mother, my grandmother, who also was a huge Hawkeye fan. Every single week, we'd all sit in the kitchen and listen to the Iowa Hawkeye football game, where Frosty Mitchell would do his play-by-play. My dad would be out in the field working and wouldn't be able to listen. When my mom's dad and my dad and several uncles were out in the field picking corn during games, my mom would put a white flag out on the peak of house when Iowa scored a touchdown. There was also a red-colored flag up there as long as Iowa was ahead. If Iowa was down, they put a different flag in this window. So these guys were out in the field, and the only way they could tell about the game would be to look up and see that colored flag. KGRN was where she got her Hawkeye Fever and then she passed it on to us with the Musical Scoreboard.

My mother had her teams that she really, really liked, and teams that she despised. She liked Notre Dame because she was Catholic and Irish. That never passed on to any of the rest of us because I can't stand Notre Dame. When they'd win, KGRN would salute the Fighting Irish. They'd play the song and give the score during the song. She knew every fight song there was. She liked all the Big Ten teams because she liked their music. She didn't like Iowa State. We never listened to their games or read the things in the newspaper about them.

One time, she said to me, "Of all the fight songs, I'll bet you can't find five Iowa State fans who would know their own fight song." To this day, I'll be at a rally where there will be Iowa State fans. They'll start playing their song, but these fans don't know the words. They can't sing it. Then, here we were, little kids who knew "The Iowa Fight Song" by heart. I suppose it's just ingrained in you somewhat. Back then, neither Iowa State nor Iowa got to play their fight song very much because neither won very much. She didn't care for the USC song either, probably because of the Notre Dame rivalry.

I would like for radio stations to go back to the musical scoreboard shows. Now they have people call in and vent about the coaching and do all that sort of thing. That is fine, but I think you could incorporate some music and some talk and scoreboard together. That old Musical Scoreboard show was the most unique thing ever. It was something else. You'd sit there and listen for the score, and they'd salute the school with a fight song, and it was a neat, neat deal. I've got a CD burned with all of the Big Ten schools and have a lot of the Big 12 songs. We listen to them from time to time and it just brings back all those memories—sitting at the kitchen table—nine brothers and sisters.

—**DAVE GALLAGHER**, DJ at Iowa Bowl game parties

To me the best part of being a Hawkeye fan is the anticipation, the excitement and the expectations of the teams. This is something I do in an ongoing fashion. When I go to bed at night, I used to try to solve problems while I was going to sleep, but I found that kept me awake. Now, I try to think of only positive things. I review the Hawkeye football team and their potential and also the basketball team, I'm very much aware of them. I get information through the Voice of the Hawk-  eyes and, of course, the Hawkeye Report Internet Service.

I used to listen to Jim Zabel on the radio, and it would fade in and out, and I'd have to twist it around. A friend here was a big Hawkeye fan and had a big dish, and I was able to follow the team at his house. When I got my own dish, I was in heaven, and I'd buy all those packages each year and wouldn't miss one for the world.

Jim Zabel had wonderful enthusiasm, and I loved that, but I didn't always know where the ball was when he was doing the game. Gary Dolphin, the current radio broadcaster, does a really good job.

—JIM COLSTON, 75, Salem, Virginia

Those guys who bring the radio games to the fans truly are the voice of the Hawkeyes. They're the stability. The fans know those guys a lot better than they do the players. People really follow the Hawks through their eyes. I remember when I was a little kid and would be out on the tractor, and Jim Zabel was larger than life to me at a young age. He was the guy that we listened to. I remember turning on the radio and listening to him do the games instead of listening to the TV guys because he brought so much life into the game. He made it so much more exciting than what it really even was, which was a great testimony to him. For me to able to come up to The University of Iowa, to go through that first Media Day, you're standing there getting interviewed by Jim Zabel—that was a huge deal to me.

Where we lived, our Channel 6 news guy in Davenport was Thom Cornelis. I got to meet him for the first time my freshman year at the Media Day. To go from being a fan to being interviewed by those guys is very special. What most fans don't realize is that when Brooksy and Gonder and Zabel covered the away games, those guys would ride on the same charter plane with us. So here before games and after games on these planes sitting in the back with those three guys—they've got like a hundred and fifty years worth of stories combined. They're talking about every sport and every player. If you're a fan of Iowa basketball, it was just one of the coolest things to be able to sit down and talk to those guys about Iowa sports. I got a chance to do that so many times—so many late nights flying back from Big Ten road games, talking to those guys. They were special. They treated the players so wonderfully. I miss all three of those guys. Gary Dolphin just stepped right in and has done a phenomenal job, and I know that all the guys really like him.

—JESS SETTLES, Former Hawkeye Basketball Star

The broadcasters who have done the Iowa sports are the best. I enjoyed listening to Zabel through the years and hugging and kissing the radio. I'll never forget the Marv Cook catch at Ohio State. That game wasn't on TV, and I heard Jim Zabel do the call. I don't know that I've ever been as excited listening to any radio call in my entire life. I enjoyed all the others as well. Gary Dolphin is a true pro. Iowa was so unique before when they had three sports broadcasts. So when Dolphin began, he wasn't just following one guy—he was taking over not only for Zabel but for Bob Brooks and Ron Gonder. That's tough because everyone had a favorite. He was almost in a no-win situation, but Gary's a pretty secure guy, and he knows that not everybody is going to like what he does. He's told me more than once, "I have the greatest job in the world."

—<u>TOM KAKERT</u>, Blue Grass, Iowa

Jim Zabel is my favorite Iowa announcer. I have a favorite Jim Zabel cup that I took to the Iowa-Penn State game, and they tried to throw it away. I screamed, "You can't throw away my cup." They got it out of the garbage can for me. I water my plants every day with that cup before Iowa starts their game. Jim Zabel was my favorite announcer because he's as hyper as I am. He was able to give enthusiasm to people who were thirty-two hours away. Gary Dolphin is probably more statistical, but I like the enthusiasm of Jim Zabel. After the spring game, I was able to meet Jim Zabel. I said, "Jim Zabel, can I give you a kiss?" He said, "Oh yes, I didn't know I was in for all this today."

—<u>COLLEEN SCHREIER</u>, 41, Richmond, Virginia.

Podolak is an absolute riot. You never know what's going to come out of his mouth. Dolph has really developed as an announcer doing Iowa games. He started out over at Northwestern. Once he's off the air, you never know what he's going to say. Those two guys are classic. But, if you really want to talk classics and really go back to three guys that just depict everything about an Iowa radio broadcast, it's Brooks, Gonder, and Zabel. I've met them all. Zabel's getting old now and so is Brooksy, and Gonder's not exactly young anymore. They have so much knowledge, and their memories are so good when it comes to Iowa athletics. You can sit and talk to those guys for hours, and they'd never tell you the same story twice—or even touch on the same story twice. I was real lucky when I first started covering some of the Iowa athletics, somebody introduced me to Bob Brooks. Brooks just looked at me and said, "Stay right behind me, all day, and I'll take you everywhere you need to go." I said, "Okay." And he did. And I've never forgotten it. So, of the old guys, I'd say Brooks is probably the favorite.

—MIKE ZIERATH, 41, Planet Hawkeye Web Site

In 1950, in Columbus, Ohio was the first time I actually saw television. We went to Columbus to do that game, and it turned out to be an ill fated game...that 83-21 game. They had Bert McGrane, the writer for the *Des Moines Register*, and all the media in a TV station in Columbus, Ohio. We were supposed to pick the outcome of the game. I predicted Iowa 21-14, and I was halfway right. Iowa got 21...but Ohio State got 83.

In the official Ohio State book, *Ohio State Football, The Great Tradition*," by Jack Park, under the title of "Zabel Owes Me One," there is a story about the time that I go to Columbus, Ohio—that was that same fateful 83-21 year. For some reason or other, whoever the WHO program director was at that time didn't figure on changing to the Eastern time zone. I wound up going on the air an hour early. I needed to fill time, and Jack Buck was in the adjoining booth. He was then the student broadcaster for Ohio State. I got him over, and he filled an hour with me, just talking. Years later, he would be doing a Cardinal game, and there would be a rain delay, and he'd say, "I need Jim Zabel here. He owes me one."

—JIM ZABEL, Scottsdale, Arizona

Jim Zabel—you hated him, but at the same time, you loved him. I remember listening to the Michigan game on the radio when Iowa won 12-10. One of our great kickers that day kicked four field goals-the fourth one coming with the score 9-10 and no time remaining on the clock. Zabel was so wound up that he couldn't tell us that we had scored. It was a pretty good guess, from his reaction, that it was a positive thing. He was just screaming. A guy can be running a long run back, and Zabel wouldn't ever be saying the yard numbers, he's just be going, "He's going—and he's going—and he's going." You're like, "Well, where the heck's he at? Is he close? Is he going to score?" With Jim, you never quite knew for sure whether you had won or not, but you could take a pretty good hunch that it was probably positive.

—RANDY COFFEY, 45, Des Moines, named after Randy Duncan

I really have to credit Clear Channel, the owner of WHO now, because they take a lot of heat as a company, but they really have taken care of Jim Zabel. Jim's about 82, and is still on their payroll listed as a full-time employee, and is on their medical and everything. He lives here in Phoenix most of the time, but he does a Sunday night talk show on WHO, and he still does some pre-game stuff during the football season. When he's back in town, he does afternoon sports on radio. They just told him, "Do what you want to do." It's really great when a company does that. They have taken good care of him.

—AL McCOY, Phoenix Suns announcer

Living in Ottumwa, a pretty isolated area, neither one of my parents went to college, but they're native Iowans and had always been Hawkeye fans. I remember, at eight-nine years old, listening to their games. In those days, there was hardly anything about Iowa on TV, but WHO, Clear Channel Voice of the Midwest, rebroadcast the football games at about ten-thirty on Saturday nights. I'd listen to the game during the day, when it was live, then I remember going to bed at night, taking my little portable radio with me and listening to Jim Zabel call those games again.

I remember listening to the staticy old radio trying to pull in the Cedar Rapid station or WHO. I would draw a scorecard on notebook paper and I kept score of all the basketball games. Guys like Jim Zabel and Harry Caray who really loved what they were doing, loved the sport they were broadcasting and loved the teams they were broadcasting for—I don't think they get enough credit for building that fan base, maintaining that fan base through all those terrible years when the games were not very good. The teams were not very good. I just can't imagine, with an ordinary broadcaster, how you could keep fifty thousand people in those seats. It just wouldn't happen. I know it's Iowa, and the Hawkeyes are all they have, and all that, but, still, you look at other situations like Kansas, various other situations where you have similar kinds of things, and you don't see that. Iowa was unique. Again, I just don't think people understand, especially the people at The University of Iowa, that Jim Zabel saved their program. I just don't think there's a question about it.

—<u>MIKE KIELKOPF</u>, author *How 'Bout Them Hawkeye Fans*

IOWA IOWA IOWA IOWA IOWA IOWA IOWA IOWA IOWA IOWA IOWA IOWA IOWA

Chapter 6

Tailgreat

Do You Believe in Magic?

THERE IS A REWARD FOR THE GREAT AND GRACIOUS AND THAT REWARD INCLUDES THE MAGIC BUS

Brian DeCoster

Brian DeCoster, 42, graduated Bettendorf High School in 1980. Today, he is the successful owner of Big Ten Rentals in Iowa City and former owner of the legendary "Magic Bus."

I'll tell you how it started. We were going down to see the Iowa—Miami game in 1990. I bought a bus for about a thousand bucks. We stole the name, Magic Bus, from the 1960s Magic Bus with Tom Wolfe—The Electric Kool-Aid Acid Trip—going across the country in a magic bus. Some of our friends had a pool going on what mile marker and what state we would break down in on our trip. Nobody actually picked that we would return with it. Nobody won the pool.

We were getting the bus ready, carpeting it and putting beds in, when a buddy called from Atlanta. He called me to hear Iowa stories, because his friends down there didn't believe what he was telling them about Hawk fans. I said, "Hey, you know what, Pat, I just bought a bus, and we're going to **Miami** tomorrow. We'll stop by and see you in Atlanta." Bear in mind, he called me—I didn't call him. He turned to his friends and said, "He just bought a bus, and he's coming through Atlanta tomorrow to see us." We could hear all his friends muttering in the background, "Yeah? Whatever." I said, "We really are." He said, "I know, but none of these friends here believe anything I say about Iowa."

We showed up at his house…in Atlanta…the next day. He's having a party and there are all these people there thinking they'll get to call

> **Do you confuse Miami of Ohio and Miami of Florida? Miami of Ohio was a school before Florida was a state.**

his bluff. We show up at his party, and all these people just can't believe that this whole busload of people came all the way from Iowa to go to Miami for a football game. His roommate, who was very conservative, was just overcome by all the fun of it. He said, "I'm going to the Miami game, too." He'd never been on a road trip like this. He ends up shaving an "I" in his chest and running out and tackling the Miami mascot during the game. It's funny because he'd never even been to Iowa, and here he is as one of the four guys with shaved chests spelling out I - O - W - A.

That guy from Atlanta who'd made the Miami trip with us is now a federal prosecutor. He's a really conservative jerk. When an article came out in *Sports Illustrated* about the Magic Bus, it spawned other articles. In another article, I went into that story about the origin of it. I referred to him, not by name, but by incident. I faxed it down to his office, and he pretended he didn't know me.

All buses are mechanical headaches. I don't think anybody owns one forever. It sounds pretty fun for awhile, but they're so expensive to keep on the road. On the way back from Mardi Gras one year, I had some really expensive problems with the flywheel and some other stuff. We had it fixed and finally got back to Iowa with it. I had spent way more just getting it home than it was even worth. I sold it. I figured I would never get it mechanically the way I wanted it. It wasn't really good for cross-country trips.

The Magic Bus was pretty well known. There were a lot of news articles on it. It made the *Sports Illustrated* #1 Traveling Tailgate Party in America. The magazine did a top fifty different schools for fifty different things, and Iowa was #17 for tailgating. They rated the Magic Bus the #1 Traveling Tailgate Party. They just came to Iowa City looking for a story and asked around. The way the reporter tells me it happened was he wanted to do a tailgate story, and the first three people he asked thought he should do it on the Magic Bus.

> *Sports Illustrated* began in 1954 and its first swimsuit issue was in 1964. The *Sports Illustrated* swimsuit issue has 52 million readers, 16 million of them are females…12 million more than normal.

Three different places—three different people—so he said, "I'd better find this bus."

The Magic Bus had the world's largest Tupperware party. We thought it would be fun to have a theme party. I contacted Tupperware and told them I wanted to have a Tupperware party. The gal at Tupperware who I talked to at the home office in Florida basically said, "You've got to contact your neighborhood home party planner." I said, "No, I don't want to contact my neighborhood home party planner. This is a going to be a BIG Tupperware party." She said again, "You've got to contact your neighborhood home party planner." I said, "I don't think you understand. This is gonna be a big one. We'll have 50 kegs, the whole ball of wax." She kept trying to refer me to a party planner. Finally, I said, "You don't understand. This is going to be the world's largest Tupperware party, and I would like corporate sponsorship on it, and I would like recognition." At that point is when it became the world's largest Tupperware party. We had videotape from the president of Tupperware thanking everybody for attending. We had prizes for the different ages of Tupperware. It actually was only 30 kegs, but it was the best party I ever threw." We had a couple of DJs. We had a representative from Kraft, who came and talked about the Velveeta Cheesekeeper. It was total madness. Nobody came up from Florida, but I ended up going down and meeting the president of Tupperware. He was a little confused by the whole thing. He never did "get it." It was just a great party. The "Neighborhood Home Party Planner" did attend, and she was very angry. She said she sold more Tupperware the day after at a neighborhood party than she did tailgating. They don't actually bring Tupperware to parties, they take orders. They had some samples at the Magic Bus. As soon as we ran out of beer cups, everything Tupperware that would hold beer was gone in seconds. Until we ran out of cups, they didn't sell anything. And, they didn't take many orders. It was a huge party, and it was just a blast. It was great weather, and we had a good-tempered crowd. It made ABC Sports.

We took my second bus to Columbus for an Iowa game. Rick Derringer, a Grammy award winner, was at the Ohio State game. They have a big tailgate party there with bands. I had just raffled off the bus the year before, but the rugby team agreed to let me borrow it back for Iowa Homecoming. I was going to have a big party, and I wanted to get a big band. Rick Derringer was the guy I wanted to get. I went up to him, "Hey, I want to hire you in a couple of weeks." He said, "Okay." He gave me his card, and I gave him my card. I called him, and two weeks later, here's his band on the roof of the Magic Bus. It was freezing cold out. I put a tent up over the yard, and we had it heated and had the Magic Bus inside. I had to get a crane to come in and erect the tent in place because there were 20-foot tall sides on it. Derringer played. We had a lingerie show for half-time. The Outback Bowl scouts were there. They came over wearing their green blazers, and we invited them to come on in. They said, "We can't go into a party like this. It looks crazy in there." I said, "You sure? Rick Derringer is playing." They said, "Really, Rick Derringer is playing?" So they come in, and the next thing you know, the Outback Bowl guys are drinking. I've got a picture of Rick Derringer and the guys from the Outback Bowl, a girl in lingerie, and the publisher of the newspaper, all standing together. Talk about an unlikely group. That was still mid-season, at the Homecoming game, late October, but Iowa didn't get to go to the Outback Bowl.

These parties we had were held in the back yard of a house. I would rent the yard for the game. The house changed owners about four times during the time I was renting the yard. The parties cost me about five thousand a season. I pass the hat, but nobody donates like they should. You want to hang out with older people, and it's the younger kids who are causing the most problems. I don't mind giving away some beer, but I don't want a headache to go along with it. I took my wife to one of these parties shortly after I started dating her, and I'm still not sure why she continued to date me.......

I used to sneak kegs into Kinnick in a wheelchair. They never caught me doing that, but they did catch me taking one in a duffel bag. There is a brace in the middle of the bottom of a wheel chair. With it in there, there's not much room for a keg. So we cut that brace out, and sewed a pony keg into a bag, a big canvas bag with grommets in it, and we had it laced into the bag and put it down in that bottom space. We had the keg tied up underneath. Once we got in the game, I could pull on a rope, and the keg would drop out. You could grab that handle on the end of the bag and drag it down the aisle. In '85, I actually had two kegs at the Iowa-Michigan game when we beat Michigan 12-10. I would put my leg up, and a blanket over my leg. I decorated the spokes up in black and gold crepe paper, just trying to draw attention away from the keg. I also did that at the Kentucky Derby and got away with it there.

I actually did that several times. It wasn't challenging enough. It was just too easy. When I was younger, I was a paperboy for the *Daily Iowan*, and I had a newspaper bag. You could fit a pony keg in there. It rode up on me too high and didn't look very casual, so I cut the straps off and had them extended. Then it rode more at hip level. I put a duffel bag round it with some slits in the ends of it. Then you could take a bag or a blanket or whatever you wanted into the games. But one time they caught me carrying it in. When they caught me, they didn't just say, "We caught a guy with a keg." The security guy said, "WE GOT HIM. WE GOT HIM. WE CAUGHT HIM. WE GOT HIM. WE GOT HIM."

The students used to pass people up the stands at games. Well, we passed the keg up. There was no way we were going to carry an empty out of there. So we were going to show that baby off. The people at Iowa, when they saw the keg coming, loved it.

I snuck one in the Fiesta Bowl, too, in 1985, Miami vs. UCLA. I carried it up to the third tier there. I ended up dropping it and banging a lady in the head. It didn't actually hurt her, but she said it did. It was a scam. It was me versus Judith Ann Tone, from the Arizona Sports Foundation, doing business as the Fiesta Bowl. There was a lawsuit over that. She was awarded $65,000......

When we go to other campuses, we generally enjoy it. That first road trip to Miami was a very threatening group of people. They were like, "We're going to kill you." Not like, "We're going to beat Iowa." But like, "We're really going to kill you and cut your hearts out."

Iowa tailgates like nowhere else. There's no doubt about that. Florida-Georgia may be better. When we took trips on the Magic Bus, we always picked up hitchhikers. It's kind of like a dream come true for them. Usually, they're penniless and like alcohol. Here we pull up with all the beer they can drink. We have to end up kicking them out because they don't ever want to leave.

SOMETIMES, GOD JUST HANDS YA ONE

Steve Charlton

After his freshman year at The University of Colorado in 1988, Steve Charlton ran low on funds and had to transfer to The University of Iowa. Ironically, the first football game he went to in Iowa City was against Colorado. He was mollified that at least Iowa had a strong Biology Department and was nearer his suburban Chicago home. Little did he know that tailgating at Iowa football games would lead to winning the lottery, going on the tailgating trip of a lifetime, meeting his wife and becoming a full-time Iowan. He works for Seneca Environmental Systems in Des Moines.

Shortly before graduation in December of 1991, I lived in a house in Iowa City with four guys and four girls. One of the girls, Leslie, was having a birthday. We decided we should go to a place called The Pleasure Palace for her birthday shopping. You can probably guess what kind of place Pleasure Palace is. One guy walks out of there with 18-inch, double-headed gag gift—that's how it was referred to in the newspaper—for her. The birthday comes and goes, and the gift is a big hit. She moved back to Illinois to start a teaching career. I stuck around in Iowa City to drink for a couple more weeks before I went back to Illinois to start a job. As I was getting ready to leave, I noticed this gag gift lying on the living room floor. I thought, "What kind of friend would I be if I didn't take Leslie her gift that she had obviously forgotten?" I threw it in the back seat of my car and off I went to start my after-college life.

First, I was living with my mom, and then went to live with my brother and his wife for a while. Neither of these places seemed to be the appropriate place to keep this "gift." Time went by, and I forgot it was in the back seat until I needed to get an oil change. I pulled into a

Jiffy-Lube in Warrenville, a western Chicago suburb. I went into their waiting room and started reading the "14-Point Check List" up on the wall. When I got to "vacuuming," I remembered this "thing" was in the back seat of my car. I immediately decided I was going to go get enough cash to pay Jiffy Lube, give them a fake name and just get the heck out of there. I wasn't going to give them a credit card with my name on it. I went across the street to a White Hen Pantry to use the ATM. I felt guilt to go into a store and use their ATM without buying something from the store, but I didn't actually need anything. So, I said, "Give me five dollars of lottery tickets." The next morning on the way to work, I stopped for gas and bought a newspaper. When I pulled out of the gas station, at the first red light I came to, I opened the paper and started checking the numbers. There it was. I could not believe my eyes. I drove about another 45 minutes to the office, where I worked for a civil engineering company. I worked in a big, open room at the end of the offices with five architects, all Filipino guys. I walk in and called for this one guy named Primo, "Primo, come here and look at this." Primo said, "Oh, you guess four numbers." I said, "No. No. Look at this." He looked again and said, "You win. You win." That's how I found out I was the winner. Primo takes off running down the hall, jumping up and down, yelling, "Steve quitting. Steve quitting. Steve quitting." That was the end of keeping it a secret right there. So that is how The University of Iowa and the "gag gift" was responsible for my winning the lottery.

A guy named Bob Waldstein had written a book called *Saturday Afternoon Madness*. He had gone on a tailgating trip two years prior with a friend, Phil Silverman. They were on another cross-country journey trying to sell this book, plus going to new schools to get stories for a second book. These guys had a legitimate product. They weren't just there saying, "We're here to write a book." They actually had already done one and were getting another one ready. They would call the Sports Information Director (SID) of a school before they went there and say, "We're coming to your town. What are the essential things about college football there at your school?" The SID at Iowa told them to go to the I-Club breakfast, to follow the Beer Band around on Friday night, and to go to the Magic Bus on Saturday morning. They arrived at the Magic Bus. They had their books on the trunk of their car for sale. I got to talk to them and told them, "I've got a twenty-seven-foot long RV. I've got a job I can take plenty of time off from. (At that time, I was delivering flowers for a flower shop.) I've got a fair amount of disposable income, and a trailer we can put your car on and tow it. Would you guys mind if I tagged along with you?" They kind of looked at each other and in about two seconds said, "Yeah, that would be great." I just love college football, and I wanted to see how they tailgate in different parts of the country—to go to some of the great places.

The first place we went was **Notre Dame** for an Ohio State game. I'd never been to South Bend and was amazed at how clean and tidy the campus was. Touchdown Jesus was pretty neat to see. One thing that really stuck out was when the football players parade through campus toward the stadium in their blazers and ties with everybody lining the sidewalk and cheering them on. The night before the game we went to the ceremony where they paint the helmets. We were towing around an old Cadillac, and we got the students who were painting the helmets to paint the roof of our car with the Notre Dame paint.

From there, we went to Baton Rouge. I've fallen in love with that place. **LSU** was playing Vanderbilt that night. It wasn't a very big rival game, but that game was awesome. There were only two schools these writers went back to on this second trip that they had visited on the first trip—Notre Dame and LSU. In their first book, they had written very favorably about Baton Rouge, so we were treated like kings. There is a sports talk radio guy down there, Buddy Songy, who is sort a Jim Zabel-Bob Brooks type. He's well known in Baton

When Knute Rockne and seven others were killed in a 1931 plane crash, it was the largest disaster in U.S. aviation history up until that time.

What Heisman Trophy winner has made the most money? The 1959 winner, Billy Cannon of LSU, was arrested for counterfeiting in the early '80s and spent almost three years in jail. Technically, he's the only Heisman Trophy winner to ever "make" money?

Rouge. He showed us around town and got us into boosters' dinners. The most entertaining part for me was we went to do a radio interview. We did a lot of these. Pretty much the way they would all go was, "These two guys have written a book." Bob and Phil would sit and answer questions about their book. About five or ten minutes into the interview, they'd see that I'd been sitting over there not saying a word. They'd look at me and say, "What's your job?" "I'm a state lottery winner just out on the road having some fun with these guys." Invariably, it was, "Okay, you two guys, thanks for coming." And immediately to me, "You say you won the lottery?" Then I'd have to go into the whole lottery story. On this one particular radio show in Baton Rouge, the producer said, "You know what today is?" The host said, "It's Thursday." Well, they normally set two listeners up on a blind date. They said, "Well, how about we do a little something different this week, and we give away a date with an Illinois state lottery winner. So, thank God, it was radio and not TV. The next thing I know I'm the prize in a dating game. They found a girl, and she and I went out and had a good time for a couple of nights that week. She was very pretty—not as pretty as my wife, though. Make sure you say that in the book.

LSU really had the greatest tailgating. People there had menus printed up for the whole season—what they were going to serve to eat at each tailgate. I saw people with purple and gold Cadillacs. For the sheer size of it, LSU couldn't be matched. However, I never saw one single great tailgater that could match the Magic Bus, as one single entity. The Iowa tailgating is excellent. They just are perhaps not as loony… maybe. And I'm not getting any younger; maybe I'm forgetting how crazy things were. I thought Notre Dame's tailgating was kind of quiet and reserved. We just may not have been in the right spot for that. The pageantry for Notre Dame was very special. When people realized I was from Iowa, most of them would ask about Hayden Fry…corn… pigs. Iowa wasn't really doing all that great at that time so I don't know that people had a real strong understanding of Iowa football.

From Baton Rouge, we went to Austin, Texas, and then up to Dallas for the Red River Shootout. Before the game started, we went to this bar across the street from the Texas State Fairgrounds. There was a bar in the front and a laundromat in the back. There were about half a dozen **Oklahoma** Sooner fans who were so drunk. That game was the only place we went where we couldn't get a third press credential so I actually had to go scalp a ticket to get into the game. It turned out to be too good of a game. Texas was pretty heavily favored. We had to get away to our next stop so we were taking off right after the game ended. The one thing we didn't plan for was how to meet up after a game if there was overtime. Sure enough, the game went into over-time, but I left the stadium at the end of the regulation. I went back to the bar where we had arranged to meet. When I got there, those same Oklahoma Sooner fans were still in there and still drinking. The fun-niest thing about it was that the arguments finally erupted on what turned out to be the last play of the game. The center hiked the ball just about the exact moment that first Texan took a swing at one of these Oklahoma guys. The whole bar just went crazy. I'm standing up on the back of a bench pointing at the TV where this Oklahoma guy is going to run in for a touchdown in overtime to win the game. There couldn't have been more than three people in the bar who saw that play because they were all in a brawl at the time.

After that, the other two were going up to Madison to a Wisconsin game, and I didn't go with them. The very weekend I got back, at the Magic Bus in Iowa City, I met the woman who is now my wife. It was sort of storybook-like that I got out there on the road, had one great last final run, and then found my wife. We actually met the night before, but at the tailgate the next day was the first time we spent any time together. The two people who were writing the book went to Wisconsin and Northwestern and then they got their car broken into in Evanston. Somebody stole all their notes and their pictures so the second book never did get made.

Now with the success Iowa has had in the past few years, football is the one non-corn and pig thing that people across the country know about. It's a good sort of rallying point. I like college football more than I like professional sports. You have a closer bond with it than you do in

> **The first coach with his own TV show was Bud Wilkinson at the University of Oklahoma in 1952.**

professional sports. You may have had the starting quarterback in your geography class or the defensive end might live in the dorm room next to you. It just gives you more of a family orientation. Now, especially being out here in Des Moines, I don't know when I'm getting back to Iowa City, but I know I'm getting back there six Saturdays every fall. As we get older now, and people have kids, that's the one place you can know you're going to see them again. We're probably at the age now where we don't really make too many new stories. We just sit around and talk about the old ones…when Molly Hatchet was going to be arrested if they took the stage on top of the Magic Bus…Rick Derringer and the lingerie half-time show…

Going to The University of Iowa was the best thing I ever did.

IOWA IOWA IOWA IOWA IOWA IOWA IOWA IOWA IOWA IOWA IOWA IOWA IOWA

SOME WOULD SAY THAT BOBBY KNIGHT WAS THE BACKBONE OF INDIANA. I WOULDN'T GO QUITE THAT HIGH.

BEER: MORE THAN
A BREAKFAST DRINK

Depending on the weather, depending on the score, depending on who the opponent is, people will start filtering in sometimes late in the third quarter and fourth quarter and then we're maxed out the rest of the day. If we're playing Wisconsin, it never dies down. Their fans are great. They're the last ones to leave. They always come on Friday. It's just a sea of red in here on Friday night, along with the Hawk fans. On Saturday morning, the Wisconsin fans will be out front waiting for us to unlock to get back in and start with the Bloody Marys. They're fairly close but they probably travel down here as well as anybody in the conference. We never have any problems with them. You'll even see a lot of Wisconsin people and Iowa people together, simply because of geography. Iowa State is always a big weekend. The people who travel with their teams are almost like a regular crowd. The same ones tend to come back again. In basketball, it's even more pronounced because you've got a shorter time window. We shuttle the fans up the hill to the football games and to the basketball games, but they have to walk back.

—DICK QUERREY, owner, Wig and Pen, Iowa City

Brian DeCoster decided he couldn't run the Magic Bus anymore because it was just a huge financial drain to him. He didn't run it the way we do it nowadays. He decided to raffle it off and was selling $5 raffle tickets. Three other guys from the rugby team and I pooled our money and bought raffle tickets. Two guys from Des Moines buy one ticket that day, and they won the bus. We said to them, "Whoa, whoa, whoa. Your wives are going to kill you if you drive this bus back to Des Moines." They thought about that and said, "What will you give us for it?" I said, "Why don't you just hang out with us tonight? We'll take you out on the town, and then we'll negotiate the price." So, that night, we got them absolutely stoned and drunk out of their minds. We ended up buying it off of them for two hundred bucks and giving them a couple of rugby T-shirts. We sent them home very happy. Their wives didn't have to kill them when they showed up with this piece of crappy, old school bus.

A lot of articles came out in the newspapers about the bus because the people who had followed the bus for years were interested in what was going to happen. We devised this plan where we would play live bands and have security. We're going to charge for the bands, but have free beer. For five bucks, you can come in to listen to the band and drink beer, if you want. Since we are all rugby players, we got the rugby guys involved. Every year since, we give at least $10,000 away to children's charities all over the state of Iowa. We keep a quarter of it for the rugby team. By not charging for the beer, but charging for the band, we don't have to have a liquor license. We wanted to see what we could do for the community to make the appeal of rugby a little bit better than it was in the eyes of most people.

—JEREMY FREERKS, Iowa City Rugby Team

The craziest thing I've ever seen there would be "naked mud sliding." I did not participate in that. Right behind where we tailgate at 609 Melrose, which used to be privately owned but which the University now owns, there is a small hill on the east side of the lot. One day, it was raining and you could hear the kids back there getting kind of loud. One of the guys from our group actually went back there. He'd probably had a little bit too much to drink. The next thing we know, we hear people chanting his name. We look around the corner of the garage—here he comes, down the hill, without a stitch of clothing on! But, he was wearing a see-through rain poncho so he wouldn't hurt himself. Here he is, sliding down the hill naked. We hooted and hollered for him. The women were, "Oh my God!" The guys were like, "Yeah. Go!"

I do remember the first game I ever attended—walking into the stadium, seeing how old it was and going up the tunnel that goes out to where the seats are—having that feeling, that really excited adrenalin rush—to walk out of that tunnel and see the field. That never goes away. It's the same for me every time, maybe not every time is it as intense as it was that first time—there's nothing like it.

—MIKE ZIERATH, 41, owner, Collegiate Sports store

Chapter 7

Today We Ride

On the Road Again

'TIS BETTER TO TRAVEL WELL THAN TO ARRIVE FIRST

Dave Gallagher

Dave Gallagher was raised in Grinnell, Iowa and force-fed the Hawkeyes from an early age by his mother and grandmother. His Black and Gold Hawk Bus is a familiar sight at Hawk games and at RAGBRAI stops each summer. He works in group sales for the Iowa athletic department and promotes the Hawks at RAGBRAI each July.

Iowa played at **Arizona** back in 1982. It was Chuck Long's very first collegiate start. I was in college and didn't have enough money to go out there, but yet we really, really wanted to go see this game. So we got an S-10 pickup and put a topper on it. Seven of us got in that little truck—three in the front and four in the back, and we went out to Arizona…it took us 36 hours. We had to pick a gal up in Texas, and a guy in Colorado, and we finally got out there.

We start tailgating with all these Iowa fans, just having an absolute ball. All of a sudden, the University of Arizona band is coming through to go onto their field. My cousin and I grabbed two Iowa flags, and we led the Arizona band into the stadium. We almost got on the field with these two Hawkeye flags. We got inside the stadium, but didn't make it onto the field. Security saw that we were wearing black and gold and they stopped us, but the band just kept following us. We almost got arrested and thrown in jail.

Among all seven of us, we had one credit card. We didn't have any money. We're coming back to Iowa and we nearly maxed that credit card out. We had enough money for gas. We didn't have enough

The undersection of the University of Arizona football stadium doubles as a student dormitory.

money for beer. There was a guy who had brought his piggy bank, and he paid for a case of beer in Kansas. They weren't even supposed to sell beer in Kansas on Sunday, but we talked the gal into it. We ended up paying for that beer with nickels…hundreds of nickels and pennies. Now, the seven of us could drink beer on the way home. I don't know why it took us 36 hours to get out there, but only took us 26 hours to get back. That was our first baptism into the Hawkeye faithful.

It was a great game. It was Chuck Long's first start. It was a surprise move to even have him start the game. Hayden was known to pull stuff like that. Some years later, we went to Michigan State—in that same S-10 pickup. **Dan McGwire**, Mark's brother, was supposed to start. If he didn't start, it was supposed to be Hartlieb. Well, the game starts—and here comes Poholsky. Nobody even knew who this kid was. Just out of the blue, Fry starts Tom Poholsky. The fans are just stunned, thinking, "What in the hell is he doing…starting a third-string quarterback when he's got these two guys?" He obviously knew what was going on, and it came down to the very, very, very last play. Iowa was ahead by two. George Perles was the Michigan State coach. Michigan State had a time out left, and were on the one or two-yard line. Our whole family and our friends were there. We were holding hands and praying as hard as we could. Michigan State threw that football into the end zone rather than running it and calling time out. All they had to do was run the ball, call time out, kick a field goal and win the game. They threw the football, and we intercepted. I'm telling you that stadium went absolutely crazy with Hawkeye fans. Here it had been less than twenty seconds to go and there was absolutely no way Iowa could win that game…and, they decided to throw that ball. Fans were on top of each other. That game, to me, was equivalent to the 1985 Michigan game in Kinnick Stadium where people were falling all over each other.

> **Mark McGwire's brother, Dan McGwire, once a starting quarterback for the Iowa Hawkeyes and a former #1 pick of the Seattle Seahawks, is the tallest NFL quarterback ever at 6' 8". Former NBA star and Toronto Blue Jay Danny Ainge, is the tallest MLB second baseman ever.**

About four years ago, my wife and I were talking. We wanted something different, something unique that we could take and tailgate with our family. Iowa was going to play at Kansas City against Kansas State. That spring, I thought, "What a fun thing it would be to take everybody down in one vehicle." I got a call from a buddy of mine who said, "Hey, they're selling a school bus over in Benton-Shellsburg. I think you could get it pretty reasonable." I called and they told me they were accepting closed bids for it. I put in a $2,500 bid, thinking, "Well, I'll either get it or I won't." I end up getting the thing. It probably had 70,000-80,000 miles on it. The engine was in poor shape. We got it over here to Iowa City. All my friends helped me. We painted the entire outside—spent $2,000—all black and gold. We tore all the seats out. The seats that are in there now were in the Iowa basketball locker room. When **Steve Alford** came, he wanted leather seats so they took out all the seats that Tom Davis had. A friend called and told me what they were doing and asked if I wanted the old seats. I told him, "Sure I do." They're black cloth, theater-style seats.

We took it down to Kansas City—my whole family, plus 30-35 people. At the time, the TV show "Survivor" was hot so we decided to play that game on the way down there. Everybody would put a dollar in the pot, and whoever was remaining at the end got the pot. We had everybody fill out a piece of paper and you could vote one person out of the game. Obviously, you were going to write down the person you thought would be popular within the family because you knew they had a chance to win it all so you didn't want to compete against them. We'd pass the hat around, count the votes, and whoever got the most votes was out of the game. We'd go on to the next round. When we'd make a stop for gas or restaurants or to go to the restroom, people would form alliances to get rid of someone, "Okay, this time let's all vote for Larry and get him out of there." We got it down to two or three people. By that time, the beer had kicked in, and

> When Steve Alford was a senior in high school in 1983 in New Castle, Indiana, his high school team averaged more people in attendance per game than the Indiana Pacers.

my sister ended up winning, just because she was the quietest so nobody ever thought she'd win. It was a lot of fun.

We've taken that bus to six or eight away games, Northwestern, Minnesota several times, Wisconsin several times. At Wisconsin, we pulled in, and a guy throws a football at the window. That night, we were parked at the motel, and the mirror was busted off. The taillights were both kicked in. The license plate, which said, "Hawk Bus" was ripped off. I decided that would be the last time we took it to Madison.

Two years ago, when we went up to Minnesota, there was a bad snowstorm. We took a charter bus. People were drinking and partying all the way up there. We get to the Metrodome and couldn't use the toilet in the back of the bus because it was near to overflowing. Sheldon was the bus driver's name so we kept chanting, "Well done, Sheldon." We get to the Metrodome, and Sheldon parks the bus in the snow. I have a black and gold Hawkeye Santa suit. I wore it into the Metrodome. I got escorted out because each school can only have one mascot so we couldn't have a Hawkeye Santa in there. Someone took a picture, and it was on the front page of the *Press-Citizen*. They told me if I changed clothes, I could come back into the game. So I went back to the bus through the snow and saw that the snow was all changing to a blue color. Well, Sheldon had opened the toilet container. He was emptying it onto the bus parking lot, and that stuff was just running out all over the Metrodome parking lot. He said, "Don't you say anything. I'd lose my job. I couldn't stand it any more. I'm hoping this snow keeps coming because if it does, it'll cover all this blue stuff up before everybody comes out." My wife and I get back into the game, and I'm laughing so hard and telling the whole group what had happened. After the game, walking out, sure enough, everybody had that blue stuff all over their shoes. They could not figure out what it was. I quickly got on the bus and said, "Well done, Sheldon. We're not going to take any _ _ _ _ from Minnesota tonight."

At that same time, Iowa was trying to get into the Outback Bowl. Rick Klatt, my boss, saw me in the Santa suit at the Metrodome on that Saturday. The next day he called me at home and said, "Bob Bowlsby and I want you to fly down tomorrow morning to Tampa and deliver this sack of corn in your Santa suit." Bob Bowlsby sent me down to Florida with this Santa suit to go and talk to the Outback Bowl Committee. I was carrying this huge bag of corn kernels—through the Chicago airport, where I had to go through security and put that bag of corn on the belt. Next on to the plane, and then through the Tampa airport. When I got into the cab, I put the Santa suit on and went to this committee meeting. The receptionist said, "Sir, do you have an appointment? They're meeting on the teams they are selecting for the bowl game." I had the Santa suit on, carrying the bag of corn and I said, "No, I don't." I charge into the meeting. There were about twenty people, all dressed up in business suits." I put this big bag of corn up on the table. I said, "Each kernel of corn represents a person who would buy a ticket to your bowl game if we get selected. Iowa really, really wants to come here." They ended up picking Michigan over Iowa, but it was fun, and they had a good time with it. The committee was stunned that a university would go to that extreme. They knew Iowa was special in that regard because Michigan wasn't sending anybody down. They weren't lobbying like that. The committee really laughed about it, and I think they even sent an e-mail to Bob Bowlsby and said, "Nice corn ploy."

Iowa gets 4,000 tickets for away games. In 2004, at Arizona State, Iowa sold out of their allotment. Arizona State was selling single-game tickets. The Iowa fans began ordering these tickets. Arizona State looked at the zip codes of all these orders, over 8,400, and realized they were all from Iowa. When we got out there, where we're supposed to have 4,000 fans, we had over 20,000 Hawkeye fans there. We went to ASU as an anniversary-type thing since we went out to Arizona the last time in 1982. This time it was a little different...we could afford it...we flew and did the whole thing. We had a great time, except we didn't expect to get creamed 44-7.

Our RAGBRAI Hawk Bus came about when we DJ'd for the Hawkeyes for all the pre-game parties. I'm the emcee for the Hawkeye Huddles, which we do before Bowl games. In Florida, we had over 20,000 Hawkeye fans for the Orange Bowl in this convention hall. It's a free event. When they open the doors, people just run to the tables. We were talking to the Orange Bowl rep down there. He got on the mike and said, "We've had Notre Dame here. We've had Oklahoma. We've had **Nebraska**. Nothing can match what this Iowa party is all about." They estimated there were over 20,000 people. The beer lines were 200 people long. The food lines were incredible. President Skorton played the sax. At all the bowl games, he will go and play with the band at the Huddle. He'll get on stage with the band, and he will lead the band in "The Iowa Fight Song." No place else in America would a university president get up there with their band.

We have a group of about sixty who ride RAGBRAI with us, and we play music all across the state. I call these communities and bars and restaurants and set up a chance to play music. We've been doing this for 12 years. We play The Iowa Fight Song at these events and hand out schedule cards and magnets. This year, we had 12 different events all across the state. It's a good opportunity for us to promote the Hawks. When you get to the western part of the state, a large number of those people are Cyclone fans. We always come home with absolutely no schedules and no magnets. They always request the Fight Song or "In Heaven There is No Beer" played. We usually don't play anyone else's fight song, but this year, we gave in and played one for Iowa State in Union, Iowa because of the fact it was such big Iowa State country.

When we do the Huddles before bowl games, usually the Foundation will hire me or ask me to help them out. We take our own equipment, but in the case of the Orange Bowl, the venue was way too large so we had to rent equipment down there. It's similar music to what I play on RAGBRAI. It's not the rap stuff, not the swearing words. It's pretty much wholesome music mixed in with The Fight Song. Then we play the Hokey-Pokey. At Kansas City, when we DJ'd that event, we tried to bill it as the World Largest Hokey-Pokey. I'll bet we have eight hundred people doing the Hokey-Pokey. As soon as we got done, the band came right down the center. It was really neat. They

> **Academic All-American teams have been picked every year since 1952. Nebraska leads all colleges by a wide margin in number of players selected.**

had a lot of video and photos and camera videos of it because that was Hayden's signature song for a victory.

This year, I put a new engine in the bus. It cost $8,000, and I did it just to make sure it was reliable to drive to these games. When we came back from Kansas City that time, we were losing oil so badly on the road that we'd have to stop and fill it with oil and then check the diesel. It had started to blow gaskets and we kept doing some patchwork and repair work until I finally gave up and put in the new engine. I bought the bus for $2,500 and have probably put an additional twenty grand in it. But we've got all kinds of fun out of it. As we're driving down the highway, people will roll down their car windows and give us the high sign. Once in a while, someone from Iowa State will flip us off. Mainly, people give us the thumbs up when they go by. I put on the back, for tickets, call 1-800 IAHAWKS. The license plates say HAWK BUS. The plates seem to be very popular because people will just rip them off. I've had to replace them twice. They're black and gold, and I suppose people put them on their walls.

Iowa fans have come up with some of the most creative things for their license plates. One is "FT4IA" —Fight for Iowa. Some are very unique in the way they word things and have challenged things. I looked at the book one time and there were four thousand different Iowa Hawkeye personalized plates out there. You can't duplicate them so when I was trying to get something for the Hawk bus I had to come up with something nobody else had. I thought of HAWK BUS and looked it up, and, sure enough, nobody had it. So, that was it.

IOWA IOWA IOWA IOWA IOWA IOWA IOWA IOWA IOWA IOWA IOWA IOWA IOWA

DIFFERENCE BETWEEN GOVERNMENT BONDS AND NEBRASKA ATHLETES? GOVERNMENT BONDS MATURE...

FLUSH TWICE
IT'S A LONG WAY TO CHAMPAIGN.

Walter B. Planner

Wally Planner, of Davenport, was instrumental in the rousing success of the inaugural season of the Quad City Thunder. Planner, 57, is retired and winters in Florida.

In 1987, the Quad Cities got a CBA (Continental Basketball Association) basketball team. Our general manager was a great guy from the Washington, D.C. area, but he had no idea of the power of the Hawkeyes. The team had to submit 50 dates to the league office for a 27-game home schedule at Wharton Fieldhouse in Moline. The general manager made a list of the 50 dates. Our marketing consultant took one look at it and narrowed it down to 32 dates. He eliminated all Mondays, all Tuesdays, got the Iowa schedule and eliminated every date where Iowa was playing—home or away. The general manager said, "Well, we've got to submit 50 dates." The marketing guy said, "We're going to submit 32. Tell them that's all the dates we have. If we play on any of those other dates, we'll lose at least $20,000 in additional revenue." The team averaged almost 5,000 people per game, but during one playoff game, there was a conflict in dates where the Quad City Thunder had to play the same night as an Iowa game. Instead of drawing the customary 5,000, the Thunder drew 1,600 people that night.

About the same time, the University of Illinois had a home football game where they invited 75 companies from the state of Illinois to put on a display. They could do anything they wanted in this 30' by 20' area. There had never been an entry from the Quad Cities. The team thought it would be a neat idea to have a good entry since it would impress people from the Quad Cities who went to the Illinois game that this new basketball team meant business. We created a thing called the Cham-Bana Country Club, Truck Stop, Honky-Tonk and Drive-In. We recreated the inside of a 1950s drive-in restaurant, complete with booths, tables, jukeboxes, cheerleaders doubling as waitresses—the whole deal. We brought in the Blues Brothers who performed at the Chicago Bulls games, put orange shirts on them and called them the Orange and Blues Brothers. In order to create this elaborate set, we needed a lot of lumber. We prevailed on John Schneckloth, who owned a lumberyard in Durant, Iowa. John donated all the lumber. The Friday night before the game, we're assembled behind the Greenbrier Restaurant in Moline sawing the wood and pounding boards together to create this drive-in. John Schneckloth was on all fours, pounding nails when all of a sudden, he let out this terrible scream. Everybody thought he was having a heart attack. We looked over and said, "John, what's wrong?" He said, "I f-ing hate the University of Illinois. I hate Illinois. What am I doing?" He got up. He threw down his hammer. He walked inside and never even went to the game.

The entry for the Quad City Thunder finished second out of those 75 businesses at the football game the next day. We were beaten out by some couple who got married next to a ready-mix concrete truck with the slogan that they "wanted to cement their marriage." For finishing second, we were awarded 50 tickets to the Iowa-Illinois basketball game in Champaign later that year. Of course, John was all for going to that since he had donated the lumber. So, 25 businessmen from the Illinois side of the Quad Cities, and 23 from the Iowa side went down to the game. Iowa was getting waxed at half time. Of the 50 seats we had for the basketball game, no two of them were together—all 50 of our people were sitting in 50 different locations. When the game was over, we headed to the bus. It was bitter cold. We were waiting for the bus, but there's no bus coming. Pretty soon, all the other buses pulled away, and there were about 25 of us standing in an empty, frigid parking lot. We finally figured out that the guys that weren't there were all Iowa guys. We knew Schneckloth was the ringleader so we started marching to downtown Champaign and found the bus parked in front of the biggest bar there. Schneckloth had commandeered the bus at half time, rounded up all the Iowa guys, and was downtown drinking. Schneckloth was a great guy, but he was not an Illinois fan.

VIRGINIA IS FOR LOVERS ...OF HAWKEYE SPORTS

Charlie Henneman

Charles Henneman lived in Iowa City from 1969-1983. His father, John, was a history professor at Iowa. He and his wife Laurel, live in Charlottesville, Virginia, where Charles directs the CFA Institute.

My family was from the East. My father had gone to Princeton. When they moved to Iowa City in 1969, Big Ten sports was a very big culture shock to them—the size of it, the whole spectacle of Big Ten football was something they'd never experienced. My father enjoyed it a lot. This was not a great time for Iowa football, right in the midst of the twenty-year streak of losing seasons. He got season tickets right away, and it was our big event. When we had home football games, it was always a big deal about who got to go. It was built up a lot at our house. We always got to buy a pennant. I still have a huge collect of pennants, from Iowa and their opponents. It was just a special thing to be able to go to the games. I still remember hearing the "On Iowa" horns going on Saturday afternoons after a win. I loved the whole atmosphere, the marching bands and everything. It was a carnival event. For my family, it was very different from their experience in college sports. The Ivy League football games are like a cocktail party.

I would usually go to one game with my father and one game with my mother each season. I had equally great experiences with my father and with my mother at games—and some terrible experiences, too. There were some heartbreakers in there.

The anticipation of a game was something else. We would usually park on the other side of the river and walk up over the ramp, the circular bridge, walk around the Field House, and there was a giant parking lot. I think that is now a part of the hospital. We'd walk across the parking lot, through all the tailgaters. Usually, the band was out in the parking lot playing and talking with the fans. I loved the band and the drummers and the cheerleaders. I was as interested in that aspect of it as much as the football.

My brother would do a lot of sales on game days. He'd usually have a souvenir table set up when he didn't have a ticket to the game. Or, often, he'd go buy a Knothole ticket, but I was too little to go do that by myself. We'd often see him at a table selling hats and shirts. We'd go up the ramp, find our seats and get something to eat. Then we'd just wait for the game to start.

In some ways, I've become a much fiercer fan after I left Iowa. My parents lived there until '83, but I left and went to prep school in New Jersey starting my tenth grade year in the fall of 1980. I've been on the East Coast since then, and if anything I've been a much more vocal fan since I'm so far from Iowa. I like representing Iowa and Iowa fans in a sometimes hostile environment.

After I got to New Jersey, I found that there were a couple of other Hawkeyes there, which helped. It also helped a lot that Iowa had just been in the Final Four in basketball the previous spring. There was some name recognition. That helped a lot. A lot of people who followed college sports had just become aware of Iowa.

There were a lot of fierce rivalries at the prep school. There were students from all over the country so the whole spectrum of fans was there. Verbal fights were constantly breaking out. Any time we could watch games on television, it would be in a common room. I was in a house with forty other boys, and there was one TV in a common room. Lively debate ensued around the Saturday broadcasts of whatever happened to be on. There was a lot of trash talk being thrown around, especially my first fall, when TV kept showing the college scores after the Saturday games. It was always like, "Iowa just got crushed," in almost every game that year. They ended up going 4 and 4 in the Big Ten, but they had some miserable games. They lost to Arizona 5-3, which had to have been one of the worst games ever. Ohio State just destroyed them. Every time an Iowa score went up, of course all the boys I lived with would turn around and give me the raspberry.

But the following year, which was the fall of '81, was the turn-around year. As bad as it was the first fall, it got a lot better when "Iowa 10-Nebraska 7," went up on my first weekend back at school. That was a great day.

At night, I could pick up WHO-Des Moines broadcasts sporadically so I could get some of the Iowa basketball games on the radio. I could usually get the Thursday night Big Ten games so I followed those teams very closely. I would try every trick I knew to bring the broadcasts in clearly. Sometimes, I would literally sit there and listen to nothing but static for forty minutes. I could imagine I could hear Jim Zabel in there. It would fade in and fade out usually, but sometimes it never came in. Then, other nights, it would come in like it was next door. Those were the best nights.

Jim Zabel brought me so much pleasure throughout my years out here on the East Coast that I could never say an ill word about his broadcasting style. To me, he is the Voice of the Iowa Hawkeyes. I'd be sitting there—far, far from home—and, to me, he was bringing Iowa all the way to me. He'd describe the weather and tell how cold it was outside the Field House. Because I had so much difficulty bringing in the broadcasts, hearing his voice, locking in on his voice just was always such a triumph for me. It makes me feel good now just thinking about it. I can hear his voice in my mind. In '86/'87, he started getting a little wacky with the "I love it," at the end of a big victory. I saw a college roommate almost twenty years later, who did a perfect Jim Zabel imitation based on that era.

One unforgettable game on the radio was a Northwestern contest. The game was a defensive struggle. Iowa was a young team. It was one of those games where no one seemed to be able to find the basketball hoop. In my memory, Iowa had never been in a close game with Northwestern. It was the second half, and there was never more than a one or two-point difference in the score. That was a new experience for me. There was some see-sawing and you knew one or two baskets could make the difference in the whole game. Then, with a couple of minutes left in the game, the broadcast just went out. It faded and disappeared, and I could do nothing to retrieve it. I sat there and played with the radio for five or six minutes and could get nothing. I knew the game must be over by that time. I had to go down-stairs to use the pay phone to call Sportsphone to get the score. At a prep school, where kids are far from home, you always had to wait in line for the phone. I had to wait in line for about half an hour just to put a dime in and dial to get the score of the Iowa game. I finally heard the final—Iowa by one—and I was thrilled to hear that. The next day I had early classes and I was just trying to figure out where I could go to look at a newspaper to find out how they had actually won the game. I had a break between classes so I ran to the school infirmary where I knew they had a subscription to some of the local newspapers. I grabbed one and opened it up and saw that Kenny Arnold had hit the winning shot as time expired. I'll never forget that one.

The Internet is a great thing because I love being able to listen to the broadcasts far from home. For me, as an Iowa fan, just getting access to the games, whether football or basketball, has always been a chal-lenge. Often on the East Coast, even if Iowa is televised, it may only be a regional broadcast. I've gone to great lengths on many occasions just to get access to a radio broadcast. The idea I can just click on a link and bring them into my home now is almost a decadent experi-ence. I feel almost spoiled to be able to get them that easy. I've always envied Iowa fans who live in Iowa who could just turn on the TV or flip on the radio. I'm happy to have any sportscaster in my home bringing me Iowa sports. I'm a big Bobby Hansen fan. I pat-terned my own jump shot after his.

IOWA IOWA IOWA IOWA IOWA IOWA IOWA IOWA IOWA IOWA IOWA IOWA IOWA

SHORT STORIES FROM LONG MEMORIES

When I first started, the station engineers and I used to travel by car to do the games. After that we went by train, which was a two-day trip. Travel was tough in those days, but I loved it. You spent days going and coming instead of hours. They were great days. We'd play cards, visit with everybody, have a few drinks, tell a few stories and listen to all the newspaper guys who'd been around for years telling all their stories about the great days. Football was a very romantic thing—the writers were great—it was wonderful to listen to them spin their tales. Then, of course, the airlines came in and changed everything.

—JIM ZABEL, WHO Radio-1040

The first year Coach Raveling came on board at Iowa City, I became acquainted with grad assistant, Scott Howard. Scotty brought Coach Raveling and a couple of his assistants down to the Quad Cities. At the conclusion of our function that evening, Scotty loaded them all up in their van—they were not familiar with that area of town. They pulled out through an intersection onto what they thought was a two-lane, two-way service road—turned out the road was a four-lane, divided, highway, and they were on one side of the divided four-lane, going the wrong way. He looked up, and here comes this big semi bearing down on them, blasting his air horn.

The next morning they called. I was talking to Scotty on one phone and to George on the other. Raveling said, "You're going to have to teach these friends of yours how to drive." We all laughed about it, but, of course, it was a very scary thing. George said he had visions that this was the end of his career—and life—when he saw that big semi bearing down on them. George said, "It scared me so much I turned white. Maybe now, the Iowa fans will like me."

—WAYNE COOK, Davenport I-Club

When I was lived overseas, it was fairly hard to follow the Hawkeyes. When I first went to Abu Dubai in 1994, they did not have satellite television. There were basically a couple of local Arab channels and a Hindi channel. I remember watching "I Dream of Jeannie" in Hindi. There was no Internet. There was no contact with any media. My dad used to fax me some stories out of the *Cedar Rapids Gazette* on Iowa football and basketball games and some Cubs games. Somehow, I found out about a guy back in the States who made some kind of radio for the military which they used to tune into Armed Forces Radio. I called this guy and told him where I was and that I wanted to get access to some sports and asked him what he could do for me. He actually built a special adaptation of this Armed Forces Radio that he had been contracted by the Army to build. He didn't charge anything because it was an experimental model. He sent it to Abu Dubai. I remember going up on the roof of my five-story apartment building with one of our Indian workers trying to aim it at the right angle of the sky to catch the signal of Armed Forces Radio to listen to Iowa or any other game that might be being broadcast on it.

We managed to get it to work a couple of times, but it was very difficult. We tried to mount it so we wouldn't have to manually operate it. That worked for a month or so, but it turned out to be not very practical. We went from that to, a few years later, a company called TRZ Sports from Ohio. You could call them up, and they would patch you into a live radio broadcast of your favorite college football team. In my case, I had to pay for the international call for three or four hours. It was $25 an hour. I would try to time it so I could get in and at least listen to the fourth quarter. I couldn't afford to listen to the whole football game. We tried to do that every once in a while. Then, finally, we got the Internet, and I was able to access the live broadcast. There was a ten-hour time difference so if the game was a 2:30 p.m. late game for television, it would start at 12:30 a.m. and finish at 3:30 in the morning. Then I had to get up and go to school at 6:30 a.m. It was an interesting evolution of technology.

—MIKE KIELKOPF, starting second baseman on Iowa's 1972 College World Series Baseball Team

In '93, I took the Magic Bus to Daytona Beach with the Iowa wrestling team on it. It was spring break, and it was a riot. We get down there and the bus is longer than they will allow on the beach. I pull up to the entrance, and there is a line painted on the blacktop. You drive to it, and if you're longer than the line, you can't take the vehicle on the beach.

They said, "You're too long." We had a deck welded on the back of it. I said, "Oh no, technically, that back deck is considered a bumper so you can't count it." They said, "Get out of here." So we tried another entrance. Same spiel. They said, "Get it out of here." We tried four times, and the fourth time was a charm, and we got in. We were driving it down the beach, and there were a lot of Iowans there. The bus stands out like a sore thumb. A cop freaked out about it. You can't have any beer on the Daytona beach, and we had open containers. The cop makes everybody get out and the Iowa wrestling team is spread eagle, lying in the sand. The cop was just having a cow. Beer on the Daytona beach is a huge no-no. He's calling for back up and says to me, "You got beer on there?" I said, "Yeah, I've got beer." He said, "How much you got?" I said, "A couple of kegs." He says, "You're all going to jail." I said, "Why? It's a motor home. We can have beer on there." He said, "No, you can't." I said, "Yes, we can." He said, "Absolutely not." I said, "It's totally legal. I can drive down the Interstate with beer in there." He said, "You're telling me that if I call the Florida Highway Patrol over here, they're going to tell us it's legal to drive that thing on the Interstate with beer in it." He called in the Highway Patrol. Next thing you know, the Highway Patrol cars came cruising in. People were gathering around to see us, because they saw the bus was from Iowa. The Highway Patrol comes in and the cop says, "They're telling me this is licensed as a motor home, and they can have an open container on it on the highways." The Highway Patrolman says, "Yep." He totally backed me up. The cop freaked out. He said, "I'm going to tell you what. I'm going to let you go this time, but get that thing off the beach."

Believe it or not, I've not gotten pulled over very often driving the bus down the road. We've been to most states, and I've never really been harassed. Usually, we're going way too slow to be bothering anybody.

—**BRIAN DeCOSTER**, Iowa City, former owner of the Magic Bus

Evashevski, after the "Fainting Irish game" in '53 was the maddest I've ever seen a coach. You didn't have to know what he was like; you only had to look at him. He was like a lion that had just been wounded. I had driven over to the game so wasn't with Evy and the team coming home.

I liked to go to games at Michigan. It's just a happening. It's kind of the Rose Bowl of the Midwest. Minnesota is my least favorite stadium. It was always cold there, and the press box was always cold. We were always given lousy treatment. We had a saying in those days, "In the Big Ten, nine teams do it one way. Minnesota does it the other." Their field had the biggest crown on it that I have ever seen on a football field. When you looked from one sideline to the other, and the teams were on the hash marks across the field from you, you could only see a player from the waist up. Coach Bierman always had them in uniforms which were supposed to be maroon and gold. He was a big devotee of the spin back, and he had the uniforms designed the color of a football.

Before the Iowa-Notre Dame game in 1964, we had a blizzard. I was driving with my wife, and we had stayed overnight in Chicago. It had snowed a foot or more, and there were cars in ditches all over the place. Notre Dame didn't have enough equipment to clear the parking lots and you just had to stuff your car in a snowdrift and make your way to the stadium. It was bitter cold—the high for the day was minus 10. I had a heater with me. Notre Dame had a wooden press box with open windows, a little lean-to affair for the visiting stations. I turned on the heater, and it would light up, but I could put my hands against the filaments and not feel a thing. That's how cold it was.

—**BOB BROOKS**, Iowa radio announcer since 1943

Iowa was in the Rose Bowl in 1982, and that was our family vacation. My dad and mom and my brother and I fought through a blizzard to get to Chicago O'Hare to get out to Pasadena. That was our vacation—"Let's go watch the Hawks. Let's go to the bowl game. We don't want to miss this opportunity." Mom and dad got us new Hawkeye coats and hats for Christmas. We were feeling pretty proud walking through Pasadena before the game. It's just amazing that I ended up getting to play for them.

—**JESS SETTLES**, Former Hawkeye Basketball Star

When I got married a couple of years ago, my wife wanted to get married in the fall, which, of course, conflicted with the football schedule. Many of my friends are Iowa fan season-ticket holders, and a lot of them go on the road. I didn't want to have them miss out on the wedding so we found a weekend in October that was an away game, at Indiana. Most of my friends weren't going to make the trip to see Iowa beat Indiana. Since it wasn't a home game, I told her we could get married in the parking lot at Kinnick and have a tailgater be our wedding reception. We'd have a lot more people bring us gifts, I told her. She didn't buy it. We got married in St. Louis that weekend, which was fun because the wedding was in the middle of the afternoon. My groomsmen and I and some family members all went to a sports bar in St. Louis and watched the first half of the Iowa—Indiana game before we headed down to the church to get married.

—TOM KAKERT, Davenport Native

You can never get decent seats in the Metrodome. In one end zone, there's always a large contingent of Hawkeye fans. In order to get these tickets, you have to order through a Minnesota address. Four years ago, I looked on the map and found a high school in Minnesota. We called the ticket office and said, "We're having a class reunion and want to know if we can get 500 tickets for the Minnesota-Arkansas State game." She said we could and gave us the price. I said, "What other games are available?" She read them out. Then, she'd get to Iowa, which was the last one. "Hey, that'd be fun. I think our group would enjoy that. Is there anyway we could get block seats?" We ordered over 600 tickets, and they ended up giving us a discount 'cause we had so many people. We save five or ten dollars a ticket to what we would have paid getting them through Iowa. The Cedar Rapids Elks took six or eight buses up there. This year we've ordered over 500. So far, they've never figured out that there are all these Hawkeye fans sitting there in this block of seats. Then you look up in the very top, and that's where the regular Iowa seats are...because they don't give the visiting team fans very good seats.

—DAVE GALLAGHER, Iowa City

When I came to school out here, I was just looking for something different to do. My first year at Arizona State was the year they finished #2 in the country after beating Nebraska in the '75 Fiesta Bowl. I remember coming to the first game they played that year against UCLA. It was on national TV, and I was expecting Sun Devil Stadium to be out of control. I was really excited to be going to school here and to have a good football team and follow them. I got here...and it wasn't important to anybody! It wasn't like going to a game in Iowa City where it's important! In Iowa, it is important… people have been talking about the game coming up all week. You get to the game there, and it's a big deal. There's tailgating going on. There's the excitement that revolved around the trip there. Here, people showed up for the game, casually watched it, and then they left. I was so disappointed. This is nothing. There's not the rabidness. You don't go back in time the way it does in Iowa City.

—MIKE McGREGOR, 48, Iowa native, Phoenix resident

IOWA IOWA IOWA IOWA IOWA IOWA IOWA IOWA IOWA IOWA IOWA IOWA IOWA

Alan Zazza caters to the Iowa opponents.

THE BCS BOWLS...OR AS THEY SAY iN CHAMPAiGN...PASSOVER.

Chapter 8

Hawkapalooza

Bird Watchin'

THIS LITTLE LIGHT OF MINE, I'M GONNA LET IT SHINE!

Joe Crookham

Guess what the cover story was on the sports page of the inaugural issue of USA Today, *September 12, 1982. It was about an Iowa native and a University of Iowa graduate who was about to drastically change the face of big-time college football. Joe Crookham of Oskaloosa received a B.A. degree in accounting in 1962, an MBA in 1964, and a law degree in 1968. His company, Musco Lighting devised a way to light college stadiums for night games, even though the venues had no permanent lighting system. The fact that Crookham was a pilot who loved to fly was an important factor in bringing to reality an almost impossible dream. Musco Lighting is one of eight participants in the University of Iowa Partners In Excellence Program.*

When I got out of law school, a guy came into my office one day to get a deed to a piece of property. He and another guy were interested in starting a manufacturing business. They were engineers at Pella-Clark. I said, "I've got an accounting background and a law background. I'd be interested in helping out, not on a fee-basis, just to be part of it." One guy dropped out of it after a couple of years, but the other guy, Myron, and I stayed in it and held it together.

We decided we needed to get into something where we had our own marketing control. We heard about a lighting company in Muscatine that was for sale. We bought the company and discontinued all the products they had. We shut down the foundry they had and bought the building.

We decided six products would be a good mix, a cross-section of several things. The first product we developed was a sports lighting product, to light a ball field. It was the only product they'd had which made any sense at all. That was the first product we developed. I keep telling my partner that it's twenty-eight years later, and he still owes me five products.

Knoxville, Iowa has the Knoxville Raceway, World of Outlaws, and NBC wanted to televise that race, back in '78. The lights weren't adequate to do that. The people at Knoxville asked us about possibly lighting their track for them. I met with a farmer-based board of directors who really didn't have any idea what to do with a television contract offer. They didn't want to spend money to put lights on the track. After talking with them, my partner and I were trying to figure out what would be best. I joked, "Maybe we should just put these lights up on a crane truck just for this event." As I was flying along, thinking about their problem, I remembered that remark. The more I thought about it, I decided that might not be the dumbest idea I've ever had. Myron and I figured it wouldn't be impossible. The track wouldn't have to spend the money to permanently light the track, yet they could have the one televised event.

The next time I was in New York City, I looked up ABC, CBS and NBC in the phone book. I called them and asked if they would talk to me about an idea for lighting for television. All three of them invited me to come over and talk to them. The guy at ABC said, "We've got a college football contract coming up. If that would enable us to add late afternoon and night-time games, we might be interested."

This was in the spring and summer of 1979. We had several conversations, and ABC got more serious. The only thing I knew about television was how to turn it on and how to complain about the programming. If I had a clue what we were getting into with this idea, I'd have gone and done something else. ABC was trying to decide whether or not this thing was really feasible. We made arrangements to go over to Kinnick Stadium and test it out after the football season was over.

We got one rental crane and put lights on it and the guy from ABC came out with us and we did a demonstration of it at Kinnick. ABC liked it so we took a lot of photographs of it and we started to work on perfecting it. This was only a concept of what we wanted to do.

For more than a whole year, nothing happened. Then I got a call from ABC's Don Bernstein on April 14, 1982. He said they wanted to do the Michigan-Notre Dame game that September—five months away. I asked when he'd need to know. He said Notre Dame had agreed to it, but I would need to talk with Michigan, and he would need to know "by noon tomorrow!" He said, "Any chance you can talk to them?" I said, "I guess I could fly up there. Will they be available to talk to me?"

I got out the three-ring binder we made up from pictures of the trial at Kinnick. After our presentation, they said, "We were expecting something like carnival midway lighting, but this looks very substantial." I didn't bother to tell them it didn't exist anymore. They told us they thought it would be okay, so I called Don Bernstein. At that point, all that existed was one rental truck and a theory on paper. It occurred to me as I was going out to the airport in Lansing that I had never actually seen Notre Dame and that I probably should stop by there and find out what we had just promised.

Remembering the famous game at Notre Dame in **1953** when Notre Dame faked the injuries to stop the clock, I was still mad at Notre Dame. I had not gotten over that and had no use for Notre Dame. I stopped in South Bend and went by the campus and met with the A.D. there, Gene Corrigan. One of the dilemmas I had with this whole thing is that by the time we did the first game at Notre Dame, I'd fallen in love with the place. They are such nice, nice people.

We had arranged that two weeks before the game we would go over and light the stadium and go through a trial run. We were scrambling. I called Gene Corrigan three weeks before we were going to be there, "With all that's going on here, we think we'd be better off spending the extra time getting ready to go rather than coming to Notre Dame for a trial run." He thought about it for a while, and said, "We need to talk about that. Can you come over?" I flew over there, and that was about as long as that conversation was.

> **Johnny Lattner, the 1953 Heisman Trophy winner from Notre Dame, didn't even lead the Irish in rushing or receiving that season.**

I sat down, he looked at me, and said, "What in the hell is this crap about not doing a test? I've got my neck stuck out a country mile. The alumni think I'm crazy for doing this game, and I've got everybody you can imagine all over the top of me on this, and you're telling me the first time I'm gonna see it is the weekend of the game. I don't think so." I had never seen the man even frown, he'd been such a gentleman, and I decided, "He's serious about this." He talked to me about all the security and about how they would have to redirect their traffic. We went over and did the test and everything was great. We were still scrambling wildly with it.

First of all, we had no financing for this. It was a four million dollar system, and we didn't have four million dollars. We had to borrow the money. Most of the financing we worked out was with the company that sold us the cranes. They were a large company and agreed to provide the leasing/purchase financing on the trucks and cranes. That was about half of the four million dollars. We got the rest from the bank in Muscatine. George Shepley, the bank president, was a big fan of Hawkeye football. He agreed to lend us the rest of the money, about a million and a half. George Shepley was there for the closing, and said, "I'm a big backer of my local community. I'd really like to see a Musco manufacturing facility here. If you would, I'd provide your financing." Being a desperate company in '76 when we bought this, I agreed to leave it there, and I'm kind of old-fashioned about loyalty—if you promise something, that's the way it is—so our manufacturing plant will always be Muscatine.

The parent of the crane company was the Kidde Corporation. They ended up panicking at the thought of these cranes setting up over crowds of a hundred thousand people. They decided they didn't want to sell those cranes for that use. We were halfway through the project and everything was designed around these cranes. We had to have the cranes. Their final shot was, "Well, okay, we'll sell you the crane, but we're not going to supply the financing." All of a sudden, three months into a five-month project, two million dollars in financing just dried up. When I told Shepley, he came up with the other two million dollars.

This is 1982, when banks and savings and loans were going broke. The next year, George called me and wanted me to come up immediately—the examiners had just been there. George is a really nice guy; he's got a temper, but he's a really nice guy. He called me over to his office. I went in and he closed the door. He sat down and looked at me and said, "How in the hell did you ever talk me into this? Do you know what the examiners just did to me last week over this loan?"

I told ABC we'd really like to have a promo at the start of the game. I know nothing about how that kind of thing gets done, the value of it or how to go about it. At the start of that game, they did a daytime shot from the end zone camera of Touchdown Jesus, and they zoomed down to the floor of the stadium. Keith Jackson starts out saying, "Up until now, college football has been a Saturday afternoon sport at Notre Dame," and they were showing a shot of the floor of the stadium, "but tonight we bring you the night the lights went on at Notre Dame," acknowledging Musco Sports Lighting, and they went to a wide shot of the stadium. Then they did a tight logo shot of the side of our truck and then pulled back and showed the whole truck. That was 1982. I've never had a year go by since that happened, and not have someone ask about that Notre Dame game. The risk was not whether or not we could do it. The risk was whether or not, with all the complexity of the challenge of doing it, something would fail. After the game, I took out a full-page ad in the newspaper "Thank you, George Shepley, for the help that made this possible."

CBS, who had been a foot-dragger, came to us Saturday night while we were still at Notre Dame and asked us to do the Penn State game the next week. They decided they had to play catch-up with this whole thing. We told them we would take a look at it.

On Sunday, Myron flew out to Penn State and looked at the stadium and I came back and tried to figure out how to do it. We knew they had a big, long press box at Penn State and we could set lines on top of there, and we could rent a couple of cranes and put them on the other side of it. We figured that if we manufactured a certain make-shift system and shipped it out there, we could install it "as is." We said, "We can do that." On Monday morning, we called CBS and committed.

We manufactured a complete stadium lighting system Monday and Tuesday in our plant in Muscatine with people working twenty-hour days for two days to do that. The lighting system was done by late Tuesday night and the electrical part wasn't done yet so the guys who were working on it volunteered to climb in the back of the truck, ride out there and finish the work while the truck was moving down the turnpike.

Friday night, the facilities manager for Penn State, said, "I've been at this place a long time. Look at this field stadium and press box. There used to be a track around here and the fifteen or twenty rows that are closest to the field didn't exist. I came up with the idea of jacking up the entire stadium and building fifteen rows of bleachers underneath it, and everybody laughed at me. And we did it. I tell you that by way of letting you know I believe people can do fairly amazing things if they just put their mind to do that. They told me Monday you guys were going to build a lighting system, ship it out here, install it, and we'd have lights on tonight for a test and lights for a game tomorrow night. I laughed when they told me that. I'm standing with you here now on this field. I'm looking at this, and I still don't believe it's possible."

A lot of the people are proud of what we do, and I hear people brag about the fact that we were in Athens for the Olympics. We won an Emmy for technical advancement of lighting in television in 1983. We were there 9/11 at the Trade Center. We lit the site through May of the next spring during all the search and recovery efforts. On 9/11 we were able to call four guys who were in Rhode Island. They had just finished doing the Gravity Games there for **ESPN** that weekend and were getting ready to head back. They were getting ready to have lunch out there, and we told them we really thought we should be at the World Trade Center. We said, "It's optional whether you want to go or not. There's a lot of danger involved in going down there, but, on the other hand, we think they need what we do." Without a lost beat, they said, "We're on our way."

That should be our slogan.

> **ESPN debuted September 7, 1979. ESPN2 debuted October 1, 1993. *ESPN The Magazine* made its first appearance on March 11, 1998.**

COACH ERICKSON, DO YOU NEED MORE TOWELS? NO, THANKS. MY SUITCASE IS FULL.

Alan Zazza

Alan Zazza, owner of the Clarion Hotel—formerly the Sheraton—in Cedar Rapids holds the national record for most consecutive years hosting a major university's opposing teams. Zazza is known nation-wide for his management style.

In the late '70s, when we were building the hotel, I said to my dad, "I want to go after all the Iowa opposing football teams." My dad said, "You'll never get them. They stay in Iowa City." I said, "Well, I'm going to try." It was like everything else—if you do a good job, they continue to come back. I study harder getting ready for a football team than I ever did in college.

In 2002, we hit our 150th team, and it happened to be Barry Alvarez. Iowa announced in front of 72,000 people in the stadium that we were the only hotel in the nation that has hosted every team for over 25 years. When Barry came in, he brought me a helmet. Barry wrote, "Alan, we're honored to be your 150th team. On Wisconsin! Barry Alvarez." Right now, I've hosted 157 out of 157 football teams.

Visiting fans like to stay at the same hotel with their team, but the team takes so many rooms I'm not able to get too many of them in. The parents who plan ahead of time and who know a year in advance that they're going to be staying there usually get in.

The Miami game was a night game in 1992. They were very cocky, ranked #1 in the nation. Their coach, Dennis Erickson, said, "You'll never have any problems. You can go in and change the beds and clean the shower when the boys take their suitcases." I remember they had 105 rooms and, just to be mean, about 85 of the boys stripped the beds and took the blankets, bedspreads, sheets and pillows and put them in the shower and turned on the water. My girls went in to tidy up a little bit and get ready for other guests. It was a real nightmare. We had a lot of guests who were very, very unhappy. I can't blame them. It was one of those deals when you wish you were not in the hotel business. We had to refund a lot of money. The new check-ins were there and wanted to get into their rooms and shower and change for a big wedding, but they couldn't get into some of the rooms until eight or nine that night because of what we had to do to get the rooms ready. We had to take big garbage cans and put all the wet linens in them and take them out of the rooms. It was the worst nightmare I've had hosting a team.

These teams do all their taping at our hotel, too. They don't do any taping at the stadium. I have to give them one room for offense, one room for defense, one room for taping and one room for meals.

Usually, for most of the opposing teams, after the game, I cater a meal for them in locker room. They give me passes. I take corporate customers down in our motor home and have cocktails, munchies and brats. Then about the middle of the fourth quarter, I'll leave the customers for a little bit and I'll have my staff meet me down in the locker room. We'll get the team's meal all set up. Some of the coaches will tell me to just put them in big boxes and mark them and put them on their buses. Some of them eat the meal in the locker room, and that's fun.

I've gotten to be real good friends with Archie Griffin. Last year I went out to Ohio State to meet their new coach and new staff. Archie took us out for dinner. He is one class act. No cockiness. No attitude. I can't say enough about Archie. He's wonderful.

When I feed a team, which is usually 100 people, it's like feeding a wedding for 400. I order different tables to feed them because a table that seats 10 normal people will only seat six football players because of their size and the quantity of food they eat.

NEW RULE
YOU ARE ALLOWED ONE BEER
FOR EVERY SIX MILLION DOLLARS
YOU DONATE

Kevin Krause

Kevin Krause, 43, was raised in Hampton, Iowa, graduated from Iowa and now owns The Quad City Swing, the Midwest League Class-A affiliate of the St. Louis Cardinals. While at Iowa, Kevin was Herky the Hawk. Kevin's father, Bill Krause, student manager of the 1956 Hawkeye Rose Bowl team, is a legendary supporter of the Iowa program. The senior Krause once attended 111 consecutive Iowa games—home and away. On September 10, 2004, Bill Krause donated $5 million to the University of Iowa Athletic Department—the largest gift ever.

Being Herky the Hawkeye was a great experience. I had the opportunity to go to Pasadena for the 1982 Rose Bowl. We didn't play very well against a good Washington opponent. We were down 13-0 at half time and hadn't seen much life. We started the second half and held them on their first drive, which I thought was a good start for us and would maybe give us momentum. The punt was heading toward the end zone and I was right there. I thought, "This is a great opportunity. I'll pick the ball up and run on the field. I'll get the Iowa crowd back in the game." I leaned over to pick up the ball as it was bouncing through the end zone. I looked up and saw a big "6" and "9" in gold and purple coming right at me. What happened was that one of the Washington players was trying to keep the ball from going into the end zone so it wouldn't be a touchback. He couldn't stop in time. He knocked me flat—put a great hit on me! This created an uproar with our fans. This was surely unintentional—he couldn't stop, but the fans wanted to make sure they protected their mascot. As they heard the crowd roar, Dick

Enberg, who was doing the game with Merlin Olsen, announced, "Perhaps the ball went out of bounds inside the five-yard line, and it won't be a touchback." Merlin Olsen said, "No, I believe the Washington player hit the Iowa mascot." Then, they went to commercial, and when they came back, they showed the clip of the Washington player nailing me. As I went to the ground after the hit, my beak was cracked. Enberg said, "The good news is that the Iowa mascot is all right." Merlin joked, "Someone put a jerky on Herky." One of our fans put a Band Aid on the broken beak. The Los Angeles Times had it as the best hit of the bowl games that day.

I always felt I was representing the University and didn't want to represent it in a bad light. In all situations, I would try to avoid any major conflict. You can get a feel for the other mascot pretty early in the process. When I was at Northwestern one year, their cheerleaders came over and grabbed me, and they were going to run me into the goalposts. They dropped me early and cracked the helmet. When you take it back to the athletic department, you're a little dismayed that while you were doing Herky, the costume got damaged. In a lot of venues, a particular mascot will be carried off into the goalposts and will be kind of a challenge between the two schools. I had no qualms with that.

IOWA IOWA IOWA IOWA IOWA IOWA IOWA IOWA IOWA IOWA IOWA IOWA IOWA

Hawk-eyetems

I run a Hawkeye website called Hawkeye Links. It's for people to go to who want quick access to a variety of Hawkeye links. Instead of having to flip through a bunch of search engines to find what they want, they can come right to this site. I try to keep tabs on most of the active Hawkeye sites, whether it's through The University of Iowa or whether it's other fan sites that are out there. This gives users quick access.

—JOHN LANGLAND, Ottumwa native, www.langland.org/iowa-hawkeye

In my first couple of years of doing the games, Brooks and Gonder and Zabel still traveled with us and were part of the broadcast. They would handle the pre-game, the half-time interviews, and the post-game show. Eddie and I basically would duck in and do the play-by-play and then get out of their way. We were at Northwestern on a snowy, icy, freezing day in late November. That's important because Northwestern had a very, very good team. They went to the Hall of Fame Bowl that year and played on New Year's Day. We were doing our segment where we were going around the Big Ten looking at other games. It was one of those snowy Midwestern days, where it was bad—terrible weather everywhere. Penn State was playing Purdue. We get to that game and Zabel and Brooks actually get into an argument over who would have the better attack in inclement weather—Purdue or Penn State. Well, Penn State had Curtis Enis at running back, Heisman Trophy candidate, and Purdue had Billy Dicken at quarterback. Brooks was talking about how their running game was better suited for that kind of weather. Zabel was saying, "Well maybe so, but if you're Purdue, you score points by throwing the football." They actually got at each other's Adam's apple a couple of times, sticking up for what they believed. Finally, Brooks just stops Zabel in mid-sentence, and he looks out onto the ice-laden field in Evanston and says, "Well, all I know is, on a day like today, I'd rather have an Enis than a Dicken." Honest to God, it came out that way. He had no intention of being malicious or "R" rated, and Podolak and I are standing there eating a roast beef sandwich, and, I'll never forget it, we both stopped chewing at the same time and

VOL. 1 NO. 7   SEPTEMBER 27, 1954

SPORTS

ILLUSTRATED

25 CENTS

There have been over 2,600 Sports Illustrated covers. This was cover #7...
Hawkeye All-American Calvin Jones. Iowa has been featured just
twice on the SI cover.

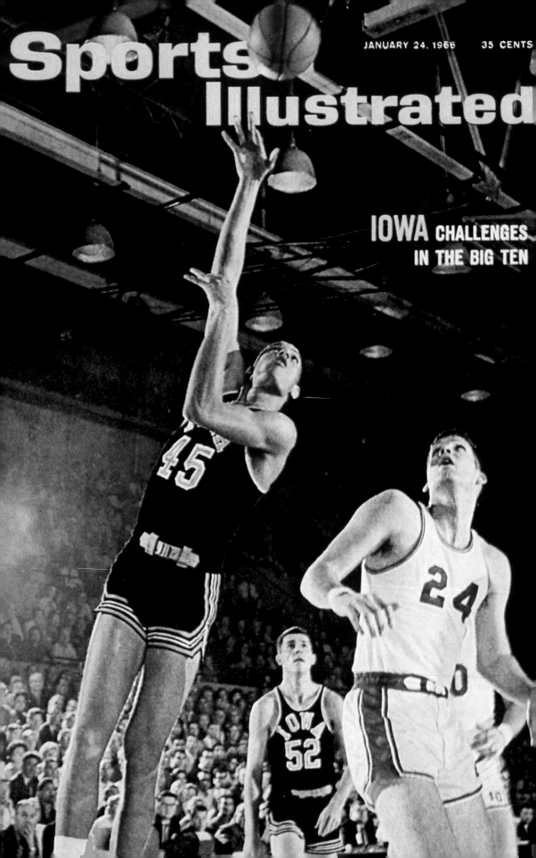

JANUARY 24, 1966   35 CENTS

Sports Illustrated

IOWA CHALLENGES IN THE BIG TEN

It's good to be the King...of tailgating. Brian DeCoster (above right) is delighted with the results of his "Miss Tupperware" idea. (Below) Tailgating fans enjoy the Miss Tupperware contest.

Perhaps the finest coaching staff in the history of college football: (Back row) Bill Snyder, Del Miller, Kirk Ferentz, Hayden Fry, Carl Jackson, Don Patterson, Bill Dervrich. (Front row) Bernie Wyatt, Barry Alvarez, Bill Brashier, Dan McCarney, Bobby Stoops.

The Settles family of Winfield, Iowa get ready to catch a Hawk road game. Parents Mary and Steve are on the couch with 13-year-old Jake. Jess Settles, 11, is wearing his Hawk colors.

Ruth (Mrs. Forest) Evashevski with legendary WMT-Cedar Rapids announcer Tait Cummins.

This is what happens if you miss just one issue of *GQ*... The whole fashion world passes you by. At the 1975 Football Awards Banquet: (left to right) Mark Wilson, Alex Karras, Earl Murphy, and Head Coach Bob Commings. It is not known how long they had to wear these outfits before they won the bet.

Building Iowa Stadium, 1928. Note horse-drawn carts.

Homecoming would not be the same without the Magic Bus.

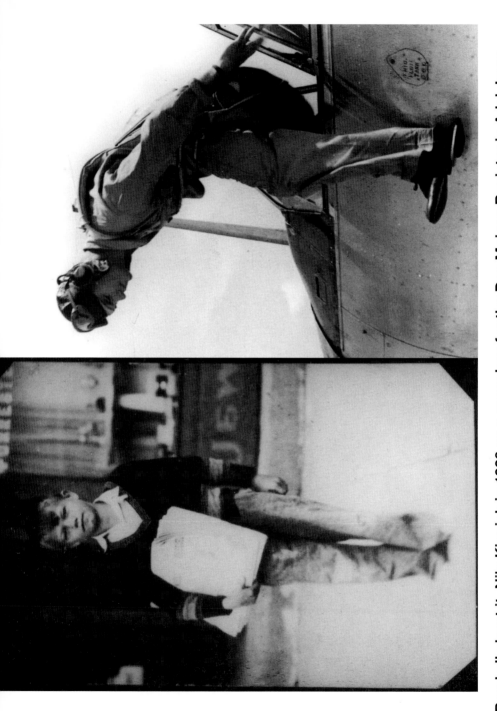

Read all about it. Nile Kinnick in 1926 as a paperboy for the Des Moines Register in Adel, Iowa. (Right) Nile Kinnick as he prepares for his last flight, June 2, 1943.

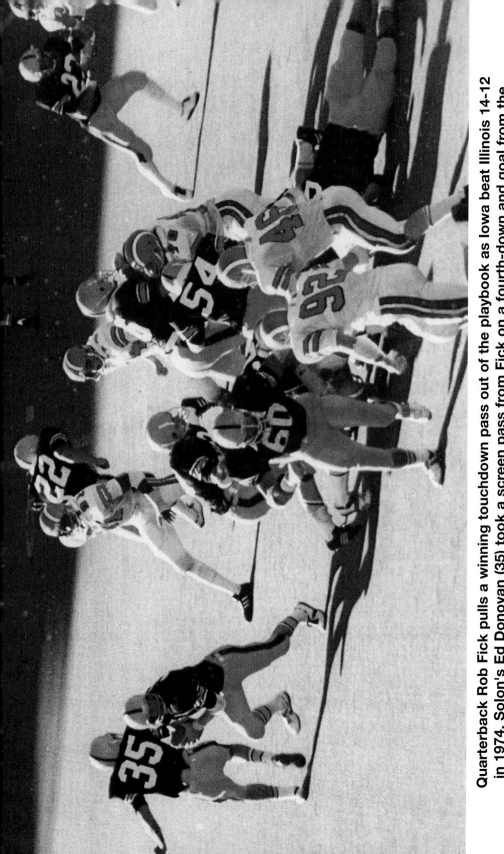

Quarterback Rob Fick pulls a winning touchdown pass out of the playbook as Iowa beat Illinois 14-12 in 1974. Solon's Ed Donovan (35) took a screen pass from Fick on a fourth-down and goal from the Illinois eight with 17 seconds to play. Dan McCarney (60) throws a key block.

Now, let's meet the quarterback of your 1950 Baylor Bears, Hayden Fry.

If youth knew, if age could do. (Above) Jess Settles at age 4. (Below) Hayden Fry in September, 2004 with young Iowa fan.

Merry Christmas from the "real" Santa.

looked at each other and almost choked on our meat. You could just read it in our eyes. You didn't have to say anything, but we were reading each other's mind, "Did he really say what I think I just heard him say? I'd rather have an Enis than a Dicken." Zabel breaks out laughing. Gonder is on the floor. It mushroomed from there. We had to go through two or three commercial breaks before we got everybody settled back down again. This is what I loved about Bob Brooks—he never cracked a smile once. He went right on, a consummate professional. I don't know, to this day, if he knew how it came out on the air, but Brooksy didn't care. He's made his point. He felt he'd won the argument with his long-time rival Jim Zabel. That's the first time, I think, in fifty some years that Zabel's been speechless. That's a true story.

—GARY DOLPHIN, Voice of the Hawkeyes

One of my favorite things that ever happened was when Rick Derringer played at Homecoming. Every week, we have this local radio station, KRNA, out of Cedar Rapids. They do live broadcasts from the Magic Bus, which is right across from the stadium. At the end of the day, it was bitterly cold for the first week of October, and it was miserable. The DJ at that time is a fairly large man. He pulls up in his KRNA company van to load up his equipment. He's sitting there B.S.-ing with us while they're loading up his stuff. He turns around, and the van is gone. He's brand new at the station at the time. He begins to break down, "What did you guys do with my van? Where is my van?" We were like, "What are you talking about? I don't know where your van is." Someone from the Magic Bus had decided that would be an easy way to get home. So…they stole the radio station's van. The DJ goes live on air begging for the van and then they call all the bars downtown asking them to announce over their loudspeakers, "The KRNA van has been stolen. If you see it, please let the police know where it is." It turned up the next day. It had been parked way out in the middle of nowhere. I found out later that a couple of guys decided to steal the van because they couldn't get a taxi home. The DJ actually called the mobile in the van and tearfully said, "Would you bring me back my van?" They said to him, "Is this the fat ——— DJ?" "Yes, this is the fat ——— DJ. Please bring me back my van." He didn't get fired, and he's still doing live broadcasts.

—JEREMY FREERKS, Clarksville, Iowa native

We had a friend named Moose, who is a fairly legendary Iowa tailgater. He's the size and shape you'd imagine from a guy named Moose. My friend, Brian, as part of the World's Largest Tupperware Party had a contest to name "Miss Tupperware." The Magic Bus has a deck on top of it so everything was being orchestrated from the top of the bus. There are lots of pretty girls up there vying for the title of Miss Tupperware. You had to come up with a "best use" for Tupperware, too. I came up with what I felt should have been the winning slogan. I had a little Tupperware cup that I had tied a string to and hung around my neck. I gave this to a girl who asked me what she should tell them she did with it. I told her to say that it was to ......You say this to a bunch of drunken college guys at a Tailgater, and the crowd just erupts. They loved it, and I thought we had a sure-fire winner until Moose got up there. He took his shirt off, and he had a giant Velveeta box stuck on his head as a hat. In disgust, people voted for him just to get him to put his shirt back on.

Moose actually passed out, just like a beached whale, after the tailgate. My wife, Mary, and our friend, Jack Noble, were kind of dragging him along because he was puking on himself. Our friend, Frasier, comes up and says, "I can see you've clearly messed up. You haven't figured the 'puking per square foot' equation properly." They were going to run out of space that they could drag him through. Brian walks up and looks at Moose and says, "I always suspected Moose was bulimic."

—STEVE CHARLTON, Des Moines, 35

I named my son Gable Hawk Fowler because Dan Gable inspired me so much. I thought it was a very unique name. My ties to being a Hawkeye fan made me feel it was an appropriate thing to do.

The doctor who was present at my son's birth was standing at the foot of the bed and going through all the regular procedures. As Gable is crowning, the doctor tells me to come down to his end. I'm there watching the delivery. He asked me what we were going to name him and I told him, "Gable." He said, "Oh, you must be an Iowa fan." I'm standing there in a Hawkeye T-shirt and Hawkeye shorts. I laughed and said, "Yes." He said, "Well, obviously you know some wrestlers." I said, "Yes, I know quite a few, just not personally." He said, "I know Jeff McGinness pretty well." I said, "How's that?" During all this, my wife's there giving birth. I was wondering how she was going to react to my standing there talking to her doctor about wrestling since my dedication to Iowa wrestling gets on her nerves at times. So I'm checking her out to see how she's doing because she knows I'm going to want to pump him for all the information he has. He goes on to tell me that his wife and Jeff's wife were real good friends in college and that just a few months ago he had gone to McGinness' wedding in Chicago. It took everything I had not to continue that conversation even more. For once in my life, I just let that go because I was unsure if my wife was going to be okay with our continuing that conversation. Of course, I did plan to later! Then, there was the birth and by the time I figured I could go talk to him some more, he was already gone.

—**KEVIN FOWLER**, Assistant Principal, Hannibal (Mo.) Middle School

The last time they had the NCAA wrestling championships in Iowa City, the Republican party wanted to have a reception at the Wig and Pen. The Speaker of the House, Dennis Hastert, is a big-time wrestling fan and a big Dan Gable fan. Hastert was a high-school wrestling coach in Illinois.

These championships are a three-day deal. It goes all day long. They have sessions. You might have two or three wrestlers you want to follow, but you don't sit through the whole thing. You just go and see them and drift in and out. Down here, we were jammed from morning until night with people just coming back and forth. It was very busy. At three o'clock in the afternoon, they wanted to have a reception here for Dennis Hastert, along with Dan Gable, and both were going to speak. I told them we would be happy to do it. At the time, I didn't know how we were going to handle it. I can tell you this—leading up to it, I had a house full of people at two o'clock in the afternoon, all wrestling fans from all across the country. We're packed, outside and inside, even though it's March.

I'm down here thinking, "I'm going to shoot myself because there's just no way I'm going to be able to clear this place out and get their deal started at 3:15." We were going to try to start clearing people out at about three o'clock for about a half-hour reception and speeches by Hastert and Gable. I was thinking, "I'm stupid. There's no way we can do this. These people are going to be upset." We printed up a flyer and after one o'clock, everybody we'd seat, we'd hand out this flyer personally and apologize for the inconvenience that would be forthcoming—that they would have to leave their seats because we had to shut down for a reception." The security people were looking at everything. As it turned out, the fact that Dennis Hastert and Dan Gable were involved in it, it was almost like, "My God, you shouldn't even have to ask. We'll do it for these people. Don't worry about it." It took us about ten minutes to clear the whole place out. Even the fans helped move tables. They went outside and stood there—I'm talking 150-200 people—and waited for this to take place. When it was all said and done, they all came back in and picked up right where they left off. There was not a hitch in the whole thing. They helped us put the place back together. It really was a testament to the wrestling fans themselves and the respect they had for Dan Gable and Dennis Hastert.

—DICK QUERREY, owner, Wig and Pen Restaurant, Iowa City

There was a band who played a song, "Flirting With Disaster," and they were pretty big in the 70s and 80s. There was one original band member left. Brian loved to have a big band come play on top of the Magic Bus, so he got the band, Molly Hatchet. The city of Iowa City has been trying to get rid of Brian forever and had done everything they could to try and shut down his parties. The rules apply to everybody. Alums can have big parties, and he was an alum, but he wasn't an alum who was giving them a hundred-thousand dollar check every year. The police tried to shut that party down, even though the Magic Bus was synonymous with tailgating and with Hawkeye games. I'll bet you that fifty percent of the people you would ask about tailgating would know about the Magic Bus. The band hadn't even played yet, but the police came and told Brian that he was in violation of the noise ordinance.

Now this was on a football Saturday, across the street from the stadium. There are 70,000 people in the stadium going nuts. You can hear them from a mile away…but they tell Brian he's in violation of a noise ordinance. The police told Brian that if the band plays, they are going to arrest him. The band is there, and Brian has paid good money to have them come there. He decides to do them one better. There's this old police officer in Iowa City who a lot of people would describe as less than virtuous. He'd had it in for Brian for ages. Every time they'd written Brian a ticket for anything, Brian would always take it to court and beat them. The police came up and told the band, "If you play, we're going to arrest all of you." The band didn't want to get arrested so they decided to pretend like they were playing. At halftime, the band came out, and instead of plugging in their instruments and playing, they just played a tape of the band and they lip sync-ed to it, which was enough to get the police to come and shut the whole thing down. They gave Brian a ticket for disturbing the peace—on a football Saturday. The police got up on top of the bus to tell the band to shut it down, and then they realized that they weren't playing. Absolutely brilliant! That's Brian. Celebrating Hawkeye football wouldn't be the same without him.

—AARON WHALEN, Durham, N.C., grad student

The first Poinsettia Bowl had an attendance problem in 1952. NBC Sports was scheduled to televise the game from San Diego's Balboa Stadium. The only problem was a daylong torrential rain forced most fans to stay home. NBC officials didn't want to go on the air with an empty stadium, so they sought the help of the Navy Shore Patrol. The Patrol raided bars, cafes and movie theaters issuing orders for all servicemen to go to the game. The soldiers—that could be found—huddled into one section for the benefit of televised "crowd" shots. One of those fans was Hayden Fry. "We heard we were there to play the crowd scene," Fry said. "But at the time, none of us knew why we were sitting there in a downpour. The Shore Patrol just picked us up, took us to the stadium, and told us to enjoy the game. Some enjoyment."

Fry's Iowa fans find their own ways to enjoy the games. Among them is stealing the helmets from visiting quarterbacks. In 1995, thieves got away with opponents' headgear in consecutive weeks, against Indiana and Penn State. According to Penn State QB, Doug Ostrosky, "It was on the bench, and I turned around and it was gone. I saw a guy flying up the stairs of the stadium with my helmet." The Indiana QB said his helmet was setting under the Hoosier bench.

But Fry had other things to complain about. He was disgusted with Iowa fans who threw beer cans, liquor bottles and animal parts on the field during games. "Lock 'em up," Fry said, "It's just ridiculous. The police need to come down on them. Lock their tails up. The more they get away with, the more they're going to do. It's really gotten dangerous. I imagine if I got hit upside the head with a beer can, I'd probably want to go up in the stands and offer the beer right back in their mouth." Police arrested ten at one game vs. Penn State and ejected another 41 fans.

Fry also complained that football crowds have become too noisy. He's suggested the use of sound meters to determine if the home crowd is disrupting the opponent. In one Iowa game, *Sports Illustrated* took sound readings and determined that the Hawkeye crowd reached 102 decibels, the equivalent of a circular saw.

That's not nearly as bad as the noise in an Iowa-Iowa State game in 1905. Iowa's engineering students rigged a steam engine that emitted a piercing whistle. With cotton in their ears, the engineers blared their whistle every time Iowa State had the ball. None of the Cyclones could hear their quarterback's signals, and Iowa State failed to score the entire game. After the Iowa win, officials confiscated the whistle, and it was never used again.

—**From the Author's book**, *Sports Fans Who Made Headlines*

The *Voice of the Hawkeyes* had a Student of the Week, nominated by the University. We would publish a page about him or her, list their accomplishments, and do a nice profile. The award was sponsored by the Toyota of Iowa group. We had a gymnast, tennis player, a swimmer—and there was never a complaint. And then we had football player, Nick Bell, who overcame some learning disabilities, had a three-point GPA and was a star on the football team. The NCAA suddenly took interest and told us we had to stop that because we were too close to the advertisers that were promoting it. They didn't care about the minor sports, but once you named a football player and recognized him for his accomplishments they took notice. The page that showed the athlete and listed his accomplishments also showed the names of the sponsors, and

Who was the only Major League Baseball player to grace the cover of the college football edition of *Sports Illustrated*? Bo Jackson? No. Kirk Gibson? No. Rick Leach of Michigan? Yes.

the NCAA said you couldn't do that...that was a violation...we continued the feature without a sponsor.

We would contact former Hawkeye athletes, find out what they are doing now, and interview them. You can find out that Eddie Vincent was mayor of Long Beach and find out what others were doing. Then somebody said, "What are we going to do when we run out of these heroes?" Don Norton said, "We're making them right now. We've got Chuck Long." He started naming off a few. We realized that ten years later, we'd have had another group...and we did.

Voice of the Hawkeyes was a good investment and a fun investment. It was made with love. Jim Murray one time remarked, "Newspapers, like all great institutions, are but lengthened shadows of the men who built them and loved them." That's the way we all felt. We wanted the paper to be a certain way and it was. It reflected our feelings about Iowa sports.

—JEFF STOUTNER, former co-owner, *Voice of the Hawkeyes*

When Iowa went to the 1982 Rose Bowl, Alex Crutchfield, who was one of the charter members when they started the Fiesta Bowl, told me, "No problem. I can get you tickets." When Iowa-Washington was announced, everybody thought, "Who the hell wants to go to that game?" It turned out to be one of the biggest demands in a long time. In his mind, he thought he could get me a couple of tickets. He asked me how many I wanted and I said, "Twelve." He's got a lot of contacts so he's calling everybody and finds the demand is incredible. He ends up getting me twelve—literally on the fifty—sitting behind the governor of Iowa. He still laughs about that today.

One night I was tending bar and talking with a customer about Iowa athletics. There was this man sitting at the bar in a little red windbreaker, not talking to anybody. He looked at me and said, "What do you know about Iowa?" I said, "I'm from Iowa. I'm a big Hawkeye fan. Are you a Hawkeye fan?" He goes, "Oh yeah, I'm kind of a Hawkeye fan, I guess." It turned out to be Wayne Carpenter, a huge benefactor and supporter of the Iowa program, and after Roy Carver, probably the biggest benefactor. He was a very wealthy, but very humble man...a great guy, and we became good friends.

I met a great guy one time, Tim McAllister, a big Illini fan, who used to call me from Hawaii, "Let's bet on Iowa-Illinois." It didn't matter what sport—basketball, football, whatever. He was extremely wealthy and would call from Hawaii, probably a $40 phone call, and want to bet $5. One time, I said, "I'm tired of making these $5 bets." He said, "Okay. Let's bet a million dollars." I said, "Well, Tim, you know Iowa's gonna win, but what if they lose? I don't have a million." He goes, "Don't pay. Don't worry about it." Iowa won the game. The next time McAllister called, I told him: "We have an old saying in Iowa…'Fast pay makes fast friends.'"

—CHUCK McGREGOR, El Chorro Lodge, Paradise Valley, AZ

I remember going to basketball games in the old Field House when they had wooden benches. We really dressed up in high heels and nowadays you don't see women going to games dressed up. And the students are still students—they can be pretty raunchy sometimes. They just are having fun. It was a lot more fun going to games in the old Field House than it is now in Carver-Hawkeye arena. You were much closer. Everyone enjoyed basketball—that was the big thing at that time. Ralph Miller was coaching and they had an excellent team. The place was always packed. I remember children would crawl up on the top and climb down through the ceiling and sneak in free. Football was on the downhill path—they were rebuilding.

—HELEN HOHLE, 82, Iowa City

We took sweet corn out to the coaches at the university every year when they were in the Field House. We'd fill the back of our truck to the top, we would be outside the old Field House at a certain time. Everybody would bring their paper bags and plastic bags and grab all the sweet corn they'd want. Gable still to this day will ask me, "Do you still have that sweet corn?"

One year I took it out there, and Kathy Gable, Dan's wife, showed up and said, "Dan couldn't come—he's exercising." The following year this happened again, and I went to his house. I walked up and Kathy said, "He's down exercising, and we don't disturb him." I said, "That's fine. Here's your corn." That same year, Lute Olson was out of town, and I took a bunch of sweet corn in a bag and laid it on his front porch. I knew he was going to be gone for over a week. When he got back two weeks later, you can imagine what the corn looked like. The next time he saw me, he said, "Stueland, you didn't happen to drop some sweet corn out here, did you?" I said, "I put some in the

216

mail box." He said, "No, you didn't. You put it at my front door, didn't you?" I said, "Why would you think that, coach?" He said, "It was rotten."

—PAUL STUELAND, 57, Tipton, Iowa

Being in the band really made you feel a part of the school, of the atmosphere. Everywhere we would go, everyone wanted us to play The Iowa Fight Song. On Friday nights before a home football game, we had a "beer band" go all around to all the bars. It was exciting. We got free beer everywhere we went. When I was in high school, I hadn't really considered being in the Iowa band. My whole family is very musical. People would say to me, "You're going to be in the Iowa Marching Band, aren't you?" I said, "Well, I hadn't really thought about it." They told me to go try out so I did. It was great. It does take a lot of time. I had never even been to an Iowa football game before I went to school there. Before that very first time on the field, there was such an adrenaline rush. To get on the field, we had to do a high step. It's a workout. Every August, before school started, we had what's called "Hell Week." It was just an intense week of drills held at the practice field.

—MELANIE LUSK, West Lafayette, Indiana

In Manson, high school football games were really a big deal. We had a population of about 2,000 and for a big game, we'd have 3-4,000 people attend. Then, there'd be one college game on TV on a Saturday, and that was it. Occasionally, Iowa would be on. Iowa was playing at Oregon State in 1962. We didn't have color TV so a neighbor kid and I rode downtown to his uncle's store, Zehr & Goeders. They sold all sorts of things, including RCA televisions. They had a couple of color TVs in there. Dean Zehr, the kid's uncle, was one of the owners, and he gave us permission to come down and watch the game on color TV. That was a big deal! From watching games on black-and-white TV, to watching it on a color TV was very exciting, but nothing compared to that first time walking into the stadium and seeing the green grass and the color of the uniforms and the atmosphere you felt.

—**MIKE McGREGOR**, on growing up in Northwest Iowa

Gary Kurdelmeier came in to my section one day and told me that Roy Carver wanted to speak with me. There was a little side office where he was sitting. I went in and sat down, and I said, "You wanted to speak to me?" Carver said, "Yes, I want you to walk over to the hospital and pick up Isabelle and bring her back." Isabelle was his girlfriend. I looked at him and said, "I don't run errands for you." And, I got up and walked out. It was embarrassing to me because Kurdelmeier hadn't told me what Carver wanted because I would have had Gary go tell him to "jump in the lake."

—**HELEN HOHLE**, Retired, Iowa Wrestling Department

Bobby Knight had his likes and dislikes. Number 1: he doesn't really like the media. He knows he needs them, but he doesn't like them. Number 2: he really is kind of a bully. Number 3: Bob Knight always wanted to be the top dog. He always to come out on top in an argument. Number 4: In my case, I did the "Lute Olson Show." He hated Lute Olson because Lute Olson beat him two out of three times in Bloomington, five out of eight times overall. He couldn't stand that. He didn't like me from the beginning. I always had an adversarial relationship with him. When Lute was still there, and I'd try to interview Knight, it was always a mess. He'd start out doing an interview and then all of a sudden, he'd start swearing and cussing. I've got some tapes that would burn your ear off.

—**JIM ZABEL**, WHO Radio 1040

The old Field House is still my favorite basketball arena ever. I went to my first game there, back in Lute's early years, and I remember going in there the first time, and the thing that caught my eye was the giant flying hawk on the wall. It was so cool. We sat in the bleachers and the place just rocked. I remember once when Iowa played Marquette in the Field House, and Marquette had Doc Rivers on their team. That place was really exciting that night. I remember seeing Bob Knight and Indiana come to the Field House and nothing brought out the vocal chords of the fans more than when Bob Knight did his walk onto the floor. When Michigan State came with Magic

Johnson, seeing Ronnie Lester and Magic match up was just something I'll never forget—the two best guards I've ever seen play in the college game. I like Carver-Hawkeye arena, but I loved the Field House. There's nothing like it. It was just a special place.

I like the way Carver is set up because there's no obstructed view. It does get loud there, and it's a fun place, a nice venue. I enjoy going to games there because it's put together well. It's built right. It's a first-class place. I've seen some great games there. The emotion that first game after Chris Street passed away was just something I'll never forget. It will be there a long time—it's built for the long haul.

There's nothing like Kinnick in college football. I've had the opportunity to go to a lot of different places, primarily Big Ten stadiums. There are some good places, but, to me, there's nothing like Kinnick on a football Saturday in the fall with a temperature of about fifty degrees, a little breeze and some sun, and the smell of brats, with cold beer around you—there's just nothing like it. There's so much excitement and pageantry and the tradition of Iowa football. Even though I'm part of the media, at least once a year, I try to go and just sit in the stands as a fan because it's so much fun to be around other Iowa fans and spend time with them and get the feel for the game. My job affords me a lot of great opportunities to be in the inner circle of Kinnick a little bit. I get down on the sidelines from time to time, and there's nothing like it—hearing the players talk, the coaches yell, the hits.

I remember talking to some old-timers who talk about taking the train to Kinnick Stadium with memories of their parents bringing them to a game on the train. Throwback is in these days and it's fun to see the retro jerseys. The players are just as excited about it as the fans are. Tradition is a good thing. Remembering tradition and trying to include some of those traditions is a good thing. I like that sort of stuff. I'm one of those people who probably isn't as huge a fan of the Tiger Hawk as I am of the old Herky or the flying hawk. That's just me, and I'm sure probably seventy-five percent of other Iowa fans are more identifying with the Tiger Hawk. A lot of them have the tattoo of the Tiger Hawk.

—TOM KAKERT, Rivals.com Reporter

I remember one wrestler we had, Ray Brinzer. He had a real different style about him. He had this floppy, curly hair and wore glasses. He was a studious kind of guy. There was a joke about him, "Ray Brinzer, the best chess player on the wrestling team, the best wrestler on the chess team." We printed up a bunch of T-shirts, "Ray Brinzer Fan Club." He wrestled at Oklahoma State for a year and then transferred here. This was about '94.

—CHUCK JOHNSON, 32, Ankeny, Iowa

Dave Triplett, director of planned giving at The U of I Foundation, was once a grad assistant along with Dan McCarney. When you travel with a sports team, everything is precision. When they say one o'clock, you'd better be there at ten minutes to one. When the bus leaves at five, you'd better be prepared for the bus to leave at quarter to five. Nobody's ever late.

One time we were on the plane going to play at Ohio State. The team always boards out on the tarmac and doesn't go through the terminals. The bus drives right out on the tarmac to the plane. We're sitting on the plane, and we're waiting...and waiting...and waiting. Nobody can figure out why we're waiting so long. Up comes the security car out on the tarmac and out gets Dave Triplett. Everybody on the plane saw him. Hayden sits in the front seat of the plane so, of course, Dave had to walk by Hayden to get to the back of the plane. Everybody just gave him all kinds of hell for being late. Triplett is a great guy, but we love reminding him of that day.

Today, however, we do have to go through security. They set up a temporary security system out in the hangar that we walk through, just like you would do going through the airport terminal. It used to be we could get off the bus and just walk up the stairs to the plane, but now we all have to go through the security procedures.

—MARK JENNINGS, U of I Foundation

Growing up in Lisbon, Iowa, I used to hitchhike to the games and look for an endzone ticket, which was about two bucks. But then I learned that if you were a Boy Scout, in uniform, you got to help with the ushering and got in free so you could see the games. After all the people got in, and the game got started, they would let us go down on the sidelines and stand to watch the game. We'd probably be about twenty feet off the sideline. It was Bob Ferguson from Ohio State who ran a play toward where we were standing. He got run out of bounds, and we all got plowed under on the sidelines. It was all I could do to keep from tripping him as he ran by. I used to do garbage clean up after the games. That was great. It was a treasure trove. You found all the programs so we never had to buy one. We'd find booze bottles, food, magazines, and paperback books.

One funny thing that came out of the ushering at the football games, two or three years later when I was in high school, at Lisbon, we had a guy who had been a trainer. He was involved with the Iowa football team in those days and later became a coach. He knew I was a big Iowa Hawkeyes football fan, and one day he gave me a jock strap, which he claimed was Mac Lewis' jock strap. Lewis was a gigantic Iowa lineman who looked like Andre the Giant. The jock strap was huge. It was big enough to fit over the head of a cow. The trainer said that he was sweeping out the locker room once, and he found it. He threw it in the washer and claimed that it was Mac Lewis'. I remember keeping that thing for a couple of years. I even kept it hanging from my bulletin board when I went away to college. It was huge—I used to tell everybody it was mine.

—MIKE CONKLIN, *Chicago Tribune*, Lisbon, Iowa native

When I was 13, I started asking my parents to buy me season tickets for my birthday every year so I've been a season-ticket holder at Iowa since 1961. I think, in that time, I've maybe missed two home games. During the Bob Commings years at Iowa, we had a jet and we would fly all the coaches' wives to every out-of-town game. So during that period of about four years, I went to every game – home and away – which got kind of old because we were getting the crap beat out of us.

My last year of college at Iowa, Larry Lawrence, the quarterback from Cedar Rapids, was one of my roommates. I think he was the best quarterback that's ever been at Iowa. Nobody could convert third downs like Larry. He was a coach's son. He knew football. He knew how to read defenses. He was just a great student of the game, and he could really move the football. Nagel's teams led the Big Ten in offense every year Nagel was there, and Larry was a big part of that. He had a heart transplant last year.

—RANDY WINEGARD, 56, Burlington, Iowa

The Cyclones give it the old college try. They get drunk, pass out, and say they'll finish it tomorrow.

BURY BOBBY KNIGHT 10 FEET UNDER...DEEP DOWN, HE'S A GOOD GUY.

Chapter 9

Iowa State— The Last Refuge of Scoundrels

Ames: That Toddlin' Town

WIT HAPPENS

Spurrier DeLugé

Spurrier DeLugé, 44, is the vital cog in that well-oiled Holmes-Murphy machine in Des Moines.

My best friend and a couple of other guys and I were coming back from an Iowa football game in Iowa City. This was the year Iowa State's Troy Davis was a senior, and he was getting all the hype for the Heisman. Hayden had said, "Yes, Troy Davis is a good back but there are two or three backs in the Big Ten that are every bit as good." Iowa State was trying to hype Davis and, basically, Hayden meant that we were not going to prepare for him any differently than we prepare for any of the other top two or three backs. I think Ki-Jana Carter was a senior that year. The Iowa State fans were screaming that it was a conspiracy and that Fry was trying to keep Davis from getting the Heisman.

"Sound Off" is a program on WHO which Jim Zabel used to chair. It was on every Saturday after games, a call-in show, when people, from across the state, call in and comment on the games that day.

After the game, I called in to "Sound Off" that night on the way home and identified myself as "Pete." Iowa State was playing a game that night. In the call, I mentioned that if Troy Davis was at Iowa, he'd be third-team behind Sedrick Shaw and Tavian Banks, unless, of course, Tim Dwight decided to play tailback, then he'd be fourth-team. The boards just lit up. I listened to "Sound Off" the last game of the season that year, and the Iowa State fans were still calling in all p _ _ _ _ _ off.

About fifteen-twenty minutes later, my best friend also called in, from the same car. He acts like he's an Iowa State fan, "I'm really upset. I want to refute what Pete said. I just really don't agree with what he said about Troy Davis." They put him on the air immediately, "We've got a hot fan." My best friend said, "I really think that Troy

Davis could beat out Tim Dwight for third-team." They just flipped out. It boiled again up to the top, and the Iowa State fans were so livid. Actually it was funny but it was the honest truth—he wasn't better than either one of those guys, and their pro careers have proven it. We were sitting there just throwing the bait into the water, and they just kept coming up to the bait. At the same time, it was so funny because they thought they had the second coming of **O. J. Simpson**. He got all his yards on third and twenty when they were down by forty points, and they couldn't pass it, so they just ran Troy Davis up the middle.

When we would call in, we would always call him "Tony" Davis. The announcer would say, "Whoa, whoa, whoa, whoa, you mean Troy Davis?" We'd say, "Tony, Troy, whoever." We acted like we didn't even know who he was, which really made them mad, too.

There's another kid I know who used to always say things about Iowa State, too. One time he called in and said that running indoors in that dome really helps the offensive stats for Iowa State. The Iowa State fans would call in and say, "What do you mean? That's UNI that has the dome." He'd say, "Same deal ISU, UNI—same deal." They would just get furious.

> **Ernie Banks and O. J. Simpson are cousins. Their grand-**
> **fathers were twin brothers.**

IOWA IOWA IOWA IOWA IOWA IOWA IOWA IOWA IOWA IOWA IOWA IOWA IOWA

DROVE BY THE IOWA STATE MUSEUM OF PROGRESS YESTERDAY. IT IS STILL NOT OPEN.

WHEN HE FIRST CAME TO AMES, HE DIDN'T KNOW "THE BIG 12" WAS THE NUMBER OF SCHOLARSHIP PLAYERS HE INHERITED.

Jim Walden

Long before he became the head football coach at Iowa State in the late '80s, Jim Walden was despised on the West Coast. His Washington State team would blow into Tempe, Corvallis or Palo Alto as big underdogs. Walden would be singing the blues worse than Lou Holtz and then sneak back to the Paloose with a victory.

Walden was born and raised in Aberdeen, Mississippi, matriculated on a football scholarship to the University of Wyoming. Currently, he is a color analyst on the Washington State games and is half of the "Two Guys Named Jim" show on WHO-Des Moines on Sunday nights.

Jim Walden is a fun, interesting and neat guy.

I knew immediately how big the Iowa-Iowa State game was because of the experience of Washington-Washington State games. A rivalry is a rivalry. I truly hate the Iowa-Iowa State game because of when it's played. I'm a traditionalist "rivalry-last-game" person. I grew up with the Mississippi State-Ole Miss, Alabama-Auburn mentality. All I ever knew was that rival games are played last. You put everything into those last games. When everything else has fallen, everything else has failed, you've got one last hope—the one thing that will keep the fires burning over the winter—is if you can just upset your arch rival.

When I got to Washington, the Apple Cup was last: Washington-Washington State. I get here, and we're playing Iowa the second or third game of the season! I don't know how to react. I never could get as jacked up about it. I couldn't get my players as jacked up as I wanted them to be because as soon as that game was over, you had another game. To get them that high, to put that many eggs in that basket, you could lose the next three games if you weren't careful. To do all that, and then lose it, then you really have to crawl back.

There's nothing better than having the upper hand in that series. Other than our very first game with them, the games were all competitive. They were so much better than we were. Hayden was probably in the heyday of his finest hour—the mid-to-late eighties were some of Hayden's finest, finest teams. I was unfortunate to have to get in on that. He was far greater in numbers and in talent than we were. I was more proud of the efforts I got in our games from our athletes than a lot of people realize because I did not think we had anywhere near the type of athlete. On top of that, I was going against one of the really top creative coaches in the country. When I was at Washington State, we at least had the right to have the same number of players. We were always behind the eight-ball at Iowa State and never did overcome it. That's not an excuse—it's just a fact. I'd have had a hard time beating Hayden if I'd had 90 guys, let alone trying to beat him with 45. I was very proud of our effort, but there was not very much chance that I was going to beat him. He was an outstanding coach. He had unbelievably good assistants who had been with him for a while. He had a great system. And, he had forty more guys than I did.

When I was there, the whole eight years, I don't think we ever took one guy in recruiting that Hayden wanted. There were only half a dozen really great Iowa players. The guy I got the closest to was the quarterback up there at St. Ansgar, Matt Sherman. We thought we had a shot at Sherman, but he went there instead. Seems like every great player that we would have wanted was in Clinton, Dubuque, Cedar Rapids, Davenport and that made it even harder because that's all Hawkeye territory.

In the first place, Ferentz and McCarney coached together and there's a little mutual admiration thing here, so I don't think it's as mean-spirited as it has been. I used to try to make everybody think we hated one another. Then after it was over, the coaches would go somewhere and play golf together and say, "Okay, what are we going to do next year?" Don't get me wrong. It's just as meaningful. I think these Iowa Staters would die if they could win that game. They're at the point right now where it's been give and take so it's a nice rivalry. This year's 17-10 Iowa victory could have gone Iowa State's way.

When you quit coaching, and you don't want to coach anymore, people aren't used to that. Most coaches get fired and they quickly go find another job and "get out of Dodge." Or, they get into another profession, and they do it elsewhere. I was 57 years old. My wife and I had never had the big bucks, but we'd made some nice investments and done some good things. We were financially good enough that I knew I didn't have to work, and I didn't want to, and she didn't want me to. We liked our setting here in Ames. We have a beautiful home we're proud of with about six acres right here in town. One thing I've learned is—if you want total privacy, live in a town where you've coached. You're no longer the guy. When they see you, they go, "Oh, there's coach." Or they look down at their shoes and let you walk by. You don't have to worry about anything. After about three years, they've forgotten it all, and you become a nice citizen. "Hi coach. How you doing? Good to see you, man." That's what I told John Cooper, "Stay in Columbus. You'll become the most popular guy in the city after about three years." He later said, "You're right." Now, they even like him.

We love Ames. Ames is a nice community. Iowa is an easy place to live, for several reasons. One, people are nice. Secondly, it's centrally located to everything. My mom lives in north **Mississippi** so it's a one-day drive to get down to where she lives. I can run down there and spend a long four or five-day weekend and get back. We had a lot of good friends here, and they didn't base their friendship on my title, so we just got caught up into this easy living, and that's why we stayed.

I've learned since then that you can't go anywhere—anywhere—and tell any person you're from Iowa, and they will immediately say, "Oh, I have an aunt in Dubuque, or some such town." I have never in

The speed limit on the University of Mississippi campus is 18 MPH in honor of Archie Manning's uniform number.

my life been around a place where so many people have had somebody come through here. It is overwhelming. It's amazing. It's a national phenomenon.

I think part of that is that these farmers get out of here—they're good spenders. Iowans have a great reputation in this country for spending their money. That's amazing to me. You're not aware of that much wealth in Iowa, yet Iowans have a great reputation for being good spenders. You could go down to Miami now and say, "We're from Iowa." They'd say, "Oh, we love those Iowans. They're dang good spenders." I hear that all the time.

That Bartyles & James bit was great. Johnny Orr was the tall, skinny one. Of course, I was supposed to be the short, fat one with glasses. They dressed us up very similar to those two guys in the ad. People around here hold onto those posters like they're going to be worth money. We actually wore the straw hats and tried to dress as close to those two guys as we could. It was a promotion for season tickets. We did four different promos for back-to-school for students; and for the season tickets. They were marvelous. People absolutely could not get enough of them. They tried to get all four of them, like collectors' items. There are people, to this day, that tell us, "I've still got those posters. I'm going to keep them." What Max Urick, the athletic director, wanted during that time when we were coming off the sanctions, was to put the fun back into Iowa State. He felt we had to get our dignity back, our pride, get to feeling better about ourselves. He thought **Johnny Orr** and I could do that through those commercials.

When they first presented it to me, I thought, "I love Johnny Orr. If he'll do it, I'll do it." What the heck. I've got that kind of personality. It's not going to bother me. They did it with dignity. We had people calling us and saying, "How did you come up with that idea? That's great stuff." It all turned out to be quite satisfying in a sense of doing it. Some coaches wouldn't do it, but then some coaches didn't

> **Johnny Orr is the winningest basketball coach in the history of two schools: Michigan and Iowa State University. Bear Bryant, Dick Tomey and George Welsh have accomplished the same feat in college football.**

understand what we were trying to do. After it was all said and done, I'm glad I did it. I was really proud to have been a part of it. It was a very emotional, uplifting thing for our fans. It unified our fans. That's what Max wanted. Our fans were so down after the Jim Criner deal. Iowa Staters are quite proud. They just don't deal with that cheating stuff very well.

The most fun thing about being a coach was hanging out with other coaches. It was the stories you heard and the things you experienced and the things you shared. It's a very close-knit fraternity. There aren't many of us. Most of us all have the same mentality. You get fired. Or you haven't been fired, but you're going to get fired. Enjoy it as you go. You work long, hard hours. The competition is always there. In the end, it's just the fun stories you share with each other about the crazy things that have happened in ball games. It never gets old…but we do.

IOWA IOWA IOWA IOWA IOWA IOWA IOWA IOWA IOWA IOWA IOWA IOWA IOWA

Larry Eustachy wasn't smart enough to know he's dumb…

HEAR ME NOW,
LISTEN TO ME LATER

My favorite interviews would be Chuck Long, Larry Station, and Brett Bielema when he was playing—you never knew what he was going to say. He was the one who called Walden a "Big Wussy" one time before they played Iowa State—that got a lot of play. That's when Hayden said, "I'm in charge of the propaganda here, son." Guys like that were fun to do. You find through the years that the defensive guys were more the spokesmen.

—THOM CORNELIS, KWQC-TV, Davenport

Growing up, I didn't pay any attention to Iowa State. They were more of an annoyance. I hate to say that because I've got friends who are really good people who are their fans. They were kind of like the junior team. I never took them seriously. Even recently, when they were on their five-year streak against us, I couldn't deny they had some good teams, but it was kind of like "they just don't get it." You go to a game in Ames, and it just isn't IT…. "You guys don't get it, and you probably never will." Manson was only about seventy-five miles from Ames, so there were certainly more kids from our high school that went to school at Iowa State than went to Iowa. Even a lot of families that had kids who went to school at Ames were still Iowa fans. Back in those days when I was a kid, they didn't play each other.

—MIKE McGREGOR, native of Manson, Iowa

They're both great schools. A lot of great people are involved with both programs. I always thought it was a bigger game for Iowa State than it was for Iowa. The Hawkeyes get more coverage and probably have a bigger following. When you're playing, obviously it's the game you want to win. I don't mind seeing Iowa State do well as long as it's not against the Hawkeyes.

The games between Iowa and Iowa State are more of a fans' rivalry than it is a players' rivalry. The fans really circle that date on their calendars. A lot of people who are co-workers, especially in the Des Moines area, where it seems like half the work force is Iowa State and the other half is Iowa, really get up for it. It's really a special, special game for the fans. As far as the players are concerned, we wanted to win those games more for the fans than for ourselves. It never was that big of a game for me personally, but, believe me, I knew that it was for the people in the seats.

—**JESS SETTLES**, Former Hawkeye Basketball Star

When I played against Iowa State, we really hated them. We really wanted to take it out of them, really wanted to win that game. One thing hit me this past year when Dexter Green, the great running back at Iowa State during the seventies, died. He and I were offset running backs against each other during those years, and Dexter was much better than I. He was All-American at Iowa State and was a great athlete. I really felt bad for the Iowa State fans. I've always wanted Iowa State to do well when they weren't playing against Iowa. When Dexter died, I sent an e-mail to an Iowa State website, if you can believe this, and said, "From an Iowa Hawkeye..." I just tried to tell them how I felt for the Cyclone fans. It was amazing because I got e-mails back from people that said, "Hey, classy move for a Hawkeye fan." There is a deep respect for schools in that rivalry but I do think the respect gets strong when you're older, when you're not in the heat of battle.

Beating Iowa State in 1977 rekindled the rivalry. There was a span of thirty-two years, or something like that, where Iowa and Iowa State didn't play each other. So, going into my sophomore year, we were starting this new rivalry again with Iowa State. Iowa State had some pretty good teams. They were still going to some bowls back then. We, of course, we were the team they just hated hearing about. We beat them 12-10 in Iowa City before a packed house. Chris Schenkel was one of the announcers, and it was just a fun, fun game.

—**JON LAZAR**, Iowa Back, 1975 -78

What's the toughest thing about being a Minnesota fan? Explaining to your father why you're ga,

Chapter 10

The Write Stuff

How 'Bout Them

Hawkeye Fans!

$14.95

"One thing is for sure. There were 105,000 fans cheering at the University of Michigan, but they don't make half as much noise as the 60,000 fans in Kinnick Stadium. I've said it before. The Iowa fans are the greatest!"
— HAYDEN FRY, head FB coach, At the Cedar Rapids Airport after the Hawks beat Michigan, 9-7. Oct. 18, 1981.

by Mike Kielkopf

and

The Hawkeye Fans Themselves

A Hawkeye Reader For Hawkeye Readers

IS THIS HEAVEN?
NO, IT'S IOWA CITY
ON A FOOTBALL WEEKEND.

Bob Wood

In 1988, Bob Wood traveled to every Big Ten campus to experience a football weekend. At each stop, he made lengthy entries into a journal. The following are his thoughts on his visit to The University of Iowa.

I finally found it—the very friendliest place on the face of the earth! Iowa City, Iowa. A town in the state that Professor Harold Hill conned into a seventy-six trombone boys' band, without knowing even a single note! A town in a state that has the best version of a pro football team—none. And where its own football team, the Iowa Hawkeyes, wears on their helmets a tribute to the American farmer. A friendly place, a place filled with good people, people who when they ask you, "How's it going" honestly hope you'll answer "Great!" That's Iowa City, and The University of Iowa, at the end of Iowa Avenue, along the rolling banks of the Iowa River. Sounds kind of cornball, doesn't it? Every place should be so cornball.

I should've guessed—Iowa City wasn't just any normal Midwest town on my drive in. About fifteen miles outside the city limits, cruising along on Interstate 80, I passed a silver corn silo with a big gold square painted on it. GO, HAWKS in bold black letters screamed from the square to passing cars. All right, I figured, so folks are loyal. Or maybe I should've noticed that things were just a little off when I reached town and pulled up to a stop sign, in front of a crosswalk. The lady standing there waiting to cross, before she crossed, nodded, waved, and thanked me for stopping. Okay, so they're polite too. Or maybe I should've gotten the hint that Iowa City was not your run-of-the-mill college town at the corner gas station. The guy at the inside register, a guy who spent forty hours each week answering stupid questions, wasn't bothered when I asked mine. He said, "Hello," gave me my directions, took my traveler's check…and didn't even ask for ID. A trusting place too? The final straw, the moment I realized that this Iowa City hospitality was just regular everyday Iowa City stuff, came during my four-minute stay inside a Hawks Spirit Shop. Four minutes at a place that survived on the sale of Hawkeye T-shirts. Four minutes, just enough time to turn a one-dollar bill into phone change. And I didn't even browse. But as I left to find a pay phone, the girl behind at the register called to me, "Thanks for stopping."

I gave up, turned around, and answered, "You're welcome."

Iowa rubs off on you. It rubs off on the people who visit the college for four years. And although it's mostly made up of Iowans, the university brings in a lot of students from a lot of other places. When a college of thirty thousand students is located in a town of forty-five thousand people, there must be some imports. Chicago high-school students learn manners and how to be Hawkeyes at the same time. New Yorkers ought to get in-state tuition rates and be required to attend—just to learn how to smile. Regardless of where they come from, people who leave Iowa City—maybe four years later, maybe five, or as in my case just a couple of days—if nothing else, leave with a little better handle on the words "please" and "thank you."

I ran into my first Hawkeye transplant, just a kid, a junior majoring in education, working in a Hallmark card shop. No other students were anywhere around. Midterm week at The University of Iowa, kids study. Townsfolk weren't cramming the place either.

The Hallmark junior was from Chicago. "Most of my friends went to Champaign," she said. "They give me a hard time for going to school here. Whenever I'm home, they ask if I'm still gonna be a farmer."

"But I don't care. It's nice, really nice here. You'll see."

People aren't all that's neighborly in Iowa City. So are the buildings and the homes, even the campus. Tucked into a pleasant little valley off I-80, Iowa City breaks a bit with all the corn that frames it. Quaint neighborhoods fill in the cracks all about town. Big Victorian homes sit back amid oaks and maples and big grassy front yards. Pretty homes. Tidy homes. Nice places—places that don't pop to mind when you think of student housing. And they bump into the campus all over the place. Up above the river, on the west side, the Iowa band and neighborhood soccer teams share the same practice field. Just a grass field at the end of a bunch of quiet, uncurbed streets. Five o'clock drilling of The Iowa Fight Song joins families sitting around the supper table. It brings a touch of quaintness to the supper table and to band practice. Big old Greek houses, the frat and sorority kind, pop up in the middle of otherwise normal-looking Iowan houses. And always there seems to be an art center or some other school building someplace you wouldn't expect it. But someplace that it seems to fit.

The university campus is nice too. And friendly. A rolling, kind of sleepy campus, it's not what you'd call gorgeous. Rather, it looks and feels lived in. A place where you don't need a car to be cool, where a good bicycle will do. And a place where there really isn't much to worry about, except maybe getting to class on time. Catching it in the middle of October didn't hurt either. Reds and yellows were peaking. Brick walkways winding below the west-side dorms and footbridges over the river provided nice, quiet picture-postcard strolls. A breath of fresh air, the Iowa campus looks like a good place to kick back and concentrate on college life, before hitting the real world.

Up above the river, across Clinton Street from downtown, the Pentacrest best catches that college flavor. Made up of five big old stately buildings, the Pentacrest serves as the heart of the university. At its center sits the original state capitol, built in 1842. Topped by a golden dome, with white columns, the old capitol stares down Iowa Avenue. And while it used to greet legislators, now that it's refurbished, just tour groups drop by. The other four buildings house classrooms and, like the legs of a table to the golden-domed centerpiece, anchor the old capitol. Trees and shrubs and old-fashioned lampposts dot the grass and walks in front. Together the five serve as the student hub. It's where from noon to one, each day that the sun's out, Iowa City political statements are made. It's where, if you want to sell anything for any cause, you get your best response. The Pentacrest, a place where nobody minds if you walk on the grass, is to the campus what sunglasses are to Hayden Fry.

Finally there's the megalopolis—downtown Iowa City. All four or five square blocks of it. Across Clinton Street from the Pentacrest, downtown exists for the university. But it's not just a college town. In fact, it looks like something you might find somewhere off any Iowa highway—with just a touch of college thrown in. Three-storied red-brick buildings dominate the downtown area. The same buildings, maybe with different signs out front, that have dominated downtown Iowa City for decades. Pizza Hut and Burger King blend in quietly with the homemade-ice-cream parlors. Bars, a lot of 'em just holes-in-the-wall, get a good mix of townsfolk and students. A couple of old movie theaters still feature the old marquees. And a beautiful little redbrick plaza marks the city center.

Under the shadow of the Holiday Inn, hidden from the Pentacrest by the Clinton Street shops, the pedestrians-only plaza takes the place of streets. Young trees, growing up out of tidy squares of dirt and wood chips, dot it. Wooden park benches provide places to sit and rest. A fountain tosses water in the air, and then lets it trickle down its side. Throughout the day, the red brick teems with activity. Kids walking to class, or stopping and sitting it out, depending on the weather. At night, particularly on the weekends, the place is a hub of excitement. Lines from the Fieldhouse and Vito's and other college bars intertwine. Hot-dog and brat carts and temporary taco stands kill the late-night munchies, and add a pleasant aroma to the place. A tiny Midwest town, zapped with some college life, easing out along a pleasant redbrick plaza. It's a nice place, just a really nice place.

One last feature lights up Iowa City. In fact, all of Iowa, really. And that's the Hawkeyes. Hawkeye football in the fall, but also Hawkeye wrestling and Hawkeye basketball in the winter, and probably every other Hawk sport every other sport season as well. And the townsfolk don't hide their affection. The Tiger Hawk, that gold hawk head on the football helmet, blankets Iowa City. It's everywhere! Bookstores and bar windows off the plaza almost all have at least one painted across the glass somewhere. Restaurants usually feature something, on the wall, or on the menu, that's Hawkeye-ish. Outside of town, things like the GO, HAWKS silo constantly pop up. A grain and feed storage facility, at another highway exit, gets an annual gold-and-black paint job. Cars even get into the act. Almost every other Iowa City bumper sticker features Iowa City's favorite saying, "It's Great to Be a Hawkeye."

In return for the support, Iowa grads don't just disappear. They keep coming back and contributing to the school and to the community. For instance, City High School ran into a roadblock two years ago. Its Little Hawks football team, nicknamed for Iowa University's team, wanted the Tiger Hawk decal for its helmets, but suffered from the typical public-school problem—no money. Pro football player Joel Hilgenberg, an ex-City High/University of Iowa star, stepped in and forked out for the decals. Now the Little Hawk helmets of City High match the "Big Hawk" helmets of The University of Iowa.

Farmers around Iowa City, particularly the last couple of years, have been hurting big time. Ex-athletes haven't forgotten them, either. Guys who were Hawkeye hoop stars, guys like Downtown Freddie Brown and Bobby Hansen, have come to the rescue. The last two summers they've put on a fundraiser basketball game featuring old Hawks vs other old Hawks. Proceeds went to something called the Farm Scholarship Fund. Because of it, three farm kids a year, kids who couldn't normally afford to go to college, now can. Hayden Fry's football team backs the farming community too. A couple of years ago the Tiger Hawk got a partner on the U. of I football helmet. A simple gold circle, right between the gold stripe and gold hawk. Inside the circle are the block letters ANF (American Needs Farmers), a tribute to Iowan farmers. All of this, the ANF, the Farm Scholarship Fund, even the Little Hawk football helmets creates almost a family bond between the university and the community.

There are a lot of reasons why Iowa University and Iowans get along so well. The I-Club, though, might be the main link. The idea of an I-Club is nothing new; all Big Ten schools have something similar. The Spartans have their S-Club, Ohio State their O-Club, and Wisconsin a big red W-Club. The clubs recruit alums, and their big bucks, in exchange for bumper stickers and alumni pins, invitations to golf outings, and fifty-yard-line seats. Proceeds go to help the school's sports programs. Well, in addition to all that, Iowa's captures the sincerity of a high-school booster program.

FOR HAWKEYE FANS ONLY

First off, you don't have to be an alum to be an I-Club member, just give twenty-five dollars and love the Hawks. Consequently, most of the club support comes from "just plain people" around the state. Another reason the setup is so successful is the number of clubs. Over fifty stretch across the country—Los Angeles, Chicago, Phoenix, Cincinnati, Denver—I-Clubs pop up everywhere. But the most important ingredient of the organization's success is the people involved. Mark Jennings organizes it. All fourteen Iowa head coaches pitch in, and they all work their tail off. Split into teams of seven, with Hayden Fry and Tom Davis as the headliners, each spring they comb the state of Iowa. Each seven-coach team covers fifteen towns, giving speeches and eating dinner and talking with Iowa fans about The University of Iowa. In Carroll, Iowa, 250 miles from the university, five hundred people turn out to listen to Hayden Fry talk about the Hawks. Not bad for a town of ten thousand people. And Belle Plaine can usually be counted on to deliver three hundred or four hundred. That's almost a tenth of the city's population!

The bond's amazing! Amazing that a big-time college athletic program would show up in a place as tiny as Belle Plaine. Amazing that the town would close down and turn out full force for the show. But then again in Iowa…maybe not so amazing.

For home football games, Fridays are one of the primo I-Club get-together times. I was lucky—I got an invite! Actually anybody in the world who wants to can go, but Mark Jennings thought I might have a good time.

"It starts at six-thirty," he told me. "With Michigan this week, there'll be close to five hundred folks. So you'd better get there early!" Strange, even early seemed kind of late, a Friday night dinner, with a big game the next day. "That's six-thirty a.m.," Mark corrected me. I got my answer without even asking.

A.M. in itself sets off I-Clubs from the O-Clubs and M-Clubs and W-Clubs around the college football world. A lot of alumni clubs have some kind of gathering for the home games, but not a lot have it at dawn. Usually it's someplace in town where a handful of rich people, thousand-dollar-a-year donors, come in for a noon luncheon.

Usually a Hilton or a Sheraton, underneath fancy chandeliers, accompanied by mixed drinks, chicken cordon bleu, and a tossed salad. Iowa's Friday morning bash was outside town, just off the highway, at a place called the Highlander Restaurant.

At 6:10 a.m. when I stumbled up, the line already bulged through the Highlander's double glass doors and out into the dark parking lot. I stepped in behind Rosemary Lyons. Rosemary looked like my mom, except for the fact that my mom doesn't own a gold sweater or anything with a Tiger Hawk on it. Rosemary's gold sweater had a Tiger Hawk on the lapel sandwiched between "Iowa" above it and "Hawkeyes" underneath. Rosemary was in line by herself, her friend, who she told me had been a Hawkeye football fan for twenty-five years, was inside saving seats.

My husband came a couple years ago," Rosemary noted. "Back when we had that 'real great-looking cheerleader.' Said he wanted to see her up close. That's the only way I could get him here."

The "real great-looking" cheerleader had graduated. So had Rosemary's husband...from the Friday morning I-Club, anyhow. He was still a big Hawkeye fan, just not at six in the morning. "He thinks I'm nuts," she added. "But I still drag him here once a season. Usually Homecoming, in case the 'real great-looking' cheerleader comes back."

For Rosemary, and for her seat-saving friend Pat, the Friday morning I-Club is a six-times-a-season event. A necessary stop off before the eight-to-five shift at the university hospital. For them and the other three or four or five hundred that pack the place, eating breakfast and listening to Hayden Fry talk Hawk football isn't only a loyalty test, it's fun too!

"Pat says the social season here in Iowa starts in the fall." Looking around at the hundreds cramming the place, I'd say she was right.

By the time we hit the pay line in front of the buffet, Rosemary and I were talking all about Hawkeye football. She told me about the I-Club, that she'd been coming to these Friday morning gatherings for last five or six years, and to Hawk games since '74. She said Pat had been coming a lot longer. We talked about the Michigan game too. And the Hawks' chances on Saturday. From the buffet table, with a cram-it-on-your-plate sausage, potatoes, eggs and bacon breakfast (no quiche at the I-Club), I could make out the sights and sounds from the big dining room ahead. It sounded like a half-time show—a jam-packed half-time show.

Luckily, Rosemary's friend had saved an extra seat. The round tables, ten seats apiece, were all pretty well packed. Latecomers just squeezed in wherever there was room, which meant that not everybody at each table knew one another. But since it was an Iowa get-together, by the end of breakfast, most everybody did. My table was filled with women. All dressed in something gold or least something with a Hawk pin sticking to it. In fact, almost everybody there was dressed in something that matched the Hawks. And a lot of the fans inside were women, mostly mothers and grandmothers, some with their husbands, some without. All week long they kept popping up, and not just at the predawn breakfast either. Walking in the shops, and Saturday around the tailgates and at the game, Iowa women "love their Hawks." It's actually a refreshing change of pace, and a great way to learn about football. Women possess a loyalty that men don't! A loyalty that transfers nicely over to college football. If the guy's a bum, be he player or coach, moms normally find a good side to him. Or feel sorry for him, that he's not better. Well, our table was full of loyalty. Conversations carried the tone of a mom talking about her kid on the high school football team. The boys usually got mentioned by first name, and Hayden, definitely not Hayden Fry, coached the Hawks. No better place to listen to Hawk talk. Even a season that had so far been a so-so one sounded pretty good!

Around the place folks woke up, worked on breakfast, and discussed the big Saturday game. Herky, the Hawk, a kid with Hawk football pants, jersey, and shoulder pads, and a huge plastic Hawk head, flitted through the crowd. Up in the corner, at the front of the room, the brass section of the Hawkeye marching band blared out The Iowa Fight Song. Cheerleaders, unfortunately minus that "real great-looking" one that lured Rosemary's husband, lined the speakers' tables in front. They smiled and jumped and shook their pom-poms. Even the Iowa twirler did her thing. She spun and danced and twirled about in front of the room. And talk about precision. She'd toss her baton twelve feet up, just high enough to graze the ceiling, turn a cartwheel, and catch it. All without bumping into a single table. An Iowa Hawkeye football breakfast celebration and I'd completely forgotten the *Today* show was still an hour from starting!

The speakers' table brimmed with Iowa dignitaries. A big old gold banner filled with block IOWA letters was tacked on the wall behind it. A bright yellow block "I" about a foot or two tall, made out of yellow carnations, perched at the end of the table. A couple of big-time alums—an ex-governor ("the best this state's ever had," according to Rosemary) and a priest dressed in, you guessed it, a black Hawkeye sweater with a gold collar—rounded out the table. Only the center seat was empty.

"Here he comes! Here he comes!" shouted the brass band's drum major.

And as the weekly master of ceremonies, resurrector of the Iowa football program and one of the world's smoothest speakers, strolled in, the Iowa band blasted out another rendition of The Iowa Fight Song. The crowd pushed away from their coffees, stood, and clapped. Hayden Fry, complete with sun glasses, nodded his thanks. I-Club Friday morning was complete.

And let the festivities begin!

The priest in the Hawkeye collar took care of the benediction, and ended it with "Lord, give the Hawkeyes strength tomorrow." Then came the weekly raffle...for all sorts of Hawkeye stuff. Gold Hawkeye jackets and black Hawkeye jackets. Gold Hawkeye shirts and black Hawkeye shirts. A voice from the microphone at the podium asked for all persons please to check their ticket stubs. The voice would call the winning ticket's first three numbers. The band in unison would ask, "Yes?" The voice would call the last three numbers. And the band in unison, if no band member won, would issue a groan. The happy winner, dressed in a Hawk sweater, would jump up and hustle to the speakers' table to accept another Hawk sweater, while everybody, band included, clapped. The biggest cheer came when Herky, then minus his plastic head so he could put away some potatoes and eggs, won the big yellow carnation I at the speakers' table.

"I've never won a thing here," Rosemary sighed, and was seconded by a couple of other dedicated ladies.

Speeches followed. The best ex-governor of the state talked for a while, and then introduced the best Hawk football coach ever. And each speech was filled with Hawkeye jokes, and Hayden jokes, and roast-everybody-at-the-table type jokes. The crowd got into it. We laughed when something was funny and clapped when something was important.

After Hayden tossed a few return cracks at the ex-governor, he got down to business. And when he does that, wherever it be, you're in for a treat! Hayden Fry is one of college football's finest speakers. I'd caught his act in Seattle at a Coach of the Year Clinic a couple of years earlier. Coach of the Year Clinic is where junior-high and high school football coaches get to listen to the big-timers tell how they made the big time. Most of the speeches are filled with X's and O's. What's the best offense and what's the best defense? How do you really block the sprint draw? Not Hayden's. He never once mentioned a play or a strategy. Or even a particular game. He talked about life. About motivation and about people. When he was finished, I'd decided if I was ever reincarnated as a college football player, I'd be at Iowa in a heartbeat!

Part of being a good speaker and a good coach is being a good sandbagger. And being a six-and-a-half-point underdog to the tough Michigan team, Hayden was at his sandbagging best.

"This is the best Michigan team I've ever played against," a Hayden specialty, was met with a drawn-out groan from Rosemary, Pat, and all the other loyal Hawks. Then for about fifteen minutes, the Iowa coach went down the Michigan starting lineup position by position, like he was pushing each for the Heisman. Still he ended with a "We'll give it our best." Rosemary, I'm sure, felt at least a little better.

But before Hayden thanked all the loyal folks for showing up, he said he had a story to tell. "I want to share with you something that happened to me," he said, "perhaps the most inspirational thing I've ever witnessed in my life." Folks who'd intently listened to the Michigan Heisman balloting got more intent. They enjoyed Hayden's stories.

This one was about a funeral from which he and some of his assistant coaches had just returned, the funeral of the father of three of Hayden's players, all of whom had worn the number 41 black and gold of Iowa. One of them, Mark Stoops, still played at Iowa. Another, Mike Stoops, still coached there. The third, Bobby Stoops, had gone to two Rose Bowls with Iowa. Hayden talked about the man, Mark's and Mike's and Bobby's father, Coach Stoops, who'd died the week before. He told the story of how he'd died—on the sidelines of a Youngstown High School football game. He told how, even though Coach Stoops was hurting, he'd refused to leave the game. How he'd coached his team till the final whistle of their overtime victory. How he'd called the game's last defensive play, then walked to the end of the bench and collapsed into a coma. He also told us of Coach Stoops' life. It was the story of a man who never missed a game for twelve years while his sons participated in the Hawkeye program. A man who every fall coached his Youngstown team on Friday, loaded the family into the car, and drove through the night to get to Iowa City. He told us how early Sunday morning after the Iowa game, he'd load everybody up again and make it back in time to grade the high-school films. He talked with great respect about a man dedicated to his team and to his family.

"The funeral," Hayden said to a very quiet I-Club, "was the most beautiful funeral I've ever seen. Thirteen priests and all the nuns were present...." People had lined up outside in rainy 40-degree weather to attend. "It really was beautiful."

Even so, the Iowa coach solemnly revealed, after the ceremony, something was wrong. Mrs. Stoops wasn't satisfied. Hayden told us why: "As honorary pallbearers, we had the opportunity to be present when Mrs. Stoops told us something just didn't seem right. Not until we'd walked in with an Iowa jersey, black and gold, a number forty-one on it. The number that each of her kids had worn...." The number that Coach and Mrs. Stoops had religiously followed for twelve years across the Midwest. Hayden handed that jersey to Mrs. Stoops.

"Ladies and gentlemen," he continued, "she had her children prop Coach Stoops up and put that jersey on him. Right there. Bobby Stoops took his Rose Bowl ring off, he had two…and he put one on Coach Stoops' finger. And that's the way that gentleman was buried."

Hayden paused and reflected for a moment. "The family was so happy, so delighted that they knew that their father was at peace. That he was comfortable." Mrs. Stoops told her husband, "Now you'll always be warm…." He paused again. "Afterwards she had a smile on her face. She told us, 'Now everything's all right!'"

We all took a long deep breath. Hayden finished up. "I told you this because I wanted you to know there are a lot of people out there that love Iowa football." And he stepped away from the microphone. The quiet crowd, still envisioning that number 41 jersey being pulled over Coach Stoops, stood. Everybody clapped. The band broke into one last rendition of the Fight Song. Recovered, the loyal I-Clubbers said their goodbyes and headed off to work, a Hawkeye jersey and a coach in a casket on their minds for a long time to come. Hayden Fry stayed and shook hands. He was the last one out the door.

If this Friday morning celebration ended eerily, Friday night's was gonna be a blowout. And I had another Iowa invite. This time to the Pentacrest for the weekly home game march of the Hawkeye Marching Beer Band. "It's a trip! You gotta come!" So at 9:00 p.m., I was on the Pentacrest sidewalk, while advancing pieces of the Iowa Marching Beer Band rolled in.

Kids with horns and drums and saxes crammed the sidewalk. Others were on the way, most in twos or threes, some by themselves.

Each got a "how's it going?" from somebody already standing around and waiting. The music was totally unorganized; a dozen recitals of tunes bounced about, none of them more than a few stanzas. A little Dixieland, a trombone warm-up of "The Iowa Fight Song," freshman scales renditions, and drums knocking out some modern-day rock-and-roll beat. A Friday night campus stream of cars whooshed by. They passed in bunches, according to the light change. Occasionally one would honk or somebody would yell out the window. Most were answered by a da da da dat da da-charge salute.

"You made it! Great!" Erin, a junior trumpeter, dressed in your basic blue jeans with the now-stylish rip in the knee, plus a big gray Iowa sweatshirt, saw me.

"You really gonna go beer-banding with us?" another trumpeter, a friend of Erin's, asked. My "As long as I get free beer" answer was met with a chorus from two trumpeters: "No problem."

While the girls described the setup, that the beer band was not the official Iowa University band policy, that they did it on their own six times a season, that it'd been going on "forever," Tony walked up. He was carrying a big box.

Tony's a crew-cut, marine-looking guy, and conductor of the Hawkeye Marching Beer Band. A regular trombonist on Saturday afternoons, besides conductor Tony was also beer band's secretary-treasurer and T-shirt orderer. And the order was in, hot off the press. Beer banders gathered around.

"Cool"—a voice popped out of the group.

"Awesome."

"Tony, they look great!"

The official beer band uniform—a white T-shirt with all sorts of beer band symbols—passed with flying colors. On the front, "Party Naked" was crossed out and in its place was "March Naked." A beer stein sat next to the naked march, and "Chug 'n' Go—HMB Beer Band" below that. The back listed in order the ten stops for the night.

"You want one?!" Tony looked my way. Besides being a beer band director, Tony was a salesman. Beer band, like any other band, needed funds, if nothing else than to pay for T-shirts. The cost was only eight dollars, and the cause was good. So I donated, and with my official shirt became an honorary beer band member.

Tony kept selling. He spread around more shirts for more bucks, till half the group was uniformed and beer band was itching to get going. "Let's go," he yelled. The forty or so kids that'd shown assembled at the curb. Tony took his place at the front. He blew his whistle three times, and the Hawkeye Marching Beer Band blasted out their first of what would be close to fifty-three renditions of "The Iowa Fight Song." On the last note, we all crossed Clinton Street, at the same time starting up "In Heaven There Is No Better Beer." We were off on the world's greatest Friday night barhopping there ever was!

Joe's Place on Iowa Avenue—in any other town on earth just another corner bar, but in Iowa City, on Friday night before the Michigan game, Joe's had the honor or being beer band stop number one.

"Remember," Tony commanded at the doorway, "this may be a beer band but its Iowa's beer band, and it's gotta be good!" Cheers answered him.

And at 9:10 p.m., pumped for the tour, the band flooded Joe's. Song number one at stop number one brought the house down. The beer band, consisting of mostly horns, a handful of drums, three kazoos, and a couple of clarinets, so crammed that trombone rods couldn't find an open space to shove to, shook Joe's with The Iowa Fight Song. Patrons joined in if they knew the words, and the bar sounded like a happy Christmas Eve sing-along, just with a different theme.

At each bar, The Iowa Fight Song led without a breath to "In Heaven There Is No Better Beer," the band's fight song. The beer song always included a short break in middle. While some of the band kept time, the rest locked arms and polkaed and sang. Each "beer song" also ended in a beer band eruption of cheers.

"That's our favorite," Erin yelled. "But Bump won't let us do it at the game." Erin was referring to Bump Elliot, the Iowa athletic director, who'd probably never caught the Friday night beer band in action, and who'd probably never hung out at Joe's or Mickey's or even Tuck's Place.

Meanwhile, Joe got the rest of the song list. Tony, standing on a table, flashed hand signals for selections. A time-out T meant "Tequila."

An index finger up for 1, or I depending on how you looked at it, kicked off "The Iowa Fight Song." An upside-down three fingered M called for the **Michigan fight song**—if not the cleanest, then certainly the most imaginative tune of the night. Give or take a line, it's the same song every college kid at every college that's ever played the Wolverines has joined in on. No musical accompaniment, aside from the three kazoos, is even needed. Thirty-six beer band voices rolled off a "Hail to the Victors" rendition filled with all sorts of rhyming, nasty, and degrading verses. Bar patrons loved it! The final verse, a "Hail, Hail to Michigan, the Cesspool of the East," was always met with hooting and hollering and wild applause.

With the last of five songs, whatever the fifth happened to be, beer band chanted, "BAND WANTS BEER! BAND WANTS BEER!" Bartenders at each stop obliged. Joe's already had the plastic cups out and the free beer flowing by the time the first chant was rolling. Ten minutes of gulping and revealing to all the interested patrons what the actual words to the Michigan song were and it was time to hit the road. Tony got back on the table...three sharp whistle blasts, one last long loud band-filled chant—"ONE, TWO, THREE...THANKS, JOE'S!" —and beer band marched to the exit. Off to Mickey's—stop number two.

Each stop along the way was greeted with cheers, the band's as well as the packed house's. Each stop along the way had a song the customers wanted replayed. Some yelled out, "TEQUILA! WE WANT TEQUILA!" For others it was "The Iowa Fight Song." Most fans yelled for the revised version of "Hail to the Victors." At each stop, or on the way to each, other little bits of beer band trivia, like the reason for the presence of three kazooers, surfaced.

"We're in the flag corps," a freshman kazoo player revealed, on the way to stop number three. "Flags don't fit in the door." Good point. They didn't.

"So these are our instruments!" And she reeled off a stanza of "Tequila."

> **The man who wrote the Michigan fight song, "(Hail to) The Victors", lived in South Bend, Indiana on what is now the site of the College Football Hall of Fame.**

To reach stop four, beer band detoured across Iowa Avenue and marched through a corner of campus. The route ran the sidewalk, between Seashore and Van Allen halls. Drumbeats marked the cadence and echoed between the tall buildings. Beer banders yelled letters in unison: 'I-O-W-A, IOWA! IOWA! IOWA!" Cheers followed chants, then started over again. Cars on Iowa Avenue stopped and honked. People at the corners stopped and cheered. Roaming cops even cracked smiles.

Stop number four, Tuck's Place, is the sentimental favorite. It's the band hangout, because as an excited flutist yelled out on the way, "Tuck's awesome. He has our picture on the wall."

Tuck's is another Iowa City hole-in-the-wall. With a twist. It has a long skinny bar that's usually bellied up to by a host of old folks. Beer band burst in. From the sidewalk outside, at the band's tail end, I could hear an eruption of cheers.

"Where ya been?" Somebody at one of the booths yelled out.

A horn in the back countered with da da da dat da—charge.

No standing and playing out with the patrons at Tuck's. The kids, as many as could, crammed in behind the long skinny counter—shoulder to shoulder to shoulder, all the horns tilted up and facing out to the cheering crowd. Those that couldn't fit behind the bar sandwiched folks bellied up to it. Tony, who'd found a chair to stand on, flashed the 1 to signal The Fight Song, raised his hands up like a conductor's and beer band rolled. "Iowa," the beer song, "Hail to the Victors," and "Tequila." Patrons toasted each song, sang along when they knew the words, and provided pretty wild applause when each ended.

"One more time on the beer song." A plump, old, gray-haired guy wanted to hear the beer band theme again. It was Tuck! The band cheered, and played it again. Even louder. Tuck's wife, meanwhile, turned on the taps. Cups full of Pabst circulated.

Before Tuck got his "ONE, TWO, THREE…THANKS, TUCK" salute, a presentation was made.

"Quiet, everybody," Tony yelled.

A couple of voices echoed Tony's "Quiet."

"To beer band's favorite bar. And beer band's favorite bartender—Tuck. Your very own beer band T-shirt." The place erupted.

"Tuck's awesome," a voice yelled out. Some of the kids hit the beer song one more time—a tribute to a great bar. Tony gave the awesome bartender his own brand-new "March Naked" beer band shirt. Tuck pulled it on. Flash bulbs popped. And beer band headed outside, off to inspire the rest of campus.

After a Quick Stop grocery store serenade, and a roll back through Seashore and Van Allen halls, by the time we got back to Iowa Avenue a second time, Friday night campus crowds had thickened. Streets were hopping with roaming kids and alums. Some were looking for a place to stop and have a brew. Others browsed shop windows. Most though, were just having a pleasant stroll on a warm October night. The echoing, I-O-W-A-ing beer band shattered the warm October quiet. Beer band hit the red-brick plaza, destination: the Sports Corner.

The Sports Corner is the halfway point, and a good place to catch a second wind. Beer band had been rolling for almost an hour. Some of the lips that had blown out barroom medleys five times already took a break. Inside, Sports Corner shook with brass and cheers.

"This is the greatest," Todd, a big junior horn player, revealed. He was sitting and leaning against the window. Most of all, he was resting. "Last year I didn't go out for band. I blew it. This year I did, and it's the best time I've ever had. Especially this." He pointed his horn toward the inside noise.

Another less sentimental member, late, ran past us, through the door into the Sports Corner. "It's a cheap way to get drunk."

"That too," Todd noted. "But I've got to rest. I've got to pace myself. I'm wiped. Last week I came out here and gave it all I had. Played all night long. And I couldn't even get through the Saturday half-time show, my lips were so tired."

Erin, meanwhile, was just beginning to roll. "She's crazy." The freshman kazoo player filled me in on Erin. "She'll play anything." Down on the corner a group of alums were clapping along to . Erin, probably one of the band's best trumpeters, stood in the middle and blasted away.

"Last week she got *three bucks*," the freshman shrieked, "for 'My Funny Valentine.' *Three Bucks!!!* Over there across the street." The freshman pointed to Mickey's. "People in that room above the bar threw it down to the sidewalk. *Three bucks* for 'My Funny Valentine'! She's crazy!"

Erin bounced up. "Sixty cents for The Notre Dame Fight Song. That's it! I can't believe it, a lousy sixty cents. It's all they'd give me." She stopped and lit up. "So I took it." Inside, the beer song got a second go-round.

A beer band fan, just a normal Iowa City lady out and about, joined us on the sidewalk outside the Sports Corner—Erin, the freshman kazoo flag corps marcher, Todd the big junior, and me.

"My daughter loved that beer song," the lady piped up, like she'd been with us all night long. She was short and plump. The kids gathered around and looked down at her.

"When she was in junior high, she heard you kids playing that beer song. And she said to me, 'Mom I want to go to Iowa.'"

"Did she?! Did she?!" Everybody wanted to know.

The plump lady sighed a sigh that only mothers sigh. And only when they talk about their kids. "She was valedictorian of her class. She got a thirty-two on her ACT. And Iowa, in all of its infinite wisdom, wouldn't give her any money." Mom stopped, probably silently hexing Iowa. "So she went to Western Illinois."

"OH, NO," the four of us groaned.

Mom went on, "And every day she asks the Western Illinois band director why can't they play the beer song." Groans turned to cheers. The kazoo joined Erin with a beer song rendition, on the house! Todd, the big junior, still pacing himself, rested.

Behind us, filing out of the Sports Corner, beer band trucked on. "Pre-game at the fountain," Tony yelled.

"What the hell for?" a voice from the rear shot back.

Tony sometimes gets that kind of response. Sometimes the soldiers think Tony, a volunteer drill sergeant with no MPs to back him up, is on a power trip. But usually they listen to him. He conducts. They follow. He keeps things under control. Even as the empty beer cups accumulate, the band members stay cool. All night long. They play their tunes. They chant their 'BAND WANTS BEER!" They chant their "ONE, TWO, THREE...THANKS." They make sure that Iowa Marching Beer Band is the best marching beer band in the NCAA...without any violations. And they keep it sharp. Especially on show, at the fountain.

The fountain is Iowa City's hot spot. At the center of the red-brick plaza, in the shadow of the Holiday Inn, it's the place where every-body who's out walking on a pleasant Friday night ends up at least three times. It's just a block from Sports Corner. Just a block from about a hundred Iowa City bars. The band trucked over in twos and threes, some serenading folks along the way. At the fountain they reassembled. Horns up, beer band came to attention on the redbrick steps facing the water. Tony climbed up the fountain. Standing on the water's edge, about twelve feet up, he pointed a 1 and raised his hands. Crowds of people, alums and high-school kids, college kids too, slowed down and gathered for the show.

Tweet tweet tweet. Beer band rolled. This time, though, since it was in public, and not in front of beer-guzzling Wolverine haters, Michigan's filthy fight song was omitted. No problem—public support was great! A group of high-school girls clapped and danced along to "Tequila." The Iowa Fight Song got alums joining in. When the beer song rolled, more than just the beer band polkaed. And when they finished, everybody standing around the fountain, especially the band, cheered for the band...and it was on to the finale.

And what a finale! The jam-packed Fieldhouse, beer band's stop number ten, is Iowa City's favorite Friday night hangout. It's beer band's second favorite...after Tuck's.

Normally, squeezing in the Fieldhouse door, especially at eleven o'clock on a Friday night, calls for a two-buck cover and at least a thirty-minute wait in line. Not for the Iowa Marching Beer Band! The dance floor was waiting. Straight through the front door, past the bouncers, the band assembled at the back-end lower level. Everybody cleared the way. Cheers thundered as the marchers hit the lower level. Beer banders, all present and accounted for, crammed the floor. A mirror behind them reflected their backs, and all the clapping patrons squeezed off to the side. It looked like a billion people crowded together. Tony found a makeshift conductor's barstool, set it up, and jumped on top. Trombones and trumpets and flutes pointed up toward him. Some rested on the head of the kid in front...but they all fit. Tony blew his whistle. The kids hit the cycle one last time. The Fieldhouse erupted. After one repeat of "Hail to the Victors," the barroom deejay turned up the rock and roll, and the trumpeters with their trumpets, the trombonists with their trombones, even the kazooers with their kazoos just started dancing, swarmed by the mob crammed onto the dance floor.

And the beer band stars of Iowa City, Tuck's favorite band, Erin the marching street musician, Tony the conductor-marine, and Todd the big junior once again became normal college kids on the dance floor. Harmless—except for the slide of an occasional boogieing trombone. All I could think was: My God, what would happen if Iowa's beer band got together with the University of Wisconsin Marching Band, someday, somewhere, for somebody's Fifth Quarter? Music would never be the same again...maybe the world, either!

A fire at the University of Illinois Library destroyed over 1,000 books and half of them had not even been colored in yet.

What are 3 things that will soften your brain?

Rootin' for the Cubs, Rootin for Iowa State, and a Crowbar...

TO BE CONTINUED!

We hope you have enjoyed the first annual *For Hawkeye Fans Only*. You can be in next year's edition if you have a neat story. You can email it to printedpage@cox.net (put "Hawkeye Fans" in the Subject line) or call the author directly at 602-738-5889.

Or, if you have stories about the Chicago Bears, Iowa State, Kansas City Chiefs or Notre Dame, email them to printedpage@cox.net (put the appropriate team name in the Subject line).

For information on ordering more copies of *For Hawkeye Fans Only,* as well as any of the author's other best-selling books, go to www.fandemonium.net.

Note: There were no actual Iowa State fans harmed during the making of this book.

Iowa sophomore quarterback Randy Duncan gets his 1957 Rose Bowl Christmas wish with Jayne Mansfield. They may have been young, but they each had a good head on their shoulders. Randy still does.